GLOBAL MANDATE:
Love of God and Neighbor

CORNEL SIMMS, D.MIN.

GLOBAL MANDATE:
Love of God and Neighbor

Seraphina Press
Minneapolis, MN

Copyright © 2011 by Cornel Simms, D.Min.

SERAPHINA PRESS

Seraphina Press
212 3rd Avenue North, Suite 290
Minneapolis, MN 55401
612.455.2293
www.SeraphinaPress.com

All rights reserved. No part of this publication may be reproduced, stored in a retrieval system, or transmitted, in any form or by any means, electronic, mechanical, photocopying, recording, or otherwise, without the prior written permission of the author.

ISBN-13: 978-0-9840355-0-2
LCCN: 2011931158

Cover Design and Typeset by Melanie Shellito

Printed in the United States of America

To Mom and Dad

CONTENTS

Preface v
Acknowledgment vii
Prologue vix

Part I: Love Imperative 1
Love is the greatest principle and highest virtue

Chapter One: Theology of Love Imperative 3
Chapter Two: Ethics of Love Imperative 17

Part II: Human Proclivity 31
Human nature is doomed without love

Chapter Three: Human Nature 33
    A. Original Sin
    B. Egoism
    C. Natural Law

Chapter Four: Happiness 49

Part III: Christian Faith 57
Christian Faith is about love, nothing else

Chapter Five: Conversion 59
    A. Definition and Identification
    B. Classic Conversion Experiences
    C. Historicity
    D. Forms of Conversion

Chapter Six: Formation and Transformation 77
    A. Faith Development and Growth
    B. Transformational Logic

Chapter Seven: Death and Afterlife 91
   A. Mortality
   B. Immortality

Chapter Eight: Personal Spirituality and Piety 103
   A. Fruit of the Spirit
   B. Works of the Flesh
   C. Sanctification
   D. Believers' Function: Prophet, Priest, and King

Chapter Nine: Gifts of the Spirit. 113
   A. Definition
   B. Variety of Gifts
   C. Ordinary and Extraordinary Gifts
   D. Manifestation of Gifts
   E. Source of Charisms

Chapter Ten: Communal Worship. 121
   A. Theological Overview of Assembly
   B. Pentecostal/Charismatic Assembly
   C. Pentecostal/Charismatic Modes and Sensibilities

Chapter Eleven: Communal Fellowship. 137
   A. Definition of Fellowship
   B. Models of Koinonia
   C. Spirit and Koinonia
   D. Instruments of Koinonia
   E. Factors that Hinder Koinonia
   F. Elements of Koinonia

Chapter Twelve: Method 157
   A. Fivefold Gospel
   B. Curran's Fivefold Stance
   C. Wesley's Quadrilateral

Chapter Thirteen: Source and Goal. 167

Part IV: Social Action **171**
Sociopolitical action when not about love results in injustice and oppression

    Chapter Fourteen: Global Poverty 173
        A. Poverty Measurement
        B. Views of Poverty
        C. Why Poverty Persists
        D. Approach
        E. Poverty Reduction Initiative:
            1. Hunger, Education, and Health
            2. Human Rights
            3. Nonviolence & Peacemaking

    Chapter Fifteen: Church and State Relation 213

Epilogue 219
Appendix..221
        A. Responsibility and Relationality
        B. Obligation and Care
Bibliography..229
Index 245

PREFACE

God is love (1 John 4:8). Love is the essence and nature of God: Father, Son, and Holy Spirit. God's work and relationality flow out of a loving triune context (1 John 5:7). God said to God, "Let Us make man in Our image, according to Our likeness..." (Gen. 1:26 NKJV). Since human beings were made in God's image and likeness, like God, our original essence and nature must be love. St. Augustine clearly articulates in his doctrine on Original Sin that our nature became tarnished in the fall, due to Adam's disobedience (Genesis chapter 3; Rom. 5:12). As a result, humans, like God, know both good and evil, unlike God humans lack the ability to live eternally: "...for in the day that you eat of it [the tree of knowledge of good and evil] you shall surely die" (Gen. 2:17 NKJV). It appears that if Adam and his family did eat of the tree of life, subsequent to the fall, they would have lived eternally, but God quickly put them out of the Garden of Eden before they could do so (Gen. 3:22–23). Hence, in the fullness of time God sent Christ that we might have life eternal through Him, and be brought back into eternal loving relationship with God (Gal. 4:4; John 3:16; 1 John 4:9, 10). Christ who was from the beginning with God as God, out of love and for love, became incarnated in the flesh, lived among mankind for about thirty three years, for our redemption (John 1:1–3, 14). The work of Christ on earth was not to show how powerful God is, although it does, but to demonstrate God's unconditional love for humanity throughout the ages, and moreso towards those who are hurting and are least regarded. In the words of Christ this holds true: "The Spirit of the Lord is upon Me, because He has anointed Me to preach the gospel to the poor; He has sent Me to heal the brokenhearted, to proclaim liberty to the captives and recovery of sight to the blind, to set at liberty those who are oppressed" (Luke 4:18 NKJV). In the events of the cross, Christ's commitment and obedience to love won our redemption and salvation. Christ made it possible for humanity to once again live in loving relationships vertically and horizontally, respectively.

The Holy Spirit helps us to live this love that God made us to be and that Christ died to restore. The untoward force behind the world's systems and structures constantly pressures us to choose evil, contrary to who we were made to be. The love at the core of our original nature seeks to only do good, but the evil that we know, due to the fall, seeks to hinder the good we ought to do. The Apostle Paul testifies of this ongoing struggle between good and evil, within him (Rom. 7:19). Thomas Aquinas' theory of Natural Law maintains that to do good and avoid evil is the natural human predilection—not otherwise—through Christ this is made possible even the more. The fruit of love is all good. The Genesis account indicates that when God, who is love, was creating the world, He often paused to admire the goodness that results from His work—goodness is the sole product of the work of a loving God (Gen. 1:12, 17, etc.). Simply put, love only produces good.

Humans, therefore, should yield to the command to love (Mark. 12:29–31; 1John 4:10), which perfects our innate inclination to love. The weakness in our nature gravitates to evil, but this can be overcome by yielding to the predisposition to love—which produces good. An ongoing sanctified life keeps us in right or loving relation with God and neighbor. If John Wesley's point holds true that an entirely sanctified life is perfect love—this end we must strive toward, daily. The eschatological discourse in John's Gospel (chapter 14) paints a picture of Christ as a loving parent that went to a better place to prepare the way for His children, and will soon return to be reunited with them. Although they are in the care of the greatest caregiver, guardian and instructor—the Holy Spirit—still, Christ misses being with them in person. Consequently, He vows never to leave them again when He returns, and therefore made accommodations for them to dwell, inseparably, with Him, forever!

Cornel Simms, D.MIN.

ACKNOWLEDGMENT

The task of writing any project usually is not a solo endeavor. It involves facilitators, reviewers, critics, and encouragers. When I was a graduate student at Barry University, Miami Shores, Florida, some of my former professors and classmates gave listening ears to some of the thoughts discussed in this book. Dr. Mark Wedig, Chair of Barry University Theology and Philosophy Department, supervised my Doctoral Thesis Project. Much of the material in this book was adopted from my Doctoral Thesis Project, with significant revisions. Dr. Cheryl Johns, my former professor, from Pentecostal Theological Seminary (formerly Church of God Theological Seminary), Cleveland, Tennessee, provided a general feedback. Several persons offered personal and professional editorial critiques. Charismata Church of God, the church I was senior pastor from May 2004 to December 2010, provided a faith context for this work. Family members and friends offered moral support and positive reinforcement, but I particularly single out Wolly for being a constant encourager.

PROLOGUE

The heart of Christianity is love of God and neighbor. Section I articulates that the love imperative[1] is the central thought and core of Christian theology and praxis; this understanding is the bedrock and fundamental thesis of this book. Chapters One and Two are the theological and ethical basis of the love imperative, respectively. They present love of God and neighbor as summary and core of Christian theology and morality. Section II, Human Proclivity, engages human nature in light of the double love command. Chapter Three shows that our nature is intrinsic to our existence—it is at the core of who we are—and it has the ability to produce both good and evil. Chapter Four articulates that happiness is the goal of human nature. We are always seeking to be happy, or have fulfillment in our whole-life endeavors. When not guided by love of God and neighbor, human nature will influence us to seek happiness, even to our own demise.

Section III is about Christian Faith and themes significant to that end—spans from Chapter Five through Chapter Thirteen. These chapters engage significant themes of Christian faith and spirituality in light of love of God and neighbor: Christian conversion, formation and transformation, death and afterlife, personal spirituality and piety, gifts of the Spirit, and communal worship and fellowship. Chapter Twelve provides a theological framework for Christian decision-making; and Chapter Thirteen articulates that Christ and the Spirit are the source of the elements of Christian faith and praxis discussed in the preceding chapters of this section. These themes help to sustain us in our walk with the Lord, individually and corporately; the goal of Christian faith and praxis is love, nothing else. Although some of the thoughts expressed in this section are from a Pentecostal/Charismatic[2] perspective, this work has far reaching implication.

Section IV, Social Action, shows that the love imperative results in concrete loving action toward neighbor. When people are truly guided by the principle of love, they cannot ignore the pain and suffering of millions living in extreme poverty around the globe. Love obligates us to care, even for distant others. A serious contemporary poverty reduction initiative, therefore, must involve education, hunger, health, human rights, and peacemaking efforts. An authentic relationship between the church and state, for the common good of all considered, can significantly debilitate some of the contemporary global challenges. Therefore, the double-love imperative should be at work in human nature, faith context, and efforts to solve contemporary global crises.

Christian theology affirms that faith in God restores fallen human nature—that God through Jesus Christ provides redemption for all people. Salvation in Christ redeems mankind from sin that once separated us from God's love and impaired our ability to love God and neighbor. In order to come to faith in Christ, a person must first respond to God's love, which converts from sin to grace. The one converted to loving relationship with God grows and develops in the faith by ongoing formation and transformation, which occur throughout a person's life cycle. Death is that which ends a person's life cycle, but it is also a passage into the eternal bliss. Personal spirituality and piety help to keep a person in right or loving relation with God and neighbor. The sanctified believer lives out the fruits or virtues of the Spirit, and negates the works or vices of the flesh. Through the agency of the various gifts of the Spirit, believers perform Christian service for the edification and building up of one another. The communal worship setting is a context for corporate outpouring of love for God. Communal fellowship bonds people together in love. Methods used to influence practical theological decision-making should lead to love. The source and goal of Christian theology and faith praxis are Christ and the Spirit and the love imperative, respectively. Christianity must be about love, nothing else. The tangible manifestation of this is seen in unconditional care and benevolence done for the common good of others. Altruism and greedlessness are basic distinguishing traits of this double-love command. Anyone who heeds the fundamental goodness of their human nature—as perfected by the double-love imperative—can emanate these traits.

Notes

[1] Throughout this book "love of God and neighbor" is used interchangeably with love imperative, double-love command, love commands, maxim of love, and law of love.

[2] The Pentecostal/Charismatic movement consists of various denominations and theological beliefs. There are approximately fourteen thousand Pentecostal/Charismatic denominations, and scores of affiliated non-denominational churches. There is no worldwide organization for the Pentecostal/Charismatic movement—Jesus is seen as head of it. The Spirit guides and directs the church where the Spirit wills. Pentecostals/Charismatics have been suspicious of organized structures. Some Pentecostals/Charismatics are Trinitarian while others are non-Trinitarians. Those non-Trinitarians are often referred to as Oneness-Pentecostals. Some believe in adult baptism only, while others baptize both adults and infants. None forbids speaking in tongues, but not every Pentecostal/Charismatic believer speaks in tongues. Most Pentecostals/Charismatics believe in baptism with the Holy Spirit with speaking in unknown tongues being initial evidence of having been filled with the Holy Spirit. Some question speaking in tongues as the initial evidence of having being filled with the Spirit. The thing that generally unifies all Pentecostals/Charismatics is their belief in the baptism of the Holy Spirit following conversion. This experience empowers the believer for Christian service and holy living. This experience is always transformational. This understanding is primarily rooted in the Lukan account (as seen in the Acts of the Apostles). Like on the day of Pentecost, Spirit empowerment is always transformational. It changes the believer's life and the believer impacts his/her faith community and world in turn. The Pentecostal/Charismatic movement is just a little over 100 years old—is the fastest growing in Christianity—and have approximately 600 thousand members and adherents world-wide. It began in 1906 with William J. Seymour and 12 brethren in a cottage prayer meeting at 214 Bonnie Brae and later transferred to Azusa Street, Los Angeles, California. Seymour and his brethren were seeking an outpouring of the Spirit like on the day of Pentecost. Some trace the origins of the movement, however, to Charles Parham's Bethel Bible School in Topeka, Kansas, when Agnes Ozman spoke in tongues on January 1, 1901. The Pentecostal/Charismatic movement has its roots in the Wesleyan-Holiness revival of the mid to late 1800s—developed out of a need for greater personal piety—emphasizing Christian perfection through entire sanctification, which was central to their social and moral outlook. The Pentecostal/Charismatic believer is believed to be Spirit-filled and their community of faith is Spirit-centered, as well. The Spirit encounters and transforms believers for the effective witness of Christ in the world. The evidence of the Spirit's workings in a believer is often seen in the manifestations of the gifts and fruits of the Spirit in his/her life. *See* Land, Steven, *Pentecostal Spirituality: A Passion for the Kingdom* (Sheffield, England: Sheffield Academic Press, 2001), 19; Johns, Cheryl, *Pentecostal Formation: A Pedagogy among the Oppressed* (Sheffield, England: Sheffield Academic Press, 1998), 63-66; Seymour, William J., ed., "Azusa Street Papers," *The Apostolic*

Faith 1.1 (1906): 1; Burgess, Stanley (ed). *Encyclopedia of Pentecostal and Charismatic Christianity* (New York: Routledge, 2006); and Burgess, Stanley and Eduard van der Maas (eds.), *International Dictionary of Pentecostal and Charismatic Movements* (Grand Rapids, Michigan: Zondervan, 2002).

PART I: LOVE IMPERATIVE

Love is the greatest principle and highest virtue

This first section, Love Imperative, is the bedrock and fundamental thesis of this book, as it outlines the theological underpinnings and ethical implications of the love imperative. The love imperative is articulated here as the principal maxim and virtue that should guide human proclivity, Christian faith praxis, and social action.

CHAPTER ONE

Theology of Love Imperative

This chapter is the theological basis of the love imperative, love of God and neighbor. It could be dubbed as a theology of the double love command. In fulfilling this task, it draws upon various scholars with diverse views. For instance, Karl Rahner sees love of God and neighbor as one and the same, while Karl Barth views love of God as superior to love of neighbor. The central thesis of this chapter, therefore, is that the love imperative is the crux of Scripture, theology, and faith praxis.

The central commands, according to the teachings of Jesus, are to "Love the Lord your God with all your heart and with all your soul and with all your mind and with all your strength" and to "Love your neighbor as yourself" (Mk. 12:29–31; Matt. 22:37–39; Lk. 10:25–28 KJV). In fact, Jesus emphasized that all the laws and prophets hang on these two commands. Wolfgang Schrage points out that in Jewish tradition, people in that community followed myriad commands, but there is not a single command that was seen as summarizing all the commandments, as Jesus articulated. Although Hellenistic Judaism has laid the foundation for this double-love command, Schrage concludes that the summary of the law in the commands to "love thy God" and "love thy neighbor" is probably unique to the teachings of Jesus. This double-love command, seen in the Synoptic gospels, goes back to the Torah, but in the Torah the commands to "love God" and "love neighbor" are itemized among a series of other imperatives, whereas in the gospels these are depicted as the greatest imperatives and summary of all commands.

Furthermore, Schrage's argument indicates that these commands to love are seen in the gospels as the measure by which the Torah should be interpreted and judged. In the gospels, the law of love is the crux of the Torah; it transcends the Torah, and those cultic regulations and rituals seen in the Torah are subordinate to the law of love. Hence, the law of love is a sign of the "in-breaking" of the kingdom of God. It replaces death with life and is the primal criterion for the human conduct in this life. This all leads to the question: who is my neighbor and how do I express love for my neighbor? The Hebrew word translated as "neighbor" (Lev. 19:18) is primarily restricted to the Hebrew covenant community, even though in a very limited way it encompasses foreigners living among the ancient Israelites.[1]

In the tradition of Jesus, love of neighbor means loving *all* people, even enemies. Christ's notion of the love of neighbor is exemplified in the story He told about the Good Samaritan (Lk. 10:30–37). In this passage, Jesus castigates the Jewish religious leaders who did not help the wounded Jewish man, and applauds the Samaritan for stopping by and administering care to this wounded person, even though in those days Jews and Samaritans were enemies. Passing the wounded by the wayside for Jesus meant violation of the love command.

Clearly, Jesus meant for the law of love to transcend ethnic, cultural, religious, and class disparities. The law of love encourages love of enemies (Lk. 6:35; Matt. 5:44), and those who inflict harm on us and hate us (Lk. 6:27–28). The demand of the law of love radically contradicts the natural inclination that teaches humans only to love those who love us and to hate those who hate us. I concur: the fact that we are encouraged in Christ's teachings to love those who have done and wish us evil shows that the love command is not contingent upon how personable another is. This is unlike the sinners and pagans, for whom Jesus says love is based on mutuality and reciprocity (Matt. 5:46–47). Jesus' model of love allowed Him to love even those who appeared undesirable to the customs of his day, people like tax collectors and sinners (Matt. 11:19).

Here the law of love is more than mere emotion; it is concrete action that makes the life of our neighbor better. In the case of the Good Samaritan, he not only bound up the wounds of the Jewish victim (who was supposed to be his enemy culturally), but also carried him to a place where he could be cared for, and paid in advance for his health and lodging expenses. Jesus demanded that we demonstrate love of neighbor through concrete action and involvement in the lives of people (Matt. 25:31–46).[2]

Another aspect of Jesus' concept of love of neighbor is that we should not love our neighbor for self-aggrandizement, as the Stoic and Hobbesian school of thought advocates, but for the neighbor's sake. The phrase "as yourself" in the love command (Mk. 12:31) and the "golden rule" (Matt. 7:12) means "instead of yourself." Hence, we are to love for the well-being of neighbor, not oneself. One cannot love God without loving one's neighbor, because the love of God is concretely manifested and proven in loving the neighbor as well. Hence, we demonstrate our love for neighbor through our unconditional service to neighbor, such as enacting the goodwill of the Good Samaritan and caring for the "least of the brethren" (or vulnerable populations) (Matt. 25:31–46). Clearly, in loving the "least of the brethren," we are demonstrating love for God, as, according to Jesus, whatever we do to them, the least of the brethren, we do to Him. In return, we will receive rewards for helping those in need, and punishment for ignoring them. This understanding, however, shows God as immanent and incarnated in the poor and oppressed, not just as transcendental and looking at them from above. Therefore, those who desire to find God can also do so in their attending and interacting with the marginalized and oppressed.[3] (This point I will further discuss shortly in considering related ideas of Rahner.)

Schrage maintains that love of God is not necessarily equivalent to love of neighbor, however, because the Synoptic tradition does not put both laws of love on the same plane. According to Schrage, love of God is first and love of neighbor is second. Still, it is impossible for one to truly love God and hate people. Love of God implies obedience to God and all that God commands. God is always first and above all, but the Apostle Paul told his audience that all the commandments "…in the second half of the Decalogue" can be reduced to love of neighbor as one would love oneself (Rom. 13:9).[4]

Rudolf Schnackenburg, however, argues that the Apostle Paul did not use Jesus' double-love-command formula in his writings—because Paul only speaks of "love of God" and "love of neighbor" separately. Schnackenburg also reveals that Paul did not make much reference to "love of God" (Rom. 8:28; 1 Cor. 2:9; 8:3; 2 Thess. 3:5), but more to "love of neighbor." One should note that Paul sees love as the highest of all virtues (1 Cor. 13:1–3, 8–13; 8:1) and the greatest of all the gifts of the Spirit (1 Cor. 13). Paul, like Jesus, advocates for love of enemies (Rom. 12:14–21). Furthermore, Christ died for us when we were enemies of God (Rom. 5:8, 10; 8:32), and God and Christ loved us first, even before we loved God. The love that God has for His children made His children inseparable from Him, regardless of the challenges they faced, because "…neither height nor depth, nor anything else in all creation, will be able to separate us from the love of God that is in Christ Jesus our Lord" (Rom. 8:39 NIV). Hence, Paul admonishes Christians to demonstrate Christ's self-sacrificing love by loving each other (Eph. 5:2, 25).[5]

St. Augustine states that the "…fulfillment and the end of all the law and of all the divine scriptures is love."[6] Augustine does not seem to applaud any notion of self-love, but he emphasizes the otherness of love: "…love of the thing which is to be enjoyed, and of the thing which is able to enjoy that thing together with us, because there is no need for a commandment that we should love ourselves."[7] Clearly, for Augustine, love should be for God and neighbor, not necessarily self. Probably, Augustine thinks that by loving God and neighbor, you in turn love yourself. Augustine contends that anyone who fails to understand that love of God and neighbor is the essence of Scripture is ignorant of it. According to him, "…so if it seems to you that you have understood the divine Scriptures, or any part of them, in such a way that by this understanding you do not build up this twin love of God and neighbor, then you have not yet understood them."[8]

Also, Augustine thinks that love is intricately woven with faith and hope:

> If you fall from faith, you are bound also to fall from charity; it is impossible, after all, to love what you do not believe exists. On the other hand, if you both believe and love, then by doing good and complying with the requirements of good morals, you ensure that you also hope to come eventually to what you love.[9]

Hence, "…faith gives way to sight, which we shall see, and hope gives way to bliss itself, which we are going to arrive at, while charity will actually grow when these other two fade out."[10] In the words of St. Paul, "...abideth faith, hope, and charity, these three, but the greatest of these is charity" (1 Cor. 13:13 KJV).

Now we turn to Karl Rahner, who concludes that love of God and neighbor are one and the same reality, and therefore they are equal.[11] It is through this unity of love of God and neighbor that we exist and know God and Christ. According to Rahner, "...the love of God and the love of neighbor are one and the same thing, and that, in this way and in this way alone, we understand what God and his Christ are, and that we accomplish what is the love of God in Christ when we allow the love of our neighbor to attain its own nature and perfection."[12]

Rahner acknowledges that the Synoptic expression of the double command to love God and neighbor is the core and summary of the message of the law and prophets (Matt. 22:40). Rahner cautions, however, that one should not ignore the "eschatological discourses about judgment" in Matthew's gospel, which imply that "love of neighbor" is the only explicit maxim by which people will be judged (Matt. 25:34–46). Furthermore, Rahner highlights that in Pauline thought, though, "love of neighbor" is seen as the touchstone of all commandments, the fulfillment of the law (Rom. 13:8, 10; Gal. 5:14), the bond of perfection (Col. 3:14), and the most excellent way (1 Cor. 12:31–13.13). Rahner articulates that in the tradition of St. John, love of neighbor is seen as the "totality of Christian existence," because humans were first loved by God and Christ (Jn. 15:12) in order that they would love each other (Jn. 13:34). Rahner maintains that love of neighbor is the "new commandment of Christ." The love that God displays toward us, humanity, is not done in order to be returned vertically but horizontally, that we might in turn love one another (1 Jn. 4:7, 11). The essence of God is love (1 Jn. 4:16), and God can only be reached through love. Hence, when we love neighbor, we love God. Therefore, if one cannot love neighbor, who is conspicuous in one's eyes, is it not impossible for one to love God, who is invisible and transcendental (1 Jn. 4:20)?[13]

Rahner believes that love of neighbor is in essence love of God, and that this understanding should be the core of Christian theology:

> The love of neighbor is not merely the preparation, effect, fruit and touchstone of the love of God but is itself an act of this love of God itself; in other words, it is at least an act within that total believing and hoping surrender of man to God which we call love and which alone justifies man, i.e. hands him over to God, because, being supported by the loving self-communication of God in the uncreated grace of the Holy Spirit, it really unites man with God, not as He is recognized by us but as He is in Himself in His absolute divinity.[14]

This leads to Rahner's notion of anonymous Christianity, which articulates that even if someone neither confesses Jesus Christ as Lord and Savior nor has any knowledge of Christianity, that person can still perform acts that can be deemed as expressing love toward neighbor, which for Rahner is equivalent to love of God. Hence, Rahner's argument amounts to saying that one can love God without explicitly believing in God. Love of neighbor, from Rahner's perspective, has both moral and salvific implications:

> This opinion [on anonymous Christianity] states that wherever man posits a positively moral act in the full exercise of his free self-disposal, this act is a positive supernatural salvific act in the actual economy of salvation even when its *a posteriori* object and the explicitly given *a posteriori* motive do not spring tangibly from the positive revelation of God's Word but are in this sense 'natural.' This is so because God in virtue of His universal salvific will offers everyone His supernaturally divinizing grace and thus elevates the positively moral act of man... This opinion states, therefore, that wherever there is an absolutely moral commitment of a positive kind in the world and within the present economy of salvation, there takes place also a saving event, faith, hope and charity, an act of divinizing grace, and thus *caritas* is exercised in this...[15]

Thus, as it relates to human existence and the environment in which we exist, love of neighbor, for Rahner, is the basis and core of human morality. Hence, love of neighbor should be the guiding principle for how humans respond to their own reality and surroundings, because love of neighbor "gives meaning, direction, and measure to everything else" in life. Furthermore, Rahner argues that the wholeness and essence of humanity is fully realized in one's love for neighbor, and that the medium through which God is originally experienced is that of the world and humankind.[16] Rahner maintains that the love of God is concretely manifested in love of neighbor:

> The categorical explicit love of neighbor is the primary act of the love of God. The love of God unreflectedly but really and always intends God in supernatural transcendentality in the love of neighbor as such, and even the explicit love of God is still borne by that opening in trusting love to the whole of reality which takes place in the love of neighbor. It is radically true, i.e. by an ontological and not merely 'moral' or psychological necessity, that whoever does not love the brother whom he 'sees', also cannot love God whom he does not see, and that one can love God whom one does not see only *by* loving one's visible brother lovingly.[17]

Rahner points out that the term "love of neighbor" has become a contemporary catchphrase, just as "faith" was for Paul and "conversion" was for the Synoptic authors. Hence, Rahner believes that it is through humans that God acts in this world, and that humans express their love of God. According to him, "…a natural-supernatural knowledge and love of God of an existentially authentic kind, in which the reality of God is truly experienced, is the very nature of things an act which can only be posited by man as a *whole*…"[18]

We now turn to Karl Barth, whose theology of love of God and neighbor differs from Rahner, in that Barth emphasizes love of God and Rahner love of neighbor. In this context, when Barth speaks of love it is primarily about God, while for Rahner it is about neighbor. Therefore, Barth argues that the Christian life begins and ends with love of God, and that it is love of God that brings us to faith in Jesus Christ. Barth believes that love must be interpreted and understood in light of the fact that God loved us first, which affords us the opportunity to receive God's love and in turn begin to love God. Hence, God's love for humanity precedes the Christian moral life and takes precedence over all—ourselves and interpersonal relationships. Barth further points out that humanity has the capacity to love God, because God first loved us, thus transforming us into children of love through Jesus Christ. Barth contends, however, that this does not make the person supernatural, because loving God is not a divine reality but a creaturely one—in other words, we love God in our humanness. Clearly, for Barth, the love of God—not love of neighbor, as it is for Rahner—stands at the core of the Christian notion of love. God's love for humanity, therefore, is both the basis of reality and the knowledge of Christian love.[19]

Barthian theology maintains that the love of God for us should be the basis of our love for God. While our love for God grows from God's initial love for us, God's love for us is neither conditional nor dependent upon human reciprocity to survive. God, who is love, chooses to love humans unconditionally, not because of anything that humans have done to deserve this love, but as an act of God's unmerited love as Father, Son, and Holy Spirit. This love that God has for us is demonstrated through Scripture and tradition in instances such as His action toward the ancient Israelites (Hos. 11:1, 4; Jer. 31:3; Deut. 7:8; Ps. 11:7) and Christ's action toward all people (Eph. 5:2; Jn. 15:13; 1 Jn. 3:1; Rom. 8:37). God explicitly demonstrated His love for humans in the self-sacrificing act of Jesus Christ on the cross, which gives life and hope to all people (Jn. 3:16). Barth maintains that our love for God is a direct response to God's love for us, and that this understanding should be the canon of Christian living and morality. According to Barth, it is this knowledge that the love commands in the Synoptic gospels (Mt. 22:37; Mk. 12:30; Lk. 10:27, cf. Deut. 6:5; Lev. 19:18) sought to communicate.[20]

Barth, in his exegesis of the passage that contains the love command in Mark's gospel (12:29–31; Deut 6:4, 5), points out that the phrase "hear, o Israel" indicates that the command that follows was not for all people, but it was directed to the people of God, all who are called by God through Jesus Christ. Barth argues that the phrase "thou shalt love" means "thou wilt love," thus making the command to love non-negotiable and necessary for all believers. Barth contends that the phrase "the Lord our God is one Lord" highlights the uniqueness of God. The essence of this refrain is that God, our Lord, is incomprehensible and incomparable. Thus, our Lord can do what no other can do, such as delivering humanity from curse and shame, interceding with the Father on our behalf, suffering in our place, and offering us eternal gifts and promises. Consequently, Barth argues that it is only with love that we can relate to the Lord, because love is the essence of God, and humans' only response to whom God is and what God continues to do for us must be to love God. Barth further points out that humanity can love only through recognition of Jesus Christ as Lord and our dependence on and gratitude to him as our Lord.[21]

The phrase "thou shalt" demands of humankind the fulfillment of the command with the entire being, and "thou shalt love" indicates that humankind has no choice but to love God in obedience to God. Barth believes that love requires a genuine partner, which humans only find in God, because in loving God, we also love neighbor. Unequivocally, for Barth, the command to "love God and to love neighbor" is realized in loving God. Therefore, to love simply means to love God, and to love God means to become God's, to choose God as our Lord, to follow God's commands, to understand and acknowledge God, and to allow love to define our nature and attitude. In addition, Barth points out that to love God is to seek God, and in seeking God we are demonstrating that we love God. We have all the reasons to seek God, providing all that God has done for us in and through Jesus Christ's incarnation, exaltation, redemption, reconciliation, justification, and liberation. We should also seek God because it is God's direction for us—what the love commandment demands—and it represents the fulfillment of the law. God indeed is "a rewarder of them that diligently seek Him" (Heb. 11:6 KJV). Therefore, when we find God, whom we seek, through love, our souls are nourished by the grace that awaits us in God, which is able to address the weakness in us and the need for God that is revealed to us.[22]

Paul Molnar points out some fundamental differences between Rahner and Barth. He writes:

> Rahner undermines any explicit need to believe in Christ through the Holy Spirit *before* discussing God's universal will to save. Rahner believes that a proper understanding cannot be gleaned *solely* from scripture and so he detaches grace from Jesus Christ and the Holy Spirit and locates it in our transcendentality as such.[23]

In contrast, "Barth insists from the very beginning on sticking to an understanding of the Scriptural texts and argues that love of God specifically means seeking God in Christ and that such seeking cannot occur without the miraculous intervention of the Holy Spirit imparting faith...."[24] Molnar further highlights that the main distinction between Rahner and Barth is methodological, with significant material implications. Molnar states:

Rahner begins his theology with our transcendental experience and seeks to appreciate Christian doctrines from within that horizon. Barth steadfastly refuses to ground his theology in experience, though he does not ignore human experience, as it is properly understood in the context of faith, grace and revelation.[25]

Both Barth and Rahner affirm the law of love; they just do so differently. Both Barth and Rahner, taken together, give a complete and thorough understanding of the meaning of love of God and love of neighbor. Taking side with one view in exclusion of the other will limit one's understanding of the double-love command as a whole. Nevertheless, Rahner could be accused of excessively humanizing the love command and Barth of overly divinizing it. A balance between Rahner and Barth could be very promising and useful.

The double-love command does not negate the love of self, as some would argue, but admonishes us to love neighbor as self. It is a given, in all normal circumstances, that a person would love his/herself. The Scripture commands that we should extend to our neighbor the same love with which we love self. Thus, love of neighbor requires a proper love of self. How can someone who hates self, loves his or her neighbor? Self-hate would be contrary to the double-love command, as it explicitly states that we should love others as we love ourselves. It is therefore clear that the double-love command is not advocating self-hate, as some skeptics would argue. Consequently, it is important for each person to have a genuine love of self that is consistent with the double-love command. So, it is safe to say that the double-love command is threefold in nature (as it involves love of God, self, and neighbor). What makes it appear twofold is that love of neighbor and self are one and the same, because the same love distributed to self should be given to neighbor. As mentioned, Rahner thinks that the double-love command is a singular reality, as he espouses love of God and neighbor as one and the same.

Love of self, therefore, should be translated into positive self-worth that is based on God's views of humanity and not on how society and culture often measure humans. God made us in God's own image and likeness (Gen. 1:27) and demonstrated unconditional love for us by sending His only begotten Son, Jesus Christ, to die for us to restore us to a right relationship with God (Jn. 3:16, Rom. 5:8, 1 Pet. 2:9). To God, we are a "priceless treasure, the object of His infinite love" (Rom. 8:38–39; 1 Cor. 6:20), and as a result, God gives great honor to us (Ps. 8:3–5). Contrary to how God views us, society often measures human worth based on wealth, attractiveness, intelligence, education, power, popularity, and accomplishments. As a result, when some people do not measure up to society's standards in some shape or form, they can develop poor self-worth. Other things that could contribute to poor self-worth and self-hate, according to Gary Collins, are faulty theological beliefs, unconfessed sin and guilt, childhood experiences that have taught us to feel inferior, experiences of defeat and failures in our lives, unrealistic self-expectations that we have not met, and self-defeating thoughts (or self-talk). But when people meet society's standards of worth, they can become prideful.[26] Consequently, one should counter these extremes of self-worth (inferiority and arrogance) and self-ostracism with God's view of humanity, outreach through the double-love command, and our practice of the command to love God and neighbor in our daily lives.

Concluding Remarks

Love of God and neighbor is the essence and summary of Scripture, and should be the primal maxim that informs our personal, religious, and social contexts. Hence, it should be the core principle that guides human nature, as our will and actions are influenced by our nature. The weaknesses in human nature are canceled out with the realization and constant practice of the double-love command, and the fundamental goodness in us is perfected when we "love God and neighbor." The antidote for nature's corruption is this love imperative, which restores humanity to God, diminishes humanity's evil inclinations, and buttresses the fundamental goodness in human nature. This double-love command is the foremost message that God communicated through the Torah, Wisdom tradition, Prophetic tradition, Writings, Gospels, other literature, history, reason, and experience. Whenever this double-love command is lacking in Christianity, it is relegated to merely a religious institution without its true sense of purpose and meaning, which in essence could not be considered truly Christian. It should be both the starting and ending points of what it means to be Christian. Anything contrary to love of God and neighbor is not the message of Christ and should not be a fundamental guide to Christian theology and praxis. Our ecclesial structures, when not influenced by this double-love command, can become oppressive, as we often observe. Any proposition that will guide humanity to the proper end must begin, continue, and climax in love of God and neighbor. In addition, we can never fully understand what life in Christ is fully worth, and even attempt to solve contemporary global struggles from a Christian standpoint, unless we understand the imperative to love God and neighbor.

Notes

[1] Schrage, Wolfgang, *The Ethics of the New Testament*, trans. David Green (Philadelphia: Fortress Press, 1988), 68–83.

[2] Ibid.

[3] Ibid.

[4] Schrage, *Ethics*, 84; Schnackenburg, Rudolf, *The Moral Teaching of the New Testament* (New York: Herder and Herder, 1956), 218–20.

[5] Schnackenburg, 218–20.

[6] Rom. 13:8; 1 Tim. 1:5; Augustine, St., *Teaching Christianity*, vol. 1.11, ed. John Rotelle (New York: New City Press, 1990), 123.

[7] Augustine, *Teaching Christianity*, 123.

[8] Ibid., 124.

[9] Ibid., 124–25.

[10] Ibid., 125.

[11] Rahner, Karl, *Theological Investigations*, vol. 6, trans. Karl H. Kruger and Boniface Kruger (London: Darton, Longman & Todd, 1974), 232.

[12] Ibid., 233–34.

[13] Ibid., 234–35.

[14] Ibid., 236.

[15] Ibid., 239.

[16] Ibid., 239–46.

[17] Ibid., 247.

[18] Ibid., 248.

[19] Barth, Karl, *Church Dogmatics*, vol. 1.2, trans. G. W. Bromiley and T. F. Torrance (Edinburgh: T & T Clark, 1963), 371–75.

[20] Ibid., 377–79.

[21] Ibid., 381–84.

[22] Ibid., 385–93.

[23] Molnar, Paul D, "Love of God and Love of Neighbor in the Theology of Karl Rahner and Karl Barth," *Modern Theology*, 20.4 (October 2004): 567–99, 591.

[24] Ibid., 592.

[25] Ibid.

[26] Collins, Gary, *Christian Counseling: A Comprehensive Guide*, 3rd ed. (Nashville, Tennessee: Thomas Nelson Publishers, 2007), 425–40.

CHAPTER TWO

Ethics of Love Imperative

This chapter attempts to develop an ethic of the love imperative. The basic thesis of this chapter is that the love imperative does have ethical implications, and can be used to guide contemporary ethical theories and decision-making. To accomplish this end, it recalls various theories of ethics, such as situation ethics, utilitarianism, Kantian deontological ethics, ethical relativism, and care ethics, and it critiques them in light of the love imperative.

Joseph Fletcher, in his *Situation Ethics*, sought to utilize the principle of love as an ethical methodology that can be used in contextual decision-making. He points out that the two commands in the double-love imperative are indistinguishable. According to him,

> The two commandments in the love Summary are really only one, and the three objects of love (God, neighbor, and self) unite its work; they do not divide it.... If we love ourselves for our own sakes, that is wrong. If we love ourselves for God's sake and the neighbor's, then self-love is right. For to love God and the neighbor is to love one's self in the right way; to love one's neighbor is to respond to God's love in the right way; to love one's self in the right way is to love God and one's neighbors.[1]

For Fletcher, all the laws seen in the biblical text are fulfilled in one statement, "You shall love your neighbor as yourself" (Gal. 5:14). Fletcher points out that in Christian situationism, love for God and neighbor is the only principle or law, and all other laws and principles should serve the principle of love. For situationism, in general, love is the only principle, and all other principles or maxims are relative to the concrete or particular situation or circumstances. Therefore, the most loving thing should be chosen in every given situation. Fletcher's situation ethics is fixated on six propositions:

1) "Only one 'thing' is intrinsically good; namely, love: nothing else at all."
2) "The ruling norm of Christian decision is love: nothing else."
3) "Love and justice are the same, for justice is love distributed, nothing else."
4) "Love wills the neighbor's good whether we like him or not."
5) "Only the end justifies the means; nothing else."
6) "Love's decisions are made situationally, not prescriptively."[2]

John Stuart Mill argues that the theory of the ethics of utility is consistent with the golden rule and love commandments. According to Mill, "...in the golden rule of Jesus of Nazareth, we read the complete spirit of the ethics of utility. 'To do as you would be done by,' and 'to love your neighbor as yourself,' constitute the ideal perfection of utilitarian morality."[3] That which prevents pain or hurt and facilitates happiness the utilitarian considers desirable, and is the goal of utilitarian ethics or morality.

Immanuel Kant articulates that the command to love our neighbor is practical, not pathological (affectionate). Practical love, according to him, rests in the will, and it can be commanded, but pathological love that is seated in the emotions or sympathy cannot. Hence, beneficence for duty's sake is consistent with this understanding of practical love.[4] Kant's supreme principle of morality is the categorical imperative, and the first formulation of his categorical imperative states, "I am never to act otherwise than so *that I could also will that my maxim should become a universal law.*"[5] Critics of Kant's rule-based system of ethics conclude that it is legalistic and stringent, driven by rules not results. In Kant's system, the end never justifies the means, regardless of the situation. Consequently, some of the negative responses to Kant's system of morality is that it usually perpetuates legalism, because it only focuses on the right or wrong of the situation. It does not provide exception to what he calls our notable duties toward others, such as: not to kill an innocent person, not to lie, and not to break promises. In general, following the rules is what matters. Even what some people deem as loving and responsible, if not consistent with the rules, would be considered wrong and immoral in the Kantian school of thought.

Love should inform and be the essence of laws and rules. In other words, law should be crafted and enforced in the context of love for the sake of love, as situation ethics articulates, lest it becomes legalistic and oppressive. When love is missing and is not the object of the law, it is reduced to merely "dos" and "don'ts." Law should afford justice, but when it is not about love, it could be for ill, and distribute injustice instead. Therefore, the rules should be universal, as Kant explains above, but only if they are about love of neighbor.

As it relates to socioeconomic injustice (such as poverty and human-rights issues), Kant's categorical imperative could serve as a powerful tool for developing laws to protect the marginalized and oppressed. It demands that each person considers whether his/her action could be seen as a universal law; if not, such action would have to be thwarted. For example, the inhumane treatment of oppressed peoples around the world could not constitute a universal law because their oppressors would not want to be treated in a like manner. The same is true for inequality and disparity between men and women. Affording privileges on the basis of gender, race, or ethnicity—such as paying males more than females or giving someone a job just because of the person's race—is unjust, because nobody wants to be on the other side of this continuum. Therefore, treating one gender, or race, or class superior to another cannot be held as a universal principle.

Kant's categorical imperative could provide a framework by which humans could govern their actions without prejudice and preference. Everyone—regardless of their gender, race, age, class, or creed—would have to adhere to the same absolutes, and violation thereof should result in consequences applicable to all. There cannot be valid laws, whether overtly or covertly, that favor some and disenfranchise others, and Kant's theory could help avoid this. Every person—regardless of race, class, ethnicity, or religion—should be afforded equal rights and justice, and Kant's categorical imperative has the potential to unequivocally attain this end. Love of God and neighbor, however, should be the universal principle that guides any universal law or rule. Categorical imperatives, however, when not about love, can become oppressive, too.

General ethical relativists charge that no matter how preposterous an act (such as racial bigotry, cannibalism, or cruelty) may seem to another, if it is acceptable and legal in the society in which it occurs, it is morally right. Relativists warn that foreigners' interference with another culture's practices, or any other form of ethnocentrism, is wrong.[6] Should each culture, society, or nation have its own morality or system of right and wrong? Should the laws of one nation be imposed on another? Should the determination of whether an action is right or wrong depend upon the culture and society in which it is done? Is it proper for ethical relativism to deny universal truths?

How can there be any non-ethnocentric reason for torture, rape, genocide, and oppression? How can one nation ignore the human-rights violations and abuses in another because they are acceptable in the eyes of the perpetrators? How can acts of socioeconomic injustice be just in any culture? Ethical relativism breeds selfishness and mere nationalism, and resists globalization at its best. Who or what should determine matters of right and wrong in a society? Acts of injustice anywhere are unjust everywhere. Crimes against humanity and violations of the fundamental rights of a person are wrong everywhere. Nonetheless, the sovereignty of any nation should be respected, as should its cultural peculiarities, norms, and customs. What might seem exotic to foreigners could be inoffensive and acceptable to indigenous people.

Consequently, the theories of general ethical relativism would not do much to address issues like gender inequality and other forms of oppression, because these abuses are often widely acceptable in the contexts in which they are practiced. Some societies think that it is fine for women to receive lower pay than their male-counterparts for the same amount of work done. However, such a practice is unfair not just to women, but to everyone, because when a woman earns what is rightfully due to her, the individual, family, society, and economy benefit more. Also, the relativist would think that it is fine for oppressed peoples, such as the Dalits in India, to be in the state that they are because it is acceptable in India's caste system. If these issues were to be left up to the theory of ethical relativism and unchallenged by reformers, they would continue forever as acceptable norms in the societies in which they are practiced. Consequently, ethical relativism, in many ways, could be seen as inconsistent with the double-love command, because the law of love contradicts any cultural standard that subverts freedom, justice, and basic human rights.

Now we turn to care ethics. Care ethics flows out of the female perspective, unlike other principle-oriented perspectives, focusing on fairness and justice.[7] Although the ethics of caring is feminine in nature, it can be utilized by men.[8] Also, care ethics is relational in nature,[9] with engrossment/empathy at its core—to be engrossed with someone is to feel that person's pain, hurt, and joy.[10] Nel Noddings favors engrossment over empathy; as Michael Slote points out, she views the former as receptive (feminine) and the latter as projective (masculine).[11] Slote, however, values empathy over engrossment and concludes that care ethicists should move "…beyond mere caring to the idea of empathic caring."[12] For Slote, "…empathy involves having the feelings of another (involuntarily) aroused in ourselves, as when we see another person in pain. It is as if their pain invades us…"[13]

The scope of care ethics is limited. As Noddings articulates, it is only possible naturally to care for a limited number of people, those in an immediate relational circle. This, therefore, leads Noddings to reject the notion of universal caring. She asserts, however, that while we cannot "care for" everyone, we can "care about" everyone.[14] This implies that since caring for someone is being engrossed with that person, it is impossible to be engrossed with everyone. Slote and Virginia Held differ slightly from Noddings on this point, as they think that it is possible to care *for* distant others and not just about them.[15] Slote concedes, however, that one will care more for those one is intimate with than those one is merely caring for out of moral requirement.[16]

For the most part, care ethics flows out of natural caring. Noddings highlights two forms of caring: natural and ethical. The former is done almost instinctively—without a sense of ethical demand.[17] The latter requires some effort (not out of duty, though). Noddings argues that natural caring is the most intimate form of caring, and that the impulse we heed to care for another is innate.[18] Noddings articulates that when we care, "…we are engrossed in the other. We have received him and feel his pain or happiness, but we are not compelled by this impulse,"[19] as one can choose not to respond to it.

In care ethics, moral judgments are made out of caring, for the sake of caring, not owing to the dictates of some principles or propositions. As Noddings illustrates, "...when I make a moral judgment I am doing more than simply expressing approval or disapproval. I am both expressing my own commitment to behave in a way compatible with caring and appealing to the hearer to consider what he is doing," and therefore, "...the one-caring is careful to distinguish between acts that violate caring, acts that she herself holds wrong, and those acts that 'some people' hold to be wrong," because "...the one-caring, clearly, applies "right" and "wrong" most confidently to her own decisions."[20] Noddings maintains that care ethics is not preoccupied with whether an action is justified. According to her, "...we are not 'justified'— we are *obligated*—to do what is required to maintain and enhance caring," and therefore, the caring one receives fulfillment when the cared-for receives and completes the cycle of caring not justification.[21] An ethic of caring, therefore, does not rely on set rules or principles—like universal care does, rather doing what caring dictates—being engrossed with the other.[22]

The ethic of caring is other-relating (or is caring about another). It does not separate the one-caring from the cared-for, since the former is engrossed in the latter. Noddings, however, recognizes the unique roles of the one-caring and the cared-for.[23] The ethics of care demands caring actions toward another.[24] Genuine acts of caring:

> Involve an emotional/motivational sensitivity to particular other people. One is concerned about the situation a given person is in, and one's focus is on the individual herself rather than on any abstract or general moral principles that someone might want to consult in order to determine how to act toward that individual.[25]

Finally, an ethic of care is reciprocal in nature, as it requires that one builds and maintains genuinely caring mutual relationships.[26] The one-caring requires that the cared-for receives the care. When the care given is received, it encourages the one-caring to continue caring. There cannot be a healthy caring relationship where those in the relationship do not play their role, as each reciprocates the other.

Peering through the lens of care ethics, the assumption is that love is

Chapter Two: Ethics of Love Imperative

partialistic. Care ethics, therefore, generates a model of love I call partialistic love, because it emphasizes personal care only for those in a given relational circle. Hence, care ethics would not encourage indiscriminate love, yet it does not advocate that we dislike those outside of the immediate relational circle. Therefore, it can further be assumed that partialistic love would have the following salient characteristics: 1) it would be relational in nature, rooted in engrossment/empathy. 2) It would be flowing out of human sentimentality, not rational principles. 3) Its principal and singular goal would be caring, nothing else. 4) Partialistic love would be other-relating, since at the core of care ethics is the notion of being engrossed and/or empathizing with another. 5) Since care ethics is reciprocal, partialistic love would be reciprocal in nature. 6) Like care ethics, partialistic love would not be concerned with welfare, but with relationship building.

It seems rather natural that care flows out of love and that love would be relational, as it definitely connects people and keeps them in relation with each other. It seems exotic for someone to love outside of the context of relationality. The question lingers: Is it possible to love someone and not be engrossed and/or empathizing with the person? Furthermore, having love as a principle that merely guides one's life is profound, but such a view often strips love of its intrinsic sentimentality. Love cannot be merely embedded in reason, as the Kantian school of thought articulates. It is something that is felt and then done. Caring for someone is a natural response to the intensity of love.

Love, then, is the motivation for caring, and when love is offered, it is natural that the love is reciprocated. Usually, the more love that is given, the more love that is received; love has a way of begetting love. Whenever love is not reciprocated, it gradually fades, as people do not naturally perpetuate love for those who will not love them back.

Partialistic love focuses on relationship over welfare, because in a loving relationship, it is impossible not to care about the other person's well-being. It is possible to appear to care about the welfare of others, but to do nothing about it. However, in a relationship, it is natural to protect the welfare of the loved one.

The inherent problem in partialistic love is exclusiveness. If utilized to determine social and public policy, partialistic love would be biased in its distribution of social and economic justice, equal rights, and the creation and application of laws—which would perpetuate discriminatory practices, as patriarchy does. By its very nature, partialistic love favors some and excludes others.

The universal notion of love goes back to the Christian theology of *agape*, which is amplified in the double-love command articulated by Jesus. Universal or inclusive love appears unrealistic when viewed from the perspective of care ethics. Inclusive love assumes the following: that love for everyone is humanly possible, that it is practical to love your enemy as yourself and friends, that love is an action not a feeling, and that an improbable universal vision of love of neighbor is attainable.

The argument that loving everyone is humanly possible implies that it is a human capability to love every other human being, although it does not seem to address the measure of intensity and fervor of love. Jesus Christ, to whom we attribute the Christian notion of universal love of neighbor, however, never seemed to fully realize this love in His ministry and praxis, although it is evident in His teachings and actions. When Lazarus, one of Jesus' friends, died, He wept bitterly and resurrected him from the dead; but when another man desired to follow Jesus but wanted to bury his father first, he was discouraged from doing so, as Jesus told him to "let the dead bury their dead."[27]

Apparently, even Christ appeared somewhat partialistic in His affection. On countless occasions, Jesus appeared to favor Peter, James, and John over the rest of His disciples. Furthermore, Jesus seemed to care more for the twelve who were His travelling companions than for others, as He spent more time with them, was engrossed in them, and was more involved in their personal lives and welfare. Also, Jesus showed preferential love for the poor, oppressed/marginalized, afflicted, and outcasts of society. Perhaps He did not exclude others intentionally; it was probably impossible for Jesus to extend quality care to everyone in His merely physical human body—but this was possible in His supernatural nature. Hence, probably the most He could have done among the masses was to teach and work miracles among them, but not to be engrossed with them. Also, He did not heal every sick person and attend to every need; only a select few—perhaps those who were in direct contact

Chapter Two: Ethics of Love Imperative

with Him and those with whom He was most affectionate—like most people would do naturally.

The love-of-neighbor formula that Jesus used is derivative of the Pentateuch, and as mentioned above, the usage in this context never meant that everyone was neighbor to the ancient Israelites, because only those who were members of the twelve tribes of Israel were considered neighbors. On countless occasions, the God of the Old Testament showed preferential love to the ancient Israelites, and often excluded other nations.

Apparently, both Jesus and the God of the Old Testament demonstrated love and care for those who were their disciples and chosen people, respectively. Even among their selected group, those who followed their commands were included, and those who disobeyed were often castigated and sometimes excommunicated. In Christianity, partialistic love often prevails over inclusive love. Christians are often friends with Christians, and exclude those of other religions. Christians appear even more affectionate toward those in their own congregation.

Love is more than wishing someone well; it requires relationship. It does not seem as difficult to wish everyone well, because there is distance, but to be in a relationship with everyone seems impossible. The reality is that a person may wish the best for someone, but not want to be connected with that person. Relationship building is far more complicated than benevolence. Given the complexity of relationships and that love thrives best in this context, it appears difficult to love everyone, as inclusive love advocates.

One could argue that Christ did many things that unequivocally demonstrated universal love for all people, such as securing salvation for everyone through the paschal mystery. Furthermore, the love that God demonstrated for the ancient Israelites was a shadow of God's universal and transcendental love revealed in Christ for all humanity. Specific cases where Christ and God appeared partialistic in distribution of love were intended ultimately to accomplish inclusive love, as they were mere typologies. In addition, one could conjecture that if inclusive love was not humanly possible, then Christ and God would not require it of humanity. God's love for humanity demonstrated through Christ's passion was irrefutably inclusive love, as God/Christ did this to secure salvation and liberation for everyone, even those who repudiate God/Christ.

The care that partialistic love administers is personal, whereas inclusive love is generalized humanitarian care. This is not to say that partialistic love does not seek the welfare of humanity; it is just not the primary goal. Saying that inclusive love offers both types of care is valid, because to love someone (even a total stranger) as self is personal. Fundamentally, however, it articulates that you love your neighbor not because of any personal attachment, but because you unreservedly care for the well-being of your neighbor. Care ethics, therefore, is concerned with good relationships. Thus, partialistic love would be primarily maintaining good relationships, whereas inclusive love would be more concerned with human welfare and good.

Another point is that the ethics of caring does not necessarily engage justice,[28] although proponents of care ethics, like Slote, articulate that care ethics holds much promise for justice. Inclusive love, however, is explicitly justice-oriented. For example, Fletcher points out that love is justice—they are one and the same—justice is love distributed.

Inclusive love is principle-oriented, while partialistic love is propelled by feelings. On the one hand, both loves are sentimental in nature—what love is not? On the other hand, inclusive love is developed as a universal principle, whereas partialistic love is not; rather, it is relationship-driven. From a partialistic standpoint, love is realized only in relationships, whereas from the inclusive perspective, love is always present, regardless of personal feelings. Partialistic love is realistic and attainable, whereas inclusive love (or universal unconditional love) seems improbable.

Partialistic love and inclusive love, therefore, do share some similarities that are worthy of discussion. Both emphasize unconditional love, the former for those in a relational circle and the latter for all people. There is a way in which both partialistic love and inclusive love are altruistic. Partialistic love expresses selflessness for the one cared-for, and inclusive-love expresses it for everyone, including enemies. Hence, both emphasize love for people, although partialistic love focuses its love on a limited number, whereas inclusive love embraces all people. On the one hand, it seems more practical and measurable to limit love to specific caring relationships, as it seems illusory to distribute love to everybody, as inclusive love demands. Both, however, articulate a love for people, and neither indicates nor encourages loathe for others. Both partialistic and inclusive loves emphasize caring for others and self simultaneously. The one who is engrossed with and/or empathizes with another does not do so in isolation from self. You can only be engrossed and/or empathize with another in as much as "self" is engrossing or empathizing with that person. The same is true for inclusive love: "love thy neighbor as thyself." Neither partialistic love nor inclusive love advocates self-hate, self-aggrandizement, self-disparagement, or self-deprecation. Finally, both loves are rooted in feelings, because love, whether partialistic or inclusive, is affectionate in nature. Proponents of inclusive love, like Kant, however, say that one must love out of rationality or duty even when one does not feel love. This is perhaps the only way one can humanly love one's enemy. However, is this really possible?

When viewed through the lens of care ethics, unconditional love appears partialistic in nature and renders a universal notion of love idealistic. Given the context in which partialistic love is developed, it is able to attain a deeper sense of unconditional love than inclusive love, as it is rooted in engrossment and/or empathy. In reality, this depth of love can only be humanly demonstrated to a restricted number of people. Partialistic love recognizes the human inability to love everyone. It is quite possible to love everyone if it means wishing them well and caring about their welfare, but not being engrossed with them.

Partialistic love, therefore, can accomplish a vision of universal love in the sense that if everyone maintains loving relationships—however small that circle may be—everyone ultimately will be connected by love. If everyone desire for others what they do for those in their relational circle, no one would oppress or seek to marginalize another. A danger with partialistic love is that it is merely pathological. Given the capriciousness of human feelings and sensitivity, it can be difficult for someone to continue loving another when the feeling is not mutual, but unconditional love demands love regardless of feelings.

A vision of unconditional love that intentionally incorporates relationality and welfare holds great promise for shaping social and public policy for the good of all. This integration, however, calls for conditions that secure common good and that which is most loving. The notion of universal relationality could help humanity to exist together better along the lines of gender, ethnicity, race, culture, and religion. Given the challenges of global crises, we need to find a way genuinely to relate to each other so that we can understand and live in relation with each other for the good of each other; but this would demand responsibility and reciprocity. With the inclusion of universal welfare, a just social and economic order could emerge, at least in part, which would result in peace and prosperity.

Concluding Remarks

Ethical theories should be subordinated to and fulfill the objective of the double-love command. The love imperative, therefore, should be the primary imperative that guides human action. Our choices flow out of our nature, and human nature fuels our whole life endeavor, but it needs to function in the length and breadth of the double-love command in order to achieve its proper end. The object of our love is both God and neighbor, not either/or. This love must be demonstrated both vertically and horizontally.

When love is our action, and our response to each other is for the good of each other, the challenges that we face around the world will wane. How can you wage war against those you love? How can you exploit those you love for gain, profit, or pleasure? How can one feel happy when his/her intended action has caused others to be unhappy? How can you discriminate against someone whom you love? Furthermore, both love of God and neighbor work together, so how can you say that you love God but not those who were made in God's image and likeness? How can you say that you love God but refuse to love your neighbor, whom God commands you to love? How can some claim that they love God, yet rape, torture, rob, oppress, and murder the poor and vulnerable? Are those actions not contrary to all that love is?

Finally, the love imperative, love of God and neighbor, results in concrete loving action—that is, doing the most loving thing in any given situation, as Fletcher advocates. Loving action is not contrary to, but is consistent with, righteousness and justice. The laws and rules of any context, however, should be derivative of and subservient to the law of love, because rules and laws are only right when they are serving the greater good: love. Societies, cultures, and religious groups should not just develop strings of "dos" and "don'ts" for merely legalistic and pietistic purposes, but for love's sake, because every imperative—whether of the categorical or relativistic type—should have love as its primal and only goal. Every culture and society (of whatever kind) has its own particularities that should be respected, except when they are in clear violation of love, such as oppressing and dehumanizing people, and destroying creation in general, etc.

Notes

[1] Fletcher, Joseph, *Situation Ethics: The New Morality* (Louisville, Kentucky: Westminster John Knox Press, 1966), 113–14.

[2] In his book, Fletcher explains each of these principles in breadth, but here they are just highlighted to give the reader a snapshot of the basic principles of Fletcher's system. See pages 57, 69, 87, 103, 120, and 134, respectively.

[3] Mill, John Stuart, "Utilitarianism," in *Morality and Moral Controversies: Readings in Moral, Social, and Political Philosophy*, 7th Edition, ed. John Arthur (Upper Saddle River, New Jersey: Pearson Prentice Hall, 2005), 67.

[4] Kant, Immanuel, "The Fundamental Principles of the Metaphysics of Morals," in *Morality and Moral Controversies*, ed. John Arthur (New Jersey: Prentice Hall, 2005), 58.

[5] Ibid., 59.

[6] Shaw, William, "Relativism in Ethics," in *Morality and Moral Controversies*, ed. John Arthur (New Jersey: Prentice Hall, 2005), 37–40.

[7] Noddings, Nel, *Caring* (Berkeley: University of California Press, 2003), 1.

[8] Ibid., 2, 8.

[9] Ibid., 6.

[10] Ibid., 9, 17. Slote interprets Noddings' usage of engrossment in like manner: "Someone who cares deeply or genuinely about someone else is open and receptive to the reality—the thoughts, desires, fears, etc.—of the other human being. When they act on behalf of (for the good of) the person they care about, they don't simply impose their own ideas about what is good in general, or what would be good for the individual cared about. Rather, they pay attention to, and are absorbed in, the way the other person structures the world and his or her relationship to the world—in the process of helping that person," *see* Slote, Michael, *The Ethics of Care and Empathy* (New York: Routledge, 2007), 12.

[11] Slote, *Ethics of Care and Empathy*, 12.

[12] Ibid., 16.

[13] Ibid., 13.

[14] Noddings, *Caring*, 18, 28–29.

[15] Held, Virginia, *Feminist Morality: Transforming Culture, Society, and Politics* (Chicago: University of Chicago Press, 1993), 223, *and* Slote, Michael, "Agent-Based Virtue Ethics," *Midwest Studies in Philosophy*, 20.1 (September 1995): 83–101, 97, 101, cited in Slote, *Ethics of Care and Empathy*, 11.

[16] Slote, *Ethics of Care and Empathy*, 11, and Noddings, Nel, *Starting at Home: Caring and Social Policy* (Berkley: University of California Press, 2002), 21–24.

[17] Noddings, *Caring*, 80.

[18] Ibid., 248.

[19] Ibid.

[20] Ibid., 91–92.

[21] Ibid., 381–84.

[22] Ibid., 385–93.

[23] Molnar, "Love of God and Love of Neighbor in the Theology of Karl Rahner and Karl Barth," 591.

[24] Ibid.

[25] Slote, *Ethics of Care and Empathy*, 10.

[26] Ibid., 11

[27] Still, some scholars argue that the man's father was alive and doing well at the time. This therefore allows some to conclude that the man was only avoiding a commitment rather than making one.

[28] Slote, *Ethics of Care and Empathy*, 11.

PART II: HUMAN PROCLIVITY

Human nature is doomed without love

Whenever human nature is not guided by the love imperative, its fundamental goodness is suppressed and imperiled by selfishness and callousness. Conversely, love brings out goodness in our nature that springs from the image and likeness of God innately imprinted in us. Love does not hinder nature from attaining its goal—the pursuit of happiness—it only helps nature to achieve real and responsible happiness. Love also guides nature to choose what is right and just, because whenever those are lacking, injustice sets in and brings with it nothing but unhappiness and pain.

CHAPTER THREE

Human Nature

This chapter shows that human nature is at the core of human existence, and it impacts our manner of choice and decision-making. Here, three perspectives are explored. One is Augustine's doctrine of Original Sin, which articulates that sin has tarnished human nature since the fall of Adam in the Garden of Eden. The other two perspectives, egoism and natural law, are articulated by Thomas Hobbes and Thomas Aquinas respectively. Each of the three perspectives engages human nature from a different point of view, but they all imply that human nature has a profound effect on humanity, for good or ill.

Human nature influences human reason, will, emotions, physiology, society, and culture. Etymologically, the term "nature" originated from the Latin word *natura*, which is equivalent to the Greek *physis*, which in a general sense means "…the essence of every existent which comes to it from its very origin…the principle of the development of a thing, the inner foundation of its action and passion…every existent has its own nature, including man and even God himself (but in God excluding all imperfection)."[1] Also, there is a sharp distinction between "natural" and "supernatural" in that "…the natural [or nature] includes everything that belongs to a created thing, either as an integral part (soul, body, intact limbs), or as a property, inclination or power flowing from it (intellect, will)…"[2] God, therefore, is creator of nature. In addition, nature is "…the state of man and of all visible things as this state develops by itself out of the laws of nature and as it renews itself ahistorically in the eternal cycle of generation and corruption."[3] Dagobert Runes defines human nature as "…the limited range of human possibilities. The human tendency toward, or the human capacity for, only those actions which are common in all societies despite their acquired cultural differences."[4] To what extent did sin damage human nature? Did Adam's sin affect the fundamental goodness in human nature? Does human nature have both good and evil inclinations?

A. Original Sin

Augustine, in his doctrine on Original Sin, differentiates between human nature and nature's corruption. The former is fundamentally good, but the latter is evil. Human nature comes from the abundance of our creator, but nature's corruption flows from the condemnation of humanity's origin. Human nature seeks to carry out the good will of the supreme God, but nature's corruption seeks to enact the depraved will of the first Adam. Human nature recognizes God as creator of humanity, but nature's corruption highlights God as punisher of humanity's disobedience. Nature's corruption is the product of Adam's sin, and as a result carnal generation holds humanity ransom. Thus, nature's corruption taints every person; even a child who is born to parents who have been regenerated in Christ is a sinner and only can be redeemed from his/her sins through God's grace.[5]

Augustine refutes Pelagius' and his followers' claim that Adam's sin only affected him and not his offspring (the entire human race). Pelagius' argument renders infants at birth in the same perfect state as Adam prior to the fall.[6] In contrast, Augustine maintains that regenerated parents do not give birth to faithful children, but to sinners. Only through "spiritual regeneration" can humans be liberated from nature's corruption. Spiritual regeneration is made possible through Christ's redemptive work on the cross, which is available to all people, even before they enter this world. God's grace awaits each person, and it can only be received volitionally by anyone who desires it.[7] Augustine further reasons that even those persons who were righteous or obedient to God throughout the ages, prior to the incarnation of Christ, are redeemed

Chapter Three: Human Nature

through Christ,[8] because God's grace is before the foundation of the earth.

Augustine maintains that God did not condemn humanity because of human nature, but because human nature is disgraced. Therefore, human nature is not destroyed because of its fault; it is still fundamentally good. The ill in humanity, however, is due to nature's corruption, and nature's corruption is a result of the human will to choose evil volitionally. According to Augustine:

> God, therefore, condemns man because of the fault wherewithal his nature is disgraced, and not because of his nature, which is not destroyed in consequence of its fault.... What, then, is there surprising or unjust in man's being subjected to an impure spirit—not on account of nature, but on account of that impurity of his which he has contracted in the stain of his birth, and which proceeds, not from the divine work, but from the will of man...[9]

Human nature will be completely regenerated of its corruption, however, in the eschaton (eschatological reality), the eternal reign offered through Christ. Now we are regenerated in part because nature's corruption still lingers and may cause us to perform sinful acts that plague our souls with guilt.[10]

Regardless of the dichotomy that Augustine makes between nature and its corruption, nature is still affected by corruption. Therefore, it is impractical to see how the corruption in nature does not affect nature itself. On the one hand, Augustine's argument implies that human nature cannot fully overcome its weaknesses in this life, even after it is redeemed by the grace of God. On the other hand, his argument does not assume that the grace of God is unable to redeem human nature completely in this life. Augustine's point that human nature is fundamentally good is seen concretely in human goodwill and benevolence.

Reinhold Niebuhr, in response to Augustine's doctrine on Original Sin, points out that Original Sin is not a part of humanity's essential nature, and therefore it is not out of the realm of humans' responsibility.[11] Sin, according to Niebuhr, proceeds from the defect latent in the human will (choice), not human nature. Therefore, Niebuhr argues that sin cannot be attributed to any inherent corruption in human nature, as the doctrine of Original Sin articulates. Consequently, there is a sense of responsibility that Niebuhr's argument demands humans should assume for their evil actions, as human nature is neither stained with nor predisposed to evil. In other words, a person only sins when he/she chooses to do so, but not because sin and evil is a necessary component of human nature.[12] Furthermore, Niebuhr argues that sin is not inherent in human nature, but in societal structures and contexts. Therefore, both Niebuhr and Walter Rauschenbusch think that through social action humans can transform their social structures and contexts, which perpetuate sin and evil.[13]

Anthropologist Ashley Montagu refutes Augustine's doctrine on Original Sin from the standpoint of human educability. Montagu holds that humans are the most educable of all creatures, because everything a person knows is taught to him/her. Unlike other creatures that function with little or no training due to their instinct, humans have to be educated about everything. Therefore, it is against this backdrop that Montagu makes the claim that evil is not inherent in human nature, but in human nurturing. Montagu points out that a human in infancy knows no ill, and it is through environmental influences that a person develops evil tendencies. Consequently, Montagu's argument vindicates human nature of all weaknesses, evil tendencies, and sins that many throughout the centuries widely ascribed to it and instead places the blame squarely on human nurture. Montagu argues that a human possesses two natures. Montagu calls the human nature that is from genetic endowment "primary potential nature," and this nature, according to him, is seen overtly in infants, and it is free of all evil. The human nature that is shaped by our environment, "secondary human nature," is the nature that imprints evil tendencies in people. Hence, humans, except for during infancy, mostly function out of their secondary nature, not their primary nature. For example, Montagu argues that tendencies like aggression toward another are not innate but are the product of our nurturing.[14]

Humans have to take responsibility for their surroundings, however, because they are often what we make them. Thus, the virtues and vices that we learn from parents, neighbors, society, and culture are fruits of humanity's own cultivation. Walter Brugger points out that culture is created by humans and is a product of human action. According to him, "…culture…is that which man makes out of himself and out of his environment by means of intellectual planning and shaping and it is that wherein he actualizes himself as a historical existent in order to achieve an even more perfect development."[15]

Stephen Duffy reasons that contemporary biblical scholarship and science challenge the literalistic and historicized perspective of the Genesis 1–3 account, the premise for the doctrine of Original Sin.[16] According to Duffy, advancements in genetics and DNA studies challenge the credibility of the doctrine of Original Sin. Some sociobiologists argue that the notion that humanity, prior to the fall, was in a perfect state—immune to pain, devoid of moral struggles, and immortal—is at odds with the theory of evolution because evolution sees the human "specie" as evolving and developing progressively. Therefore, this argument implies that the most perfect state of humanity would not have been in the past and lost in the fall, as the doctrine of Original Sin indicates, but it would be in the present and future, as all "species" are constantly evolving into a better state as time progresses.[17]

Furthermore, sociobiologists also argue that human proclivity to evil is not exclusive to human beings, but this tendency is also seen in nonhuman animals because they share the same ancestors (not Adam) with humans. According to this school of thought, both humans and nonhuman animals display vicious tendencies for the purpose of promoting their own survival and reproduction (the self-perpetuation of their genetic line). Sociobiologists surmise the inclination to perpetuate self that both humans and nonhuman animals share as selfishness, which they posit at the core of the existence of both humans and nonhuman animals.[18] Therefore, this argument assumes that vicious tendencies seen in human nature are not due to Adam's sin, as the doctrine of Original Sin portrays, because these predilections are also evident in nonhuman animals, which are not Adam's progeny. Hence, sociobiologists conclude that because humans and nonhuman animals share certain traits, they are both from the same "specie". This would be some "species" other than Adam, because nonhuman animals did not come from Adam.

Richard Dawkins argues that humans instinctively seek to preserve their genes, and that it is from their genes that all their behavior flows. Hence, the human being is tenaciously selfish and seeks self-preservation. Therefore, the selfishness in humans is not due to Adam's sin, as the doctrine of Original Sin purports, but is a result of the legacy of genetic evolutionary development.

This selfishness at the core of the human gene is so powerful that it supplants human freewill and desire to do good.[19] Duffy, however, rejects this claim. According to him, "...the ontology and the moral life and struggle of the human animal cannot be whittled down to genetic program," and "...neither can a narrow focus on gene survival do justice to the full range and complexity of human motivations, nor to the impact of mind and culture on behavior."[20]

Furthermore, Duffy points out that humans get their moral sense from reason, but human reason is often manipulated and distorted by selfishness and sinfulness. As a result, humans do not always do what reason dictates—that is, that which is true and good—but rather the opposite to fulfill latent selfish desires. Therefore, the moral sense in humanity, according to Duffy, is tainted by the human inclination toward evil.[21] Duffy maintains, however, that humans have the ability to transcend genetic, biological dispositions, the agenda of Darwinian natural selection, and the proclivity for selfishness and evil. This transcendence, Duffy argues, is vividly seen in human choice and the display of agape love, nonviolence, asceticism, and a preferential option for the poor and oppressed.[22] Hence, a human is not bound by the confines of genetics and reason, because these are subjected to the human will. This is so because a person can and often does manipulate and alter the dictates of reason's prudence and genetic predispositions.[23] Factors other than biological inheritance that incline a human to selfishness are finitude, superego, culture, and the distance between a human and God,[24] yet the inclination to do good is still present in humans. Thus, Duffy concludes that humans are inherently limited and subject to making mistakes and errors, and our actions to do both good and ill are influenced by the values impressed upon our moral consciousness through our orientation, parents, society, and culture.

On the one hand, sociobiologists are not entirely at odds with the Augustinian doctrine on Original Sin, because both schools of thought agree that genetics influence human nature. The sociobiologists' claim articulates that both the human and nonhuman animals share the same ancestor, while the Augustinians' claim differs. From the Augustinian perspective, the human and nonhuman animals share the same creator, but not the same ancestor. Hence, human inclinations, like animal instincts, are transferred through genes, but the two are not the same. Unlike animal instincts, human inclinations can be modified through reason and Christ's redemptive grace. On the other hand, sociobiologists' evolutionary claim that a human was not initially made a human being—but evolved into a human being over the course of time—is at odds with the doctrine of Original Sin. One cannot deny that nonhuman animals share some traits with humans, such as procreation, survival, and vital organs, but that does not annex them to the same "specie," as sociobiologists claim.

D. J. Harrington and J. F. Keenan both contend that sin is a result of human failure to love God, neighbor, and self.[25] The implication of their argument is that when the double-love command is not appropriated in human lives, we transgress against God, and repentance would be to return to love. This argument further implies that evil persists simply because people refuse to love, for, where love resides, evil is absent.

B. Egoism

Thomas Hobbes articulates that human nature possesses the qualities of good, evil, will, felicity, equality, and diffidence. Hobbes describes good as object of human desire and evil as the object of human dislike. Deliberation has to do with weighing humanity's appetite, aversion, hopes, good, and evil in light of the affirmative and/or negative consequences thereof, thus leading to a decision. The will is that which determines human action. Felicity or happiness is the product of one's success and the motivation of the will. Therefore, human beings continually do things to attain success, which brings happiness. In addition, Hobbes argues that due to the fact that all humans are created equal, each person seeks the same end, that is, the survival and conservation of self. Consequently, having the desire for the same end or resources to survive puts people at odds with one another, because each person is always trying to survive the other.[26] Hence, there is diffidence (mistrust) among humans, and this ultimately sparks war among people, as we are threatened by each other and constantly competing for the survival of self. This line of argument echoes the old adage that the fittest of the fittest survives. According to Hobbes:

And from this diffidence of one another, there is no way for any man to secure himself, so reasonable, as anticipation; that is, by force, or wiles, to master the persons of all men he can, so long, till he see no other power great enough to endanger him: and this is no more than his own conservation requireth, and is generally allowed.[27]

Therefore, Hobbes' principal causes for quarrel in human nature are: 1) competition, which is the reason a person "invades" another for gain—to succeed, prosper, and survive over another; 2) diffidence, the mistrust of others, which awakens the need for security and protection of self in an individual; and 3) glory, the reputation each person likes to build because humans like to be exalted and honored.[28]

Hobbes believes, however, that humans also possess the desire for peace, and this desire for peace comes from humans' fear of death and need for commodious living. Therefore, in order to attain peace among humans, Hobbes articulates that human action should be guided by what he calls three principal laws of nature.[29] Hobbes' first law of nature is the right of nature (*jus naturale*), or self-preservation. This principle contends that each person has the right to use his/her own power or that which is necessary for the preservation of his/her self.[30] Hobbes' second law of nature is the mutual covenant, which states "…that a man [should] be willing, when others are so too, as far-forth, as for peace, and defense of himself he shall think it necessary, to lay down this right to all things; and be contented with so much liberty against other men, as he would allow other men against himself."[31] The third principle is justice, and it is that which ensures "…that men perform their covenants made: without which [justice], covenants are in vain, and but empty words; and the right of all men to all things remaining, we are still in the condition of war," and therefore injustice is the nonperformance of covenant.[32] Hobbes further points out that in order for the laws of nature to work in the interest of all parties involved, a commonwealth is required. He defines a commonwealth as a person or assembly in which those in the covenant (a community or nation) invest their rights and authority to execute justice on their behalf for the common good of all.[33] According to Hobbes, "…covenants, without the sword, are but words, and of no strength to secure a man at all."[34] Therefore, Hobbes thinks that the following formula should be used in surrendering rights to a commonwealth:

> I authorize and give up my right of governing myself, to this man [or woman], or to this assembly of men [and/or women], on this condition, that thou give up thy right to him [or her], and authorize all his [or her] actions in like manner. This done, the multitude so united in one person, is called a commonwealth, in Latin Civitas. This is the generation of that great Leviathan, or rather, to speak more reverently, of that mortal god, to which we owe under the immortal God, our peace and defence.[35]

Clearly, Hobbes' argument indicates that a human being is intrinsically inclined to protect and preserve self, even at the expense of another human being, because humans are inherently selfish. This basic drive for self-preservation is common to all humans, which, along with other factors, could keep humans in prolonged conflict with each other. Consequently, the laws of nature need to be enforced by a commonwealth for the good of the whole. A commonwealth has both advantages and disadvantages, however. On the one hand, it could help to keep people in check and enforce fundamental principles to benefit the whole. One the other hand, a commonwealth is often imperfect, and investing absolute power in a person or assembly can be dangerous, because as the old adage says, "absolute power corrupts absolutely." Examples of this can be seen in broken governments and leaderships across the globe, where a people or nation invests its trust in a leader or assembly, and that trust is later violated for the benefit of the leader or leading core.

Therefore, while the core of Hobbesian self-preservation seems plausible, it reduces human nature to mere selfishness. It does not encourage altruism and "love of neighbor," but self-aggrandizement. Probably, Hobbes' theory is an explanation for inequity between the rich and the poor, as some who are powerful continue to enrich themselves at the expense of the weak. Some individuals and nations are "filthy rich," yet others are ravaged by absolute poverty and lawlessness.

Michael Ridge interprets Hobbes' concept of a commonwealth using public and private reason. Ridge reasons that Hobbes' idea of a commonwealth indicates that the human community would supplant private (individual) reason with public reason, which would help to avoid conflict among humans that springs from human nature. Public reason, Ridge argues, is the will of a commonwealth, public person or sovereign in which the community invests its authority to arbitrate on its behalf. This unchecked authority given to a sovereign individual, however, can degenerate into abuse of power and work to the detriment of the masses.[36] Ridge's alternative to the Hobbesian approach is the establishment of public principles that would supersede Hobbes' proposed unrestrained authority. These public principles that Ridge proposes are intended to be enshrined laws that would govern both the public leader and the people that he/she leads. Hence, both the leader of the people and the people themselves would have to subject their reason to these common principles.[37] David Gauthier also proposes modifications to Hobbes' idea of a commonwealth. Gauthier, a supporter of Hobbes' theory, proposes that this authority (commonwealth) that Hobbes favors could be most effective with some modifications that include limiting the scope and content of the authority given to the public person.[38]

Therefore, the benefits of establishing public principles over subjecting the community to the will of an individual or assembly are more rewarding because public reason should be guided by ideals that represent the best interest of the public and not the will of an individual who leads the public. Also, established principles or codes could both serve the will of the people and protect them from a tyrant that the Hobbesian idea of a commonwealth could easily create. When codes govern everyone, including public officials, clearly defined principles are available for people to reference, and there is less potential for the emergence of a dictator. In addition, the Hobbesian approach does not seem psychologically feasible, in that the public, in this approach, would have to constantly reorient itself to the changes that would take place when one public leader replaces another, because each public leader would have his or her individual reason and idea of governance.[39]

Nancy Stanlick sees friendship in Hobbesian thought, which of course is counter to the usual rendering of Hobbesian self-interest and minimalistic morality that represents human nature as warlike, brutal, envious, and selfish.[40] This friendship is demonstrated in Hobbes' emphasis on language, family, and protective associations, and the need that each person has for

Chapter Three: Human Nature 43

community. Hobbesian thought maintains that human nature has the tendency for both war and peace, and therefore Stanlick argues that language can serve to attain commodious living and cooperation among humans, and could avert war and promote peace. Stanlick further shows that family plays a significant role in Hobbesian thought, and can only be sustained through "long-term protective association" among its members, which would eventually bring the family peace and security.[41] In other words, Stanlick is arguing that humanity's survival can best be preserved through family units and associations, rather than by mere individual effort. While humans seek other associations from one another, Stanlick reasons that the need each person has for others is self-serving in the end because self-preservation is primary, and humans secondarily seek the society of others for profit or honor in business, pleasure, recreation, and so on.[42]

C. Natural Law

Thomas Aquinas posits that every human being possesses in his/her nature what he calls natural law, and that natural law imprints in humans the inclination to "do good and avoid evil." Therefore, humans should volitionally yield to this natural inclination toward good and away from evil. According to Aquinas, "…since good is grasped as always desirable, the first premise in reason's planning of action is that good is to be done and pursued and evil avoided."[43] This fundamental principle, therefore, should guide all human predilections, such as self-preservation, fulfillment of basic drives and needs, and the exercising of rational nature (which makes humans different from other animals).[44] Aquinas further points out that since humans have a rational tendency toward doing good, every wrongdoing is unreasonable and militates against human nature.[45] This innate desire in humans to do good is imprinted and stimulated by God.[46] The natural law in humans helps them to seek the common good, and natural law is influenced by God's eternal law.[47] The volition to pursue and do what is good and avoid evil is the product of human reason. Although humans are directed to attain the end of good, they have a choice between good and evil. There is no clearly defined prescription to do good, but this determination is made through the faculty of reason. The concept of good is not exclusive to an individual; rather, it is common to all and is attainable through reason.[48]

Aquinas argues that the human inclination to do good and avoid evil is demonstrated in the desire to preserve self, satisfy drives and needs (e.g. sexuality and procreation), seek the truth, and share in community. Humans share the first two goods with other creatures, but the last two are exclusive to humans. Good, therefore, should be pursued by humans rationally, deliberately, and responsibly; these demands can only be met with the aid of human rationality, which other creatures do not share because they only possess what is called instinct.[49] What Aquinas therefore means by "good" or "goodness" is that which all beings seek to attain from their actions,[50] and this is what the first principle of practical reason demands of every human being.[51] Hence, the pursuit of good is the ultimate path for humanity.[52] In concrete terms, some of Aquinas' constituents of human good are wisdom, justice, temperance, and courage—all aimed at attaining the ultimate end: good.[53] Finally, Aquinas sees two external forces operative in human action: God and Satan. God instructs humans by His law to do good, and Satan, through temptations, influences humans to do evil. Humans, therefore, have both the volition and natural inclination to do good, a tendency found in human reason in what is called natural law.[54]

Clearly, Aquinas' conception and postulation of natural law exonerates human nature of any inherent impediment. This principle assumes that human nature is fundamentally good, but it does not acknowledge the existence of evil in human nature; it acknowledges that evil exists and can affect humans negatively if chosen. Hence, in Thomistic thought, evil would be extrinsic and not intrinsic to human nature in any shape or form. The problem with Aquinas' natural law theory is that it romanticizes human rationalism, in that it does not take into consideration that just as humans are rationality inclined to do good, they are also inclined to do ill. If reason did not have an inclination toward evil, it would not be influenced by evil, only good. As a principle, the notion to do good and avoid evil is well-received. Good and evil are the only possible outcomes of human action; here it is either/or, not both/and; therefore, in every case, good should always be chosen over evil.

Concluding Remarks

The above perspectives on human nature unanimously agree that goodness exists in human nature, either in part or in whole. Augustine sees human nature as good, but also thinks that nature's corruption, due to the fall, taints human nature. Hobbes' egoism primarily sees human nature as fundamentally enslaved to self-preservation. Aquinas' idea of natural law does not see any flaws in human nature, but rather sees it as inclined to do good and avoid evil. Hence, it seems plausible to conclude that human nature has both good and evil tendencies. The good in human nature is often demonstrated in our benevolence and altruism toward our neighbor. In contrast, human nature is at its worst when engaged in acts such as war, violence, crime, discrimination, oppression, and marginalization of neighbor.

Consequently, if we change everything in and around us but do not transform human nature, nothing is fundamentally changed because our actions, which are influenced by our nature, will eventually make things revert to how they were. Real changes occur in our nature; hence, in seeking to make our lives and world better, the things we do should be those that help to change our nature for good. A transformed human nature, therefore, results in a changed self, community, and world.

In perfecting the fundamental goodness in human nature and restraining the weaknesses thereof, our nature must be transformed by love. Therefore, human nature needs to be redeemed through faith in Christ/God in order to address nature's corruption and perfects its fundamental goodness. The faith articulated here is Christian faith. The goal of human nature is happiness, and by this, I mean fulfillment, not necessarily hedonistic cravings. Human nature makes demands on us in various forms, and when these demands are met, we feel a sense of happiness or fulfillment from our actions. However, when they are not met, we often feel the opposite. There are various ways through which we seek fulfillment, as nature demands of us, and these could account for why we do what we do. Since human nature has the tendency to seek fulfillment by whatever means necessary, it must be guided by the maxim of love.

The double-love command in the teachings of Jesus should be that which guides all of nature's demands in all situations. Nature cannot be allowed to do as it pleases in every circumstance, even when it is redeemed through faith in Christ/God, because the redemption that we have is only partial, and in the fullness of time we will attain it in its entirety. Hence, love must be at the center and core, guiding human nature and subsequent actions. The double-love command is not averse to the rule of law and justice, but is consistent with them in their purest state. Socioeconomic injustice is a product of human vice, which is not a derivative of the double-love command and the dictates of righteousness and justice. One cannot deny that most people are marginalized and oppressed not because of their own choosing. Their nature desires happiness, not the unhappiness that injustice causes. Clearly, people are often marginalized and oppressed due to the greed and cruelty of others. Unequivocally, human nature yearns for happiness and freedom of self, and such goals cannot be attained through the exploitation of others. The fundamental goodness in human nature is also perfected in our benevolence and goodwill toward our neighbor, and is suppressed when we do otherwise.

Notes

[1] Brugger, Walter (ed.), *Philosophical Dictionary*, trans. Kenneth Baker (Spokane, Washington: Gonzaga University Press, 1974), 271–72.

[2] Ibid., 273.

[3] Ibid., 272–73.

[4] Runes, Dagobert D, *The Dictionary of Philosophy* (New York: Philosophical Library, 1942), 132.

[5] Augustine, St., *Saint Augustin's Anti-Pelagian Works,* vol. v, trans. Peter Holmes and Robert E. Wallis (Grand Rapids, Michigan: WM. B. Eerdmans Publishing Company, 1994), 250–51.

[6] Ibid., 237–41.

[7] Ibid., 252–53.

[8] Ibid., 247–49.

[9] Ibid., 254.

[10] Ibid., 253.

[11] Niebuhr, Reinhold, *The Nature and Destiny of Man: A Christian Interpretation*, vol. 1 (New York: Charles Scribner's Sons, 1964), 242.

[12] Ibid., 242–44.

[13] Rauschenbusch, Walter, *A Theology for the Social Gospel* (Louisville, Kentucky: Westminster John Knox Press, 1997), especially 38–94. Niebuhr, Reinhold, *Moral Man and Immoral Society: A Study*

in Ethics and Politics (New York: Charles Scribner's Sons, 1960).

[14] Montagu, Ashley, *Anthropology and Human Nature* (New York: McGraw-Hill Book Company, 1957), 28–42.

[15] Brugger, *Philosophical Dictionary*, 272–73.

[16] Duffy, Stephen, "Genes, Original Sins and the Human Proclivity to Evil," *Horizons* 32.2 (2005): 210–34, 210.

[17] Ibid., 214–15.

[18] Ibid.

[19] Ibid.

[20] Ibid., 216–17.

[21] Ibid., 218.

[22] Ibid., 222.

[23] Ibid., 224.

[24] Ibid., 225–31.

[25] Harrington, Daniel J. and James Keenan, *Jesus and Virtue Ethics: Building Bridges Between New Testament Studies and Moral Theology* (Maryland: Sheed & Ward, 2002), 93, 100–03.

[26] Hobbes, Thomas, "Leviathan: Morality as Rational Advantage," in *Morality and Moral Controversies: Readings in Moral, Social, and Political Philosophy*, ed. John Arthur, 7th ed. (Upper Saddle River, New Jersey: Pearson Prentice Hall, 2005), 2–3.

[27] Ibid., 3.

[28] Ibid.

[29] Ibid., 4.

[30] Ibid., 4–5.

[31] Ibid., 5.

[32] Ibid., 6.

[33] Ibid.

[34] Ibid., 7.

[35] Ibid.

[36] Ridge, Michael, "Hobbesian Public Reason," *Ethics* 108 (April 1998): 538–68, 538, 541.

[37] Ibid., 540.

[38] Ibid., 539.

[39] Ibid., 552–53.

[40] Stanlick, Nancy, "Hobbesian Friendship: Valuing Others for Oneself," *Journal of Social Philosophy* 33.3 (Fall 2002): 345–59, 345–47.

[41] Ibid., 347–50.

[42] Ibid., 350–51.

[43] Aquinas, St. Thomas, *Summa Theologiae*, ed. Timothy McDermott (Westminster, Maryland: Christian Classics, 1989), 287.

[44] Ibid.

[45] Ibid.

[46] Ibid., 281.

[47] McInerny, Ralph, *St. Thomas Aquinas* (Notre Dame, IN: University of Notre Dame Press, 1982), 63.

[48] Ibid., 64.

[49] McInerny, Ralph, *Ethica Thomistica* (Washington DC: The Catholic University of America Press, 1997), 45.

[50] Ibid., 43.

[51] Ibid., 42.

[52] Ibid., 46.

[53] Ibid., 47.

[54] Torrell, Jean-Pierre, *Aquinas's Summa,* trans. Benedict Guevin (Washington DC: The Catholic University of America Press, 2005), 33.

CHAPTER FOUR

Happiness

At the core of human nature is the desire for happiness. Happiness is more than mere laughter, joy, or hedonism. The word *happiness* is used in this chapter in terms of fulfillment. Humans constantly seek fulfillment and satisfaction, because when it seems like we have explored it all and attained it all, there is still more that we need to bring us the fulfillment that our nature desires. Therefore, this chapter articulates that happiness is the principal goal of human nature. When human nature, however, is not guided by the double-love command, happiness could be meaningless and destructive.

Qoheleth, the writer of Ecclesiastes, sets out to discover the goal of life, and concludes that there is nothing more to do in life but to eat, drink, and be merry. Jill Middlemas compares and contrasts Ecclesiastes with the movie *Sideways*. According to Middlemas, "*Sideways* with its exploration of the theme of the pursuit of human happiness resonates with the Old Testament quest for the same through the principle of wisdom."[1] Middlemas concludes that in *Sideways*, "…the ultimate goal of the characters was not joy, but instant gratification. It is a bleak portrait of self-absorption. In contrast, the biblical book of Ecclesiastes includes all of human activities within a divine sphere."[2] She paints a sharp contrast between the pursuit of happiness in Ecclesiastes and *Sideways*:

> Ecclesiastes insists that the recognition of the Divine is necessary to the fulfillment of life. In so doing the ancient sage of Ecclesiastes provides a much needed corrective to the modern pursuit of happiness

as characterized in the movie *Sideways* and, indeed, as found within the prosperity theology so prevalent in modern Western society.[3]

In order to fully understand Qoheleth's thoughts on responsible happiness, one has to explore his motivations and the actions that led him to the conclusion that happiness is the goal of life. In the second verse of the first chapter in Ecclesiastes, the writer points out that "everything is meaningless," and "utterly meaningless."[4] In successive verses, Qoheleth supports this claim with statements such as, "nothing changes," "the sun rises and sets," "the wind blows here and there," "the river runs into the sea but the sea is never filled," and "water flows in the river from rainfall and springs." This connects with a broader argument Qoheleth makes that nothing in life is new, because all that we see has already existed in some shape or form, as history merely repeats itself. Thus, nothing in life is truly new; we just experience an old thing in a new way.

Hence, for Qoheleth, life is not only mundane but meaningless, because the goals to which he devotes his life turn out to be futile. For example, Qoheleth devotes his life to the pursuit of wisdom and knowledge, only to find out that the expansion of his knowledge increases his sorrow, and as a result, he concludes that wisdom is meaningless. According to him, both the wise and the fool have the same fate—they both die and will be forgotten—so what is the point of wisdom? As for the pursuit of pleasure and hedonism, Qoheleth concludes that those too are meaningless. When he examines his work and all that work affords him, he concludes that it is also meaningless: for the fruit of his work that he attains with much wisdom, knowledge, and skill, he will one day leave to people who have not labored for it; they might not be good stewards, as well. This he considers both foolish and highly unjust.[5] Qoheleth concluded that everything that he attained was meaningless: wisdom, knowledge, pleasure, popularity, rewards from work, wealth, etc.

Qoheleth concluded after his mammoth task to delineate meaning in life, that life is meaningless, vain, and empty, and therefore we should enjoy life in the present for all that it is worth.[6] So what is the goal of life? What should we do each day? Qoheleth recommends "enjoyment," admonishing that there is nothing better for people to do on earth than to "eat, drink, and be merry."[7]

Chapter Four: Happiness

Various passages throughout the book of Ecclesiastes reflect this admonition to enjoy life.[8]

Qoheleth's emphasis on enjoyment led Roger N. Whybray to dub him the "preacher of joy."[9] Leo G. Perdue argues that the literary structure of the book of Ecclesiastes is constructed around the sevenfold occurrence of the phrase "carpe diem," the enjoyment passages. Perdue observes that the form of the first five enjoyment passages is declaration based on personal experience, while the last two are second and third person admonitions. Perdue attributes this shift in rhetoric from "personal reflection to admonitory tone" to Qoheleth's discovery that enjoying life is the sole value of human living and his intent to convey this truth to his learners.[10] Ronald E. Murphy points out that because Qoheleth recognizes the finality and inevitability of death, and recognizes that it is only in the control of God, he promotes enjoying life, either in revolt or acceptance of the reality of life and death.[11] Qoheleth recommends not naïve pleasure-seeking, but seasoned enjoyment in the context of companionship, feasting, and work in God.[12]

Furthermore, Qoheleth believes that happiness or enjoyment should be consistent with the creator and the creator's commands to humanity, because our central duty is to serve God and keep His commands (Ecc. 12:13). Everything—including wisdom, knowledge, pleasure, and wealth—comes from God, who gives to those who please Him. Not living for God alienates one from God, while living for God keeps one in connection with God. Life in itself appears meaningless, but without God it is catastrophic.

Some scholars argue that Qoheleth uses his poem "Under the Sun" to express that life on earth without God is meaningless, but with God it has meaning and fulfillment. By sharing this understanding that he obtained from his quest, Qoheleth sought to help his audience find meaning in life. Therefore, true meaning and fulfillment is in God and not from dependence on self.[13] Martin Shields contends, however, that Qoheleth never intended to use the meaninglessness of existence in "Under the Sun" as the basis for advocating a life of "faith in God," as some scholars assert, but that "…because God's ways are impenetrable to us, we ought to make the most of whatever situation we find ourselves in" under the sun.[14] Given the overwhelming evidence in Ecclesiastes, however, one cannot ignore that the poem "Under the Sun" aims to show what life is worth in God and how meaningless it is without God;[15] hence, the best way to live life "Under the Sun" is in God.

Aristotle articulates that happiness is the goal of life, and external things such as wealth and friendships help to complete happiness. Consequently, Aristotle believes that everything in life aims at some greater good or reality, even arts and science. Happiness is the highest of all practical goods. Happiness, however, means something different for the masses. The masses often equate happiness with "doing well" in life; personal meanings of happiness vary among the masses depending upon individuals' particular circumstances. According to Aristotle, the masses consider happiness:

> To be something visible and palpable, such as pleasure, wealth, or honor; different people, however, give different definitions of it, and often even the same man gives different definitions at different times. When he is ill, it is health, when he is poor, it is wealth; if he is conscious of his own ignorance, he envies people who use grand language above his own comprehension.[16]

Some philosophers hold that there are diversities of goods, but happiness is a fundamental good that all seek, and this is the primary reason for all goodness. Aristotle explains that members of Plato's school of thought "… have held that, besides these various goods, there is an absolute good which is the cause of goodness in them all."[17] Still, Aristotle is convinced that a person's conception of happiness is influenced by the vocation and lifestyle of that person.

Aristotle identifies three kinds of lifestyles in his day: sensual, political, and cerebral. The sensual lifestyle was practiced by vulgar persons who conceived happiness to be pleasure and sought a life of enjoyment. The political lifestyle involved persons who were seen as cultivated and energetic, and associated happiness with honor because honor was seen as the overall goal of political life. However, Aristotle thinks that virtue—instead of honor—should be the primary goal of political life. A caveat that Aristotle inserts is that a person might have political clout or virtue, but bears terminal illness; this leads one to wonder what kind of happiness such a person could really attain. The lifestyle of thought had to do with a more reasoned and balanced life of virtue. Furthermore, a life that is consumed with seeking wealth cannot be considered happy. Wealth, he argues, should only be used as a means to an end, not as the end. He contends that it would be more reasonable to take sensual pleasure, honor, or virtue as ultimate end, than wealth.[18]

There are multiplicities of goals in life, but they are not the ultimate end. For example, while the destined tangible end of medicine is health; architecture, a house; strategy, victory; those are not ultimate ends. Not every end or goal is final, but should lead to the ultimate end of happiness. According to Aristotle:

> Happiness more than anything else answers to this description. For happiness we always desire for its own sake and never as a means to something else, whereas honor, pleasure, intelligence, and every virtue we desire partly for their own sake (for we should desire them independently of what might result from them), but partly also as means to happiness, because we suppose they will prove instruments of happiness. Happiness, on the other hand, nobody desires for the sake of these things, nor indeed as a means to anything else at all…[19]

Therefore, Aristotle concludes that happiness is the supreme good. The best way to define happiness further is by determining what is considered the special or distinct function of mankind. He reasons that it could neither be life, because humans share life with plants and animals, nor nutrition or growth, because all living organisms share those. It could not be sensation, because humans share this with all other animals. The only characteristic that mankind does not share with any other living organism is our active rational faculty. Humankind's rationalism, Aristotle argues, is twofold: one part is obedient to reason, and the other exercises reason and intelligence.[20] Happiness is attained through a person's rational pursuits in life. A noble person enjoys noble actions, which are pleasant and virtuous. Acts of virtue are pleasant in themselves, and therefore "…happiness then is the best and noblest and pleasantest thing in the world…."[21]

Furthermore, happiness does not function on its own, because it requires external goods, such as friends and wealth. Aristotle states:

> For it is impossible, or at least difficult, to do noble deeds with no outside means. For many things can be done only through the aid of friends or wealth or political power; and there are some things the lack of which spoils our felicity, such as good birth, wholesome children, and personal beauty…happiness seems to need prosperity

of this kind in addition to virtue. For this reason some persons identify happiness with good fortune, though others do so with virtue....[22]

Aristotle further claims that happiness can only be attained by a mature person (not by children and animals) because it requires complete virtue and life.[23] Bad fortune and various atrocities can impede happiness, but if a person bears these with grace and dignity, such a person could attain happiness despite these obstacles. He notes, "Still, even in these circumstances, nobility shines out when a person bears with calmness the weight of accumulated misfortunes, not from insensibility but from dignity and greatness of spirit."[24] Hence, happiness is gained from what we do—that is, the noble and virtuous life we live. Therefore, a happy person is "...one who is active in accord with perfect virtue and adequately furnished with external goods, not for some chance period of time but for his [or her] whole lifetime..."[25]

Concluding Remarks

The foregoing perspectives on happiness are plausible. Where I differ slightly from Qoheleth and Aristotle, however, is that while they see happiness as the goal of life, I see it as the goal of human nature. Arguably, one can conclude that the goal of nature is the goal of life because the nature in us constantly moves us in the direction of happiness, or fulfillment, which is significant to the point of living. Although both Qoheleth and Aristotle believe that happiness is the goal of life, they do differ on how this goal should be attained. For Qoheleth, happiness should be attained through merely eating, drinking, and merriment, while Aristotle believes that it is accomplished through everything that we do: work, study, family, etc.

Notes

[1] Middlemas, Jill,"Ecclesiastes Gone 'Sideways,'" *The Expository Times* 118.5 (2007): 216–25, 217.

[2] Ibid., 221.

[3] Ibid.

[4] Ibid., 218. Qoheleth, the author of Ecclesiastes, concludes after careful examination of life that it is *hebel*, emptiness, meaningless, or even hot air. See Scripture references such as 1:2, 14; 2:1, 11, 15, 17, 19, 21, 23, 26; 3:19; 4:4, 7, 8, 16; 5:10; 6:2, 4, 9, 11; 7:6; 8:10, 14; 11:8, 10; 12:8. *Hebel* is used more than thirty times through this book in relation with the phraseology "Chasing after the wind." Other sources that explain the meaning of *Hebel* include Fox, Michael V., "The Meaning of Hebel for Qoheleth," *JBL* 105.3 (1986): 409–27, and Davis, Ellen F., *Proverbs, Ecclesiastes, and the Songs of Songs* (Louisville, KY: Westminster/John Knox Press, 2000), 166–69.

[5] 2:17–23.

[6] Middlemas, "Ecclesiastes Gone 'Sideways'," 218.

[7] Ibid., 219; 8:15; 9:7–10.

[8] 2:24–26; 3:12–13, 22; 5:17–19; 8:15; 9:7–10; 11:9–10.

[9] Dell, Katharine J., Margaret Baker, "Qoheleth, Preacher of Joy," in *Wisdom: The Collected Articles of Norman Whybray* (Burlington, VT: Ashgate, 2005), 141–52, cited in Middlemas, "Ecclesiastes Gone 'Sideways'," 220.

[10] Perdue, Leo G., *Wisdom & Creation: The Theology of Wisdom Literature* (Nashville, TN: Abington Press, 1994), 237. *See* carpe diem passages in note 8 above.

[11] Murphy, Ronald E., *The Tree of Life: An Exploration of Biblical Wisdom Literature* (New York: Doubleday, 2002).

[12] Middlemas, "Ecclesiastes Gone 'Sideways'," 221.

[13] Shields, Martin A., "Ecclesiastes and the End of Wisdom," *Tyndale Bulletin* 50.1 (1999): 117–39, 118; Murphy, Ronald E., *Ecclesiastes* (Dallas: Word, 1992), xlviii–lvi.

[14] Shields, "Ecclesiastes and the End of Wisdom," 118–21.

[15] Ibid., 119.

[16] Aristotle, "Nicomachean Ethics," in *Morality and Moral Controversies: Readings in Moral, Social, and Political Philosophy*, ed. John Arthur, 7th Edition (Upper Saddle River, New Jersey: Pearson Prentice Hall, 2005), 51.

[17] Aristotle, *Ethics*, 51.

[18] Ibid., 52.

[19] Ibid.

[20] Ibid.

[21] Ibid., 53.

[22] Ibid.

[23] Ibid.

[24] Ibid.

[25] Ibid., 54.

PART III: CHRISTIAN FAITH

Christian Faith is about love, nothing else

The love imperative is both the starting point and goal of Christian theology and faith praxis. As a result of God's love for humanity, Christ came to redeem human fallen nature from evil inclinations and restore it to its former goodness prior to the fall. God's love, when received through conversion from sin to grace, perfects goodness in our nature, as it radiates the image and likeness of God innately in us. Conversion is a response to God's love. When people heed God's love through the Spirit's convictions, they are born into God's love. The love of God in us allows us to be formed and transformed, that is, to mature and grow in the grace of God; thus, we are moved from one stage to another in perfect love. Physiological and psychological maturation does not dictate the born-again believer's spiritual growth and development, as the Spirit's working is not confined to these. This, however, does not alter humans' natural progression toward physical death, but it redeems the fallen soul. It guarantees the soul immortality or eternal life. There is a responsibility on each believer to live his/her life in the present to inherit this promised eternal bliss that God's love affords. At the core of personal spirituality and piety is that propulsion daily to live the fruits of the Spirit, avoid the works of the flesh, continue in entire sanctification, and operate as prophet, priest, and king.

The gifts of the Spirit are given to the believer to perform Christian service. We serve one another with our gifts and callings in love. There are diverse gifts and manifestations, but all are given by Christ and the Spirit to serve neighbor. When we serve neighbor, we also demonstrate love for God. The Christian believer is also called to care for and demonstrate Christ's love to all people, not just fellow Christians, regardless of their differences. Hence, an authentic faith praxis would not allow one to sit by without much care for the oppressed, victimized, and hurting around us. The temptation is to leave social issues like poverty to the state or government, or boxing ourselves into an unrealistic sacred and secular dichotomy, but God's love obligates the church to care unconditionally. Finally, the goal of Christian faith and praxis is the love imperative. All that we do in our faith persuasion individually and corporately, therefore, should be for love's sake, nothing else.

CHAPTER FIVE

Conversion

The Genesis account articulates that humanity was created perfect and that it was through disobedience of God's command that human nature became tarnished. This account maintains that humans were created in the image and likeness of God (Gen. 1:26–27), possessing attributes, such as reason, understanding, perception, ability to choose, etc.[1] God acknowledged that everything He made was good (Gen. 1:12, 18, 21, 25, 31): natural light, sun, moon, and stars (Gen. 1:3–5, 14–16); firmament (Gen. 1:3–5); sea and dry land (Gen. 1:9, 10); grass, herbs, and trees (Gen. 1:12); sea creatures and birds (Gen. 1:20, 22); earthly creatures (Gen. 1:24); and man and woman (Gen. 1:26, 28; 2.7, 21). After creating Adam and Eve, the first human beings, however, God commanded them not to "eat of the tree of the knowledge of good and evil" (Gen. 2:16–17), but they did (Gen. 3:4–6).

The consequence that followed their rebellion was severe and tarnished their nature (Gen. 3:14–19). As a result, humanity became vulnerable to sin and evil that they did not know or struggle with prior to the fall. Adam and Eve, and all their progeny (the human race) became sinners, and therefore can only be redeemed through Christ (Rom. 5:12–21). Adam's fall is the reason all people are "born in sin and shaped in iniquity" (Ps. 51:5), struggle with a carnal nature (Rom. 7:14–24), and have a need for Christian conversion.

A. Definition and Identification

The term *conversion* is rooted in the Hebrew word *subh* and the Greek words *epistrepho/epistrephe* and *metanoeo*. *Subh* means to "turn" or "return."[2] William Holladay's research on the term *subh* shows that the ancient writers, especially the prophets, made over 1050 uses of the verb *subh* or words associated with it, and that it appears more in Jeremiah than any other Old Testament book.[3] Stanley Grenz reveals that *subh* is usually used in the context of "…turning away from evil to God in repentance or the turning from God to evil in apostasy."[4] *Metanoia* means "repentance," and its verbal form, *metanoeo*, means "to repent."[5] The term *epistrepho* means a change of personal beliefs or ways.[6] Daniel Aikin points out that "…in only one case is *epistrepho* used in the NT of a believer "returning" to obedience and faith—when Peter "turned back" after denying Christ (Luke 22:32)."[7]

Grenz further suggests that in some cases, *metanoeo* and *epistrepho* are used interchangeably (Acts 3:19; 26:20), yet they are unique and distinct terms. *Metanoeo* seems to highlight "…the negative impulse of turning away from sin…"[8] And the term *epistrepho* is used in a broader sense, sometimes including the idea of faith and hence referring to the entire conversion process.[9] Both terms, however, seem to imply that repentance is a significantly volatile matter, a turning or change within human nature.[10] The *Westminster Dictionary of Theological Terms* defines the Latin word *conversion* as "turning around," and theologically defines conversion as "…one's turning or response to God's call in Jesus Christ in faith and repentance. It is profound in its effects in that it radically transforms one's heart, mind, and will."[11]

There are two general typologies of conversion in Christianity, Platonic and Aristotelian.

Platonic:
In Christian thought, St. Augustine is said to be the embodiment of the neo-Platonic school that speaks of conversion as that radical, instantaneous change that occurs in a person's nature, which suddenly takes a person from sin to grace. From reading the *Confessions*, one could get the impression that Augustine's personal conversion occurred over a substantial period of time,

Chapter Five: Conversion

until at once, it finally culminated in a dramatic experience in a particular time and place. Frank Flinn's perspective on the neo-Platonic model of conversion is that:

> [This] model is based on the idea of Plato and the neo-Platonic Augustine that the soul is something like a spiritual eye which attains perfection by turning away from the images and shadows of temporal life toward the eternal and unchanging realties ('Ideas', 'God'). This understanding of the soul lends itself to an interpretation of conversion as a sudden event and an escape from time. This model lies behind many accounts of being suddenly 'born again' and many psychological models of conversion as a climatic event resulting from some sort of life crisis.[12]

This Platonic and neo-Platonic Augustinian paradigm of conversion seems to be the hallmark of Protestant theology and praxis of conversion, which is strikingly evident in contemporary Evangelicalism and the Pentecostal/Charismatic movement. The understanding that conversion is instantaneous leads the community of faith always to expect that instant radical move of God in a person who seeks salvation. Oftentimes, persons are directed to pray a simple prayer, petitioning Christ to forgive them their sins and to enter into their hearts. Immediately after that prayer, they are often accepted into the Christian community as changed persons.

The problem with this model is that it does not emphasize conversion as an ongoing experience. Undeniably, the instantaneous model of conversion has been widely used throughout the centuries, and has yielded lasting results based on the many notable testimonies of its effect. Yet it still seems lacking, and could be balanced or strengthened with the model of ongoing conversion, in that, after that sudden or drastic change in a person's life, there is the need for further changes, ongoing spiritual growth and development. Also, prior experiences can lead a person to that conversion epiphany that could be seen as a part of the conversion experience as a whole.

Aristotelian:
This second conversion typology follows the Aristotelian school of thought and the ideas of Thomas Aquinas. Unlike the former, this model

views conversion as a process. According to Flinn:

> The second model follows Aristotle's and Thomas of Aquinas' understanding that the soul is the principle of growth in all living things by which they attain completion and fruition. In this view all living things have souls, even the lowly acorn within which resides a green 'fuse' that gives rise to the whole oak tree. The soul is not a[n] Archimedian lever for hoisting oneself out of time but the life fulfilling meaning of time itself. Conversion in this light is not a sudden event but a turn toward the next stage in the cycle of growth; it is a process of ordered stages.[13]

The understanding here is that a person grows from stage to stage in conversion, and that conversion is not an event, rather an ongoing spiritual growth process that changes and shapes the believer's life over a period of time. This is in keeping with contemporary human psychological growth and development theories. (Later I will show that human-faith development is consistent with models of human physiological and psychological growth and development, which involves various stages as well.)

B. Classic Conversion Experiences

Here I will discuss four separate conversion experiences that mirror the Platonic and Aristotelian conversion models: the Apostle Paul, St. Augustine, Martin Luther, and John Wesley. Paul was a devoted Jew who was later converted to the Christian faith, St. Augustine was a pagan who was converted to the Christian faith, Martin Luther was a Roman Catholic who became converted to a new brand of Christianity, and John Wesley was an Anglican priest who remained in his own Christian tradition as he started the Methodist movement after having a renewed conversion. Paul and Augustine were converted from outside into the Christian tradition, while Luther's and John Wesley's conversions took place within the Christian tradition, as they were already operating as ministers.

Prior to Paul's conversion experience, he was known as one of the most notorious persecutors of the church. Many Christians were massacred and slaughtered by this staunchly religious Jew. While Saul (later Paul) was on

Chapter Five: Conversion

his way to Damascus to continue his execution of Christians, he had an encounter with Jesus Christ that changed his life forever, and this is recorded in Scripture as his conversion experience. Immediately after this experience, Saul changed from a persecutor of Christians to a fellow brother and follower of Christ. Scripture records Paul's conversion experience in this manner:

> And as he journeyed, he came near Damascus: and suddenly there shined round about him a light from heaven. And he fell to the earth, and heard a voice saying unto him, Saul, Saul, why persecutest thou me? And he said, Who art thou, Lord? And the Lord said, I am Jesus whom thou persecutest: *it is* hard for thee to kick against the pricks. And he trembling and astonished said, Lord, what wilt thou have me to do? And the Lord *said* unto him, arise, and go into the city, and it shall be told thee what thou must do.[14]

After this experience that radically changed Paul's nature, he renounced his evil tendencies toward Christians and traveled around the then-world, preaching and teaching love of God and neighbor, oftentimes under excruciating circumstances.

St Augustine's *Confessions* reveals that prior to being converted, he struggled with the idea of becoming a devoted Christian, because of his sinful appetites. Hence, Augustine confesses that after he perused the hidden depths of his soul and squeezed its damning secrets from it, and placed them squarely before the eyes of his heart, a tsunami occurred within him, bringing with it a great flood of tears.[15] In that moment, as he continued to reflect on his life, he agonized and questioned the grip that sin had on him, which caused him each time to shun the conviction to be converted for another time. Hence, he constantly asked himself: why is it that he is unable to turn from a life of sin?[16] Finally, after Augustine's years of searching and attempts to be converted to God, there was this one striking moment that caused him to be converted instantly. He further describes this experience as occurring suddenly in the midst of the moment when he was weeping over his sins. He recounts hearing the singing voice of a child in a nearby house, urging him to take up the Scriptures and read. He then quickly ceased crying and responded to the divine command to open his Bible and read the first passage on which his eyes should fall.[17] As he came to the end of reading this passage, Rom.

13:13–14, it was as though a light of confidence gushed into his heart and all his sins and doubts were instantly taken away from him.[18]

Clearly, after the reading of this passage of Scripture and the experience that accompanied it, Augustine was a changed man and had no desire for the former "fleshly" things prior to his conversion. His mother, who was a devoted Christian, was overjoyed when he told her of his conversion—her prayers were finally answered, and visions she had of him came to past. He became rooted and grounded in the "rule of faith."[19]

Consequently, Augustine's strikingly instantaneous yet progressive conversion experience changed him forever into a devoted Christian. Even though Augustine emphasizes his instantaneous conversion experience in his *Confessions*, his testimony also implies that this was happening over a period of time, and at once culminated into one dramatic conversion experience.

Martin Luther's *Turmerlebnis* experience changed his life and changed the face of Christianity significantly. Luther was a Roman Catholic, Augustinian monk, and a Biblical scholar at the University of Wittenberg, and his dramatic conversion was a profound change that he referred to as his *Turmerlebnis* or "tower experience." Luther's conversion caused him to become convinced that the core of the Christian message was Paul's teaching on "justification by faith alone," and as a result, he argued that our relationship with God is not sustained by human action but by the gracious act of God in Jesus Christ. Luther's conversion and newly found conviction radicalized him to take drastic action, and consequently he prepared and posted his famous "Ninety-Five Theses," which led to his excommunication from the Roman Catholic Church. Finally, Luther's conversion experience helped to form the bedrock of what would later be called Protestantism, and raised the consciousness of Roman Catholics to the theology that justification is by faith alone, not by works.[20]

John Wesley, prior to his conversion experience at Aldersgate Street, was a fervent and devoted minister—an Anglican priest in the Church of England—yet he states that he was not truly converted until that episode.[21] Despite Wesley's commitment and Christian devotion prior to his Aldersgate experience, he recounted such as not being apart of his real conversion. For Wesley, his real conversion took place on Aldersgate Street on May 24, 1738.

Chapter Five: Conversion

Wesley chronicles his conversion experience as instantaneous. In a moment, his life was changed forever as a result of an extraordinary encounter with the Divine that Wesley describes. He recounts his conversion in accord with an evening when he reluctantly attended a meeting on Aldersgate Street. While there, someone at the meeting read aloud Luther's Preface to the Epistle of Romans, and something happened in his heart that caused him to completely trust Christ for salvation and gave him an unwavering assurance that his sins were all forgiven.[22]

This experience led Wesley to differentiate between two groups of Christians: the "almost" Christians and the "real" Christians. In a sermon he pointed out that the former excels in morality, apply the means of grace, has a genuine desire to serve God, but lacks saving faith and love of God and neighbor, while the latter does all the above.[23]

Interestingly, the conversions of Augustine, Luther, and Wesley were influenced by the book of Romans, which is believed to have being written by the Apostle Paul. Also, the underlying theology of Christian conversion in the Protestant Christian tradition is Pauline in nature.

C. Historicity

Christian conversion during the medieval era mainly evolved from Christianization of Jews and Muslims to a monastic lifestyle and to intra-Christian conversion.[24] As time progressed, however, people were not only moving from one brand of Christianity to another, but were being converted from sin to grace via the various denominations following the Reformation. Luther's disgust with the Roman Catholic practice of indulgences and its doctrine of justification put him at odds with the tradition, and this signaled one of the first major shifts in Christianity, particularly within the church in the West, which initiated Protestantism.[25] Following Luther's conversion were other intra-Christian conversions and shifts, which resulted in numerous denominations, such as the Lutherans, Calvinists, Anabaptists, Anglicans, later Puritans, Presbyterians, Methodists, Congregationalists, Baptists, Quakers, etc.[26]

As Protestantism evolved and developed, it formulated a pattern of conversion that its various denominations adopted. This pattern emerged primarily from the Reform movement in Puritan England during the sixteenth century, and in the American colonies in the seventeenth century. This pattern involves conviction of sin, acknowledgement of one's need for Christ, an experience of redemption and salvific assurance, and a commitment to live out the ideals of Christianity.[27] Therefore, one is considered to be a Christian when one experiences and heeds the conviction of the Holy Spirit, recognizing one's sins and admitting that Jesus is the Redeemer, and invites Jesus into one's life as personal Lord and Savior. This process gives the individual an assurance of faith in Christ, and this assurance ushers the new believer into living a victorious life of faith in Christ.

In some Protestant Christian traditions, conversion is used synonymously with the term "new birth." Therefore, the person who is converted is referred to as "born again," and the one who experiences this new birth is born of the Spirit, for the Spirit indwells a sanctified life in Christ.[28] Now, I will turn to the four major awakenings that occurred in the Protestant tradition in America, which have global implications and help to illuminate contemporary perspectives of Christian conversion.

The first awakening (CE 1735) sets the stage for the other subsequent awakenings, and would make an indelible mark on America's religious outlook. In other words, it can be called the primal awakening. The leaders who orchestrated this awakening were Jonathan Edwards, the Presbyterian pastor in Northampton, Massachusetts, and George Whitefield, a British Anglican pastor.[29] There are various traits that characterize the first awakening: 1) it was interdenominational, including the Presbyterians, Dutch Reformed, Lutherans, Anglicans, and Methodists; 2) it was interracial; 3) it spreads across the English-speaking world; 4) it involved the outpouring of the Spirit; and 5) its emphasis on the born-again experience helped to shape the American Protestant belief system.[30]

The second awakening, in the 1820s, was accompanied by much emotionalism and the phenomena of being induced or subdued under the unction of the Spirit. According to Flinn:

Chapter Five: Conversion

> [The second awakening] set[s] the pattern of tent revivals which still take place in the southern and western states. The triggering event was the Cane Ridge Revival in Kentucky (1805), during which there was rampant emotionalism including 'barking,' 'falling' and mass singing...The 'falling' phenomenon later came to be known as 'being slain in the Spirit.'[31]

Consequently, "...the conversions resulting from the Revivalist Awakening are properly called evangelical: salvation comes solely through the cross of Christ. While reliance on the Bible was upheld, the principal stress was and is on repentance of sins and 'standing up for Christ.'"[32] Flinn also points out that the Methodist movement played a pivotal role in this awakening, for, according to him, "...many luminaries of the Second Awakening, including [Charles] Finney himself, were much influenced by the Methodist Holiness movement."[33] This awakening's postmillennial eschatological awareness led to acts of social transformation in America and probably around the world in preparation and anticipation of Christ's second return at the end of the millennium. Flinn states that:

> The Second Awakening, like the first, was post-millennial in its belief. Adherents believed that the 'surprising work of God' had begun in America and that Christ would return at the end of the millennium spoken of in Revelation 20 and 21 to crown the work of the Spirit. Hence both awakenings contributed to the progressive and reformist spirit which marked much of the nineteenth century: prison reform, abolition, temperance and suffragist movement.[34]

The Third Awakening, in the 1880s, was marked by Christian fundamentalism, which gave rise to the Fundamentalist movement, and has its origins in the post-Civil War period that was riddled with failed hopes. Key figures in this movement were Dwight Moody, A. J. Gordon, and James Hall, who were informed by John Nelson Darby's dispensational teachings that placed human history in seven dispensations: 1) the age of innocence, when humans were in the Garden of Eden prior to the "fall," as seen in the Genesis account; consequently Christ was sent to rescue humans from Adam's sin. Darby further taught that the second coming of Christ could be anytime, which meant that Christ at any time could come and snatch away the true believers in what is called the Rapture. The millennium reign would follow, and the events of the last days, according to the book of Revelation. Then would come in the following order 2) the Antichrist, 3) Armageddon, 4) the loosening of Satan for a brief season, 5) the restoration of Israel, 6) the last (white throne) judgment, and 7) the descending of a new heaven and earth.[35]

The theological viewpoints held by adherents of the Third Awakening, or the Populist Revival, are as follow: 1) they were premillennialists; 2) "they took on strict doctrine," like interpreting the Bible literally, the virgin birth, sacrificial atonement, miracles, and so on; 3) they had a pessimistic view of the world as evil and unworthy of saving; 4) soul winning was pivotal; and 5) conversion meant saving people from this world or preparing people for the Rapture.[36]

The Fourth Awakening is said to be currently unfolding in America. There are many forms of this awakening, and aspects of it tend to reflect the postmodern mind-set that permeates the world today. Flinn points out that this awakening includes movements such as the rise of the new religions; the introduction and rise of various Eastern religions; the integration of Buddhism, Confucianism, and Christianity; and the rise of the "religious right," which can be termed as the neo-Fundamentalist Awakening. Groups that are associated with the religious-right movement, to name a few, are the Moral Majority, the Christian Coalition, Focus on the Family, and the Promise Keepers.[37] Though the neo-Fundamentalists are premillennialists, they do differ from the Darbyites:

> Unlike the first wave, the neo-fundamentalists seem to be abandoning the pre-millennialist agenda of Darby. Instead of expecting the Second Coming at any moment, they are entering the political fray (almost exclusively on the Republican side) in order to make their views a part of the social policy of the nation. A side effect is that some neo-fundamentalists are beginning to abandon the religious chauvinism and racism that marked the Populist Revival. In brief, they are showing signs of beginning to look like the reformist (and 'liberal'!) Second Awakening.[38]

Pentecostalism shares more of the traits of the Third Awakening than the

Chapter Five: Conversion

other awakenings, but finds its biblical foundation primarily in the events of Acts 2, which is referred to as the first outpouring of the Spirit upon the church. The early Pentecostals sought for an outpouring of the Spirit upon the church of their day that resembled what the early Christians experienced on the day of Pentecost. This outpouring of the Spirit on the believers is seen as baptism in the Holy Spirit, which is one of the distinguishing marks of Pentecostal conversion. The one who receives Christ as personal Lord and Savior is cleansed from sins and later receives the baptism of the Holy Spirit. Pentecostals, like most Evangelical or Mainline Protestant believers, agree that conversion is initiated by repentance and faith in Jesus Christ. Early Pentecostals may differ from other Protestant groups, however, in terms of their belief in Spirit baptism, with speaking in unknown tongues being the initial evidence of having being Spirit-filled. After being filled with the Spirit, a person is endowed with various charisms to serve in the body of Christ.

Contemporary Pentecostal understanding of conversion was initiated by the Azusa Street revivals, which William J. Seymour started in a home at 210 North Bonnie Brae Street in Los Angeles on April 9, 1906. While Seymour was preaching, seven persons received the baptism of the Spirit and began speaking in unknown tongues. The movement was later transferred to 312 Azusa Street in a former Methodist church. A wave of Pentecostal conversion in the United States and across the world followed the Azusa revivals, and today the Pentecostal/Charismatic movement is the fastest-growing in Christianity.[39] Kilian McDonnell highlights six elements that contribute to the tremendous growth in Pentecostal conversion: "ideology of experience," "closing of the ideal-real gap," "vocation to witness," congregational-missionary-activities, urgent-eschatological-emphasis, "the economics of conversion," and the "healing apostolate."[40]

Flinn points out that, "…the spread of Pentecostalism to the mainline denominations is now generally called the charismatic movement."[41] This is in part attributed to the Full Gospel Business Men's Association (FGBMA), whose meetings are attended and supported by various denominations, such as traditional Pentecostals, Baptists, Presbyterians, Episcopalians, Methodists, Lutherans, and Catholics.[42]

There is no striking difference between traditional Pentecostalism and the Charismatic movement, for, in reality, both movements are one and the same, with few minor differences, such as the charismatics' emphasis on the charism of discernment, building the body of Christ, and the psychological and personal benefits that they receive from their relationship with God. Those benefits Pentecostals emphasize as well, but probably the more striking difference is Pentecostals' explicit emphasis and praxis of *glossolalia* (speaking in tongues), and anticipation of the literal manifestation of extraordinary charisms like healing and miracles.[43]

Karla Poewe argues that many of the elements in Augustine's conversion in his *Confessions* are amplified in Pentecostal/Charismatic conversion.[44] Poewe's parallel between Pentecostals'/Charismatics' and Augustine's conversion outlines some of the attributes of the Pentecostal/Charismatic movement and allows it to find historical grounding and relevance in the life and praxis of St. Augustine, as well. Like Augustine, Pentecostals/Charismatics maintain that divine healing is available through the atonement for all believers, and it flows from God's gracious act in Christ. The Word of God is transformational, as stipulated in Scripture and tradition, and through it God shapes and transforms the events of human life and world history. Occurrences in human life should not be taken lightly, because God is constantly working through them to accomplish His greater good. This is seen in the doors of opportunities that God opens and closes at times that later become the basis of believers' testimonies. These stories are to be told and embraced, for when look closely in them, one can see the hand of God constantly at work shaping and forming him/her in God's providence.

Grenz argues that the Spirit's activity in conversion is fourfold: the Spirit convicts, calls, illuminates, and enables a person, and the Spirit's activity is vital for a person to be saved. The Spirit therefore helps people to come to God, for human effort alone is insufficient to attain salvation (John 3:5–8; Rom. 3:20; Gal. 2:16, 21).[45] Here, conviction indicates the act of a person being made conscious via the Spirit's promptings of his/her sins and need for God (John 16:8). The call is subsequent to conviction. The Spirit heralds us to God through the Word proclaimed.[46]

Illumination happens when the Spirit enlightens recipients of the gospel so that they can ascertain the knowledge needed in Scripture to receive their

Chapter Five: Conversion

salvation (2 Cor. 4:4, 6). The Spirit also enables our will to respond to God, thus making repentance and faith possible.[47] Finally, the Spirit's activities of conviction are operative in the person's Christian initiation, as well as ongoing formation and transformation throughout a believer's whole life. The Spirit brings a person to God and continues to shape and mold that person, and throughout the believer's journey, there will always be transformational moments and workings of the Spirit.

The early Pentecostals believed that their triadic conversion formula of being saved, sanctified, and Spirit-filled could radically change a person's sinful nature. In *The Apostolic Faith*, one of the earliest publications of the Pentecostal tradition, there are countless references to this triadic conversion formula, which further reveals its significance to the early Pentecostals. In one of the testimonies that William J. Seymour selected, he writes, "…a lady was contemplating suicide came to the meeting and was saved, then sanctified and baptized with the Holy Ghost. She is very happy in the Lord [after these events]"[48] The point here is that the triadic formula, when experienced, could transform a person from the most hideous situation to a pleasant life in Christ.

Christian initiation is that initial conversion experience that moves an individual from sin to grace and ushers a person into a lifestyle of faith in Christ. Upon the confession, repentance, and acceptance of Jesus as personal Lord and Savior, a person is said to be a Christian or a born-again believer. After being saved, such a person is expected to live a holy life, one that is free from sin. This is achieved through sanctification, which cleanses the believer of sins, thus making the individual holy. Sanctification further prepares the believer for a third blessing, called Spirit baptism, the outpouring of the Holy Spirit upon the believer. The early Pentecostals argued that speaking in unknown tongues was the initial evidence of having being filled with the Holy Spirit. Not all Pentecostal/Charismatic groups today, however, believe that speaking in unknown tongues is the first sign of Spirit baptism, much less the only evidence.

Spirit baptism empowers the believer for Christian service, and enables him or her to live a sanctified life. According to Seymour, "…the baptism with the Holy Ghost is a gift of power upon the sanctified life…"[49] Seymour further points out that Christ's disciples in antiquity were sanctified before the Pentecost through the Word of the Lord, and as a result, Christ's disciples today should be sanctified before they can receive their Pentecost, baptism in the Spirit. Seymour sometimes uses the terms Pentecost and Spirit baptism synonymously and interchangeably. Also, Seymour points out that the Spirit follows the blood Jesus sheds on the cross that works as the sanctifying agent; this cleansing effect in turn attracts the endowment of the Spirit.[50] Yet the act of being saved, sanctified, and Spirit-filled should not occur only at a juncture, but rather throughout the believer's life.

D. Forms of Conversion

Donald Gelpi describes five forms of conversion: intellectual, moral, affective, sociopolitical, and religious. Gelpi maintains that each person should experience all of these forms in order to be converted fully. Gelpi defines conversion generally as the choice to move from irresponsible to responsible behavior in some outstanding sphere of human existence affectively, intellectually, morally, sociopolitically, and religiously.[51] Gelpi defines affective conversion as, "…the decision to turn from an irresponsible resistance to facing one's disordered affectivity to the responsible cultivation of a healthy, balanced, aesthetically sensitive emotional life."[52] Intellectual conversion is "…the decision to turn from an irresponsible and supine acquiescence in accepted belief to a commitment to validating one's personal beliefs within adequate frames of reference and in ongoing dialogue with other truth seekers."[53] Moral conversion is that decision one makes "…to turn from irresponsible selfishness to a commitment to measure the motives and consequences of personal choices against ethical norms and ideas that both lure the consequences to selfless choices and judge its relapses into irresponsible selfishness."[54] Sociopolitical conversion is:

> The decision to turn from unreflective acceptance of the institutional violations of human rights to a commitment to collaborate with others in the reform of unjust social, economic, and political structures. Sociopolitical converts seek to empower the oppressed to demand and to obtain their rights from their oppressors.[55]

Chapter Five: Conversion

Finally, Gelpi interprets religious conversion as:

The decision to turn from either ignorance of or opposition to God to acceptance in faith of some historical, revelatory self-communication of God and its consequences. Christian conversion exemplifies a particular normative form of religious conversion. In Christian conversion, converts turn from ignorance of and opposition to God to adult faith in the God definitively and normatively revealed in Jesus Christ, the incarnate Son of God the Father, and in the Holy Breath whom they send into the world. Christian converts also accept the consequence of that decision.[56]

Gelpi's forms of conversion do share some common traits. In each of them, the convert is propelled from irresponsible to responsible practice. Conversion is not an event in each case; rather, it is ongoing. Persons are changed to act authentically and responsibly, because to do otherwise would be irresponsible, regardless of what a person professes. Where all the other forms of conversion tend to differ from the religious is that religious conversion always requires divine initiative and intervention, whereas the others can be accomplished solely through human effort.[57]

Gelpi's five forms of conversion move a person from irresponsible to responsible conduct, both initially and continually in an affective, intellectual, moral, sociopolitical and religious manner. In other words, a person's experience and emotions, knowledge and beliefs, conduct and lifestyle, social action and initiative, and faith conviction progress from irresponsible to responsible praxis.

Concluding Remarks

Conversion is not only a response to God's love, but it also restores human fallen nature and initiates a person in loving relationship with God. It involves a turning from sin to God's love. The love of God is efficacious. It radically transforms a person's nature and whole life, and ultimately, the various contexts in which the person operates. Once our nature is changed, our will, choice and actions are also changed.

Within the Christian tradition, there is an assumption that once a person is religiously converted—in this case, converted from sin to grace—that person's whole life is automatically changed. Gelpi's five forms of conversion deconstruct that notion, and reveal that just because a person is religiously converted does not mean one is automatically converted intellectually, affectively, morally, and sociopolitically. The same is true for each of these conversions: no one can suffice for the other, and one should not assume that just because someone is converted in one area, that person is converted in every area. Thus, the Christian tradition should seek for its adherents to be converted holistically. Authentic Christian conversion leads a person to love of God and neighbor intellectually, affectively, morally, sociopolitically and religiously. Through conversion, we accept the love that God has for us through Jesus Christ, which should change our lives holistically. Through formation and transformation we grow and develop in this love that we must demonstrate in our daily walk with God and neighbor.

Notes

[1] Hill, Brennan R., Paul Knitter and William Madges, *Faith, Religion& Theology* (Mystic, CT: Twenty-Third Publications, 2003), 422.

[2] Aikin, Daniel L, "Conversion," in *Holman Illustrated Bible Dictionary*, ed. Chad Brand, Charles Draper, and Archie England (Nashville, Tennessee: Holman Bible Publishers, 2003), 335; Grenz, Stanley, *Theology for the Community of God* (Grand Rapids, Michigan: William B. Eerdmans Publishing Company, 2000), 406.

[3] Holladay, William Lee, *The Root Subh in the Old Testament* (Leiden: Brill, 1958), 6, 7.

[4] Grenz, *Theology for the Community of God*, 406.

[5] Green, Joel, "To Turn from Darkness to Light (Acts 26.18): Conversion in the Narrative of Luke-Acts," in *Conversion in the Wesleyan Tradition*, ed. Kenneth J. Collins and John H. Tyson (Nashville, Tennessee: Abingdon Press, 2001), 103.

[6] Green, "To Turn from Darkness to Light", 103.

[7] Aikin, "Conversion," 335.

[8] Bauer, Walter, *A Greek-English Lexicon of the New Testament and Other Early Christian Literature*, ed. William F. Arndt, F. Wilber Gingrich, and Fredrick W. Danker (Chicago: University of Chicago Press, 1979), 512; and F. Laubach, "*epistrepho, metamelomai*," in "Conversion, Penitence, Repentance, Proselyte," *The New International Dictionary of New Testament Theology (NIDNTT)*, ed. Colin Brown (Grand Rapids, Michigan: Zondervan, 1981), 1: 353–57, *cited in* Grenz, *Theology for the Community of God*, 406–07.

[9] Grenz, *Theology for the Community of God*, 406–07.

[10] Ibid., 407.

Chapter Five: Conversion

[11] McKim, Donald, ed., *Westminster Dictionary of Theological Terms* (Louisville, Kentucky: Westminster John Knox Press, 1996), 62.

[12] Flinn, Frank K. "Conversion: Up From Evangelicalism or the Pentecostal and Charismatic Experience," in *Religious Conversion: Contemporary Practices and Controversies*, ed. Christopher Lamb and M. Darrol Bryant (New York: Cassell, 1999), 54.

[13] Flinn, "Conversion," 54.

[14] Acts 9:3–6.

[15] Augustine, St., *Saint Augustine Confessions*, trans. R.S. Pine-Coffin (New York: Penguin Books, 1961), 55, 60, 177.

[16] Ibid., 177.

[17] Ibid., 177–78. The passage that Augustine read before suddenly becoming converted is Romans 13:13-14.

[18] Ibid., 178.

[19] Ibid.

[20] Bryant, Darrol, "Conversion in Christianity: from without and from within," in *Religious Conversion: Contemporary Practices and Controversies*, ed. Christopher Lamb and M. Darrol Bryant (New York: Cassell, 1999), 185.

[21] Tyson, John H., "John Wesley's Conversion at Aldersgate," in *Conversion in the Wesleyan Tradition* (Nashville, Tennessee: Abingdon Press, 2001), 27.

[22] Ibid., 30–32.

[23] Ibid., 33–34.

[24] Conversion within medieval Christianity was viewed in two distinct ways. There were the efforts to convert Jews and Muslims to Christianity, but the more familiar context was the gradual devotion of one's life to God that took place in the context of the monasteries. With the eruption of the Reformation, new understandings of conversion began to emerge. These were centered around intra-Christian conversions, often dramatic and intense and resulting in a shift from one brand of Christianity to another and from one denomination to another. *See* Bryant, *Religious Conversion*, 185.

[25] The church dividing into Roman Catholicism and Eastern Orthodoxy was probably the first major division in Christendom. The Reformation with Luther, following Papal Schism, could be classified as the third major separation in the Christian church. Yet throughout the history of the church, even as early as in the cradle of its existence (in the first century), the church has undergone various splits due to heresies, among other differences.

[26] Bryant, "Conversion in Christianity,"186.

[27] Ibid., 187.

[28] Ibid.

[29] Flinn, *Conversion*, 62.

[30] Ibid.

[31] Ibid., 62–63.

[32] Ibid., 63.

[33] Ibid.

[34] Ibid.

[35] Ibid., 63–64.

36 Ibid., 64.

37 Ibid.

38 Ibid., 65.

39 Seymour, "Azusa Street Papers," 1.1, 1.

40 McDonnell, Kilian, "The Ideology of Pentecostal Conversion," *Journal of Ecumenical Studies* 5.01 (1968): 105–26.

41 Flinn, "Conversion", 68.

42 Ibid.

43 Ibid., 69.

44 Poewe, Karla, "Charismatic Conversion in Light of Augustine's Confessions," in *Religious Conversion*, ed. Christopher Lamb and Darrol Bryant (New York: Cassell, 1999), 196–200.

45 Grenz, *Theology for the Community of God,* 412.

46 Ibid., 414.

47 Ibid.

48 Seymour, "Azusa Street Papers," 1.4, 1.

49 Seymour, "Azusa Street Papers," 1.1, 2.

50 Ibid., 3.

51 Gelpi, Donald, *Committed Worship: A Sacramental Theology for Converting Christians* vol. 1 (Collegeville, Minnesota: The Liturgical Press, 1993), 17; *see also* Gelpi, Donald, *Charism and Sacrament: A Theology of Conversion* (New York: Paulist Press, 1976), 3–25.

52 Gelpi, *Committed Worship and Initiation*, 17.

53 Ibid.

54 Ibid.

55 Ibid.

56 Ibid., 17–18.

57 Ibid., 27.

CHAPTER SIX

Formation and Transformation

Having experienced being brought into the love of God, one needs to grow and mature in that love, so that one's love of God can be perfected. Throughout our lives, we will have need for ongoing growth and development. Oftentimes, formation and transformation appear indistinguishable, but each has its own function, yet both should attain the singular goal of perfecting God's love in us.

What is the relationship between formation and transformation? Are they separate theories or the same? How do they differ? How do they affect human nature? Andrew Grannell argues that both formation and transformation have their distinctive and unique characteristics, and that neither can suffice for the other. Grannell makes the following observations about formation:

1) Formation itself is not possible without the pervasive, central, and essential role to be played by transformative processes.

2) Formation has an inherent force of fragmentation[,] or more broadly perhaps "negation[,]" which must be attended to.

3) Formation must take into close consideration the Void and the Holy while avoiding the crucial mistake of confining itself to the self-world matrices.

4) Formation must be in something specific[,] whether it is Mohandas Gandhi in response to the Hindu scriptures or a "garden variety" Christian in response to the experience of the living Christ.

5) Formation cannot properly be understood as unilateral, unlinear, irreversible, or de-centered[,] which is the current paradigmatic view.[1]

Without the intricate processes of formation, there cannot be any transformation, because both work together to accomplish change in a person. Grannell therefore states the following salient points about transformation:

1) Transformation must be interpreted within the context of a lifelong, unending if-not-endless, and at least potentially universal process called formation.

2) The stage theory helps us to reflect upon the inherent continuities which must of necessity bind our experiences in formation together; no transformation can undo this continuity.

3) Transformation, like all other phenomena, must eventually submit to the test of empiricism and the stage theory aids us significantly in this task.

4) Finally, both formation and transformation theories must honor their inherent limits, if we are to bring them full circle back into the compass of practicing Christian educators.[2]

Therefore, Christian formation and transformation coexist, but do not necessarily have the same function. However, they achieve the same goal of helping to perfect human nature. Consequently, Christian faith should maintain both the formational and transformational poles. In a logical progression, it appears that formation would precede transformation, but this is not the same in every scenario, for there are occasions when transformation seems to precede and also interrupts formation. As a result, both transformation and formation may occur simultaneously and reciprocate the other. Finally, formation seems to shape, mold, and school, while transformation appears to be a force that interrupts or radically changes the individual and moves the formation process from one stage to another. These two dynamics, formation and transformation, coupled together, produce ongoing development and growth in a person.

A. Faith Development and Growth

Human faith appears to be inherent, yet it requires development, just like the physical, emotional, and rational faculties of humankind. James Fowler's stages of faith development provide much insight into human-faith growth.

Chapter Six: Formation and Transformation

Fowler primarily employs Erik Erickson's psychological stage-development theory as a framework for his research.[3] Both Fowler's and Erikson's faith stages and psychological stages, respectively, parallel human maturation and growth. Furthermore, these stage theories have implications for the Christian born-again experience. Scripture states that, "...anyone who belongs to Christ has become a new person. The old life is gone; a new life has begun!" (2 Cor. 5:17 NLT) and that, "Like newborn babies, crave pure spiritual milk, so that by it you may grow up in your salvation" (1 Pet. 2:2 NIV). The born-again believer, therefore, is expected to grow in Christ and become a mature believer.

As the Apostle Paul says, "When I was a child, I spake as a child, I understood as a child, I thought as a child: but when I became a man, I put away childish things" (1 Cor. 13:11 KJV). Jesus told Nicodemus that, "...unless you are born again, you cannot see the Kingdom of God." Nicodemus responded, "How can an old man go back into his mother's womb and be born again?" Jesus replied, "I assure you, no one can enter the Kingdom of God without being born of water and the Spirit. Humans can reproduce only human life, but the Holy Spirit gives birth to spiritual life. So don't be surprised when I say, 'You must be born again'" (John 3:1–8 NLT). Those passages and others point to the progression and growth that takes place in a born-again believer's life. The stages that will be explored below are infancy, childhood, adolescence, young adulthood, and adulthood.

Infancy (Pre-stage): Fowler refers to this period of faith development as pre-stage, or undifferentiated faith, where a person's faith development starts. Erickson characterizes it as basic trust versus mistrust. As the infant's caregiver attends to its physical, psychological, and emotional needs, the infant begins to develop a dependence on the caregiver to meet those needs, and as a result, trust and mutuality begin to be developed between the child and caregiver. A breakdown in the caregiver's pattern of love and care could allow the infant to develop mistrust that may later affect the infant negatively in successive stages.[4] Brennan Hill articulates that trust is not innate, but is gained or developed through the primary caregiver's response to the infant's physical, social, and psychological needs.[5] Here the faith, beliefs, and practices of the caregiver begin to "rub off" on the infant in one way or another.

The newly born-again believer in Christ could be referred to as an infant in the faith, and this does not necessarily have to do with physiological and psychological maturation, as seen in the theories of Fowler and Erickson, but rather spiritual maturation. Therefore, whatever one's age or physiological and psychological maturation may be, when one comes to Christ, one is considered an infant in Christ. As in the infancy stage postulated above, the person would begin to trust Christ through the care and love of his/her community of faith or spiritual caregivers. If the infant in Christ was mistreated or ignored by primary spiritual caregivers, it could hinder the person from forming stable and trustworthy relationships with those in the community of faith and body of Christ. At this point, the infant believer is fed with a basic understanding of God's love and care. Also, an infant in Christ begins to participate and share in the communal worship and fellowship of the faith community, and begins to practice the morals and ethics of the community, primarily through the lens and praxis of those whom they see as mature believers. At this stage, the mature believer could easily hinder or enhance the spiritual formation of the new believer and could also leave indelible marks and scars on the infant in Christ, which could retard his/her spiritual growth and development in successive stages.

Childhood (Stages One and Two): Fowler describes Stage One as intuitive-projective faith, which he thinks parallels Erikson's third and fourth stages of psychological development, autonomy versus shame and doubt, and initiative versus guilt. It seems appropriate to add Fowler's Stage Two, mystic-literal faith, here as well, which corresponds with Erikson's industry versus guilt. Here I combine Fowler's Stages One and Two and Erikson's Stages Two, Three, and Four, because these stages are closely related and somewhat interrelated, and all occurs during childhood. The child would move from intuitive-projective to a little more mature childhood faith, which is called mystic-literal. According to Fowler, "…intuitive-projective faith is the fantasy-filled, imitative phase in which the child can be powerfully and permanently influenced by examples, moods, actions and stories of the visible faith of primally related adults."[6] This stage is typical of children aged three to seven. Fowler refers to the "mystic-literal faith" developed during a child's first years of attending school as "…the stage in which a person begins to take on for him-or herself the stories, beliefs and observances that symbolize belonging to his or her community. Beliefs are appropriated with literal interpretations, as are moral rules and attitudes..."[7]

In the previous stage, the infant seems more dormant, passively responding to the caregiver's love and care or inconsistencies and neglect. In this stage, however, the child is more actively responding to and attempting to practice that which the primary caregiver or significant other does. The child is not only impressionable, but also responds to impressions in the manner observed in the caregiver. Therefore, praxis of faith and beliefs begin to be transferred tangibly to children at this point, and children actively begin to seek to put some of those beliefs into action.

In the same manner, from the perspective of the born-again believer, an infant in Christ is different from a "child" in the faith. After accepting Christ as Lord and Savior, a person (at whatever age) moves from being an infant to a "child" in Christ. Here the believer begins to put into action the practices of the community of faith, and is influenced by the things that members of the faith community do. The new believer at this point could almost be like a sponge, and persons in the faith community that he/she holds in high esteem have to be extremely careful and consistent in their beliefs, affections, and actions. They can permanently scar or enhance a believer in the childhood stage of faith, for such a neophyte actively practices what he/she sees. This stage lays the foundation for the following stages, because many of the things grasped in Stage One will be played out in successive stages.

Adolescence (Stage Three): Fowler refers to this stage as synthetic-conventional faith, and Erikson calls it identity versus role confusion. Fowler points out that, in this stage, "...faith must provide a coherent orientation in the midst of that more complex and diverse range of involvements. Faith must synthesize values and information; it must provide a basis for identity and outlook."[8] Fowler further points out that, "It is a 'conformist' stage in the sense that it is acutely tuned to the expectations and judgments of significant others and as yet does not have a sure enough grasp on its own identity and autonomous judgment to construct and maintain an independent perspective..."[9]

This stage is characterized by identity issues, as adolescents try to discover self, and in the process, question the belief system and values in which they are oriented in light of their social relations. A lot of deconstruction seems to be happening here, but not much construction. The adolescent does not yet develop a system by which he/she could construct or reconstruct a system of faith, values, and beliefs. The adolescent is constantly seeking ways to discover self, and as a result seeking people and things to mirror. Relationships with peers and mentors are crucial, particularly persons that the teens can identify with and mirror. Also, teens tend to question the beliefs and values of their parents or caregivers that they once held so dear, and they also relate these to the various relationships that they have outside of their religious community and family. At times, the values, beliefs, and praxis in which a teen is oriented might not seem consistent with the ideals of their peers; others might seem more acceptable and popular in a teen social group, and consequently teens may rebel against their traditions.

From the perspective of the born-again believer, the person in the adolescent stage of faith in Christ starts questioning the ideals and theology of the community that he/she once embraced without reservation. This person is at times referred to as critical and or rebellious, in that he/she not only questions the norms, values, and beliefs of the faith community, but may also become withdrawn, especially if the community of faith does not have a clearly defined model and praxis that is relevant, practical, measurable, and identifiable with the challenges faced by the believer in the adolescent stage of faith. It is important for the believer at this stage to be engaged properly in forums and media in which they are able to pose their questions and share their concerns, particularly in settings with mentors and persons in their stage. To individuals in this stage, persons in the previous stages can at times appear naïve and judgmental, while those in the following stages can appear transcendental. At times, persons of adolescent faith complain that the church is not ministering to them and their needs, so the church should tailor its programs to challenge individuals in this stage of development.

Consequently, believers in the adolescent stage of spirituality often question their faith and belief systems in light of their multiple relationships and associations. A person in this stage may ask, "Why do I have to believe what I believe?" They often ask such questions without a clearly defined rational basis, because faith for them is somewhat elusive.

Young Adulthood (Stage Four): Fowler refers to this stage as individuative-reflective faith, and Erikson calls it intimacy versus isolation. Fowler argues that, "…for a genuine move to Stage 4 to occur there must be an interruption of reliance on external sources of authority."[10] He continues:

> The two essential features of the emergence of Stage 4, then, are the critical distancing from one's previous assumptive value system and the emergence of an executive ego. When and as these occur a person is forming a new identity, which he or she expresses and actualizes by the choice of personal and group affiliations and the shaping of a "lifestyle."[11]

In Stage Four, persons begin to construct a system of beliefs that flows out of their own understanding of faith, morality, and theology. It is no longer just what their parents, religious leaders, mentors, and significant others think, but it is their own understanding, relationship with God, and perceived destiny that count. It is at this stage that persons usually make serious and lasting decisions about career, marriage, family, relationships, etc., many of which Erikson thinks are developed either successfully or unsuccessfully based upon how well the young adult masters intimacy. Here, intimacy has to do with one's multiple relations and associations with others, and failure at intimacy could result in isolation and loneliness, potentially for the rest of one's life.[12]

As it relates to the "born-again" experience, a Stage Four believer is considered to be a mature believer, whose faith and belief in God is based on a rational construction of faith in Christ and willing and active participation. The believer at this point partially resembles Christ in lifestyle, and is fully operating in and seeking ways to actualize his/her gifts and calling. Persons in this stage are stable and often unmovable in their faith, life pursuit, and destined path, and are able to guide others in earlier stages of faith development. These persons could be seen as prospective leaders and apologists of the faith and church, and therefore this is probably a good time for the church to look for its future leaders. Intellectually, a person at Stage Four has a proper grasp of his/her beliefs and can adequately articulate and actualize them in relation to God and neighbor in a responsible manner. The person's affections, morality, and sociopolitical and religious endeavors are also lined up with her/his interpretation of Scripture, tradition, reason, and experience.

Adulthood (Stages Five and Six): Stage Five is called conjunctive faith (midlife and beyond). Both Fowler and Erikson see this stage of life as the middle-adult era, and Erikson characterizes this era as generativity versus stagnation. Fowler describes this stage as:

> A way of seeing, of knowing, of committing, moves beyond the dichotomizing logic of stage 4's "either/or." It sees both (or the many) sides of an issue simultaneously. Conjunctive faith suspects that things are organically related to each other; it attends to pattern of interrelatedness in things, trying to avoid force-fitting to its own prior mindset.[13]

Fowler also describes the style people employ in this stage as dialogical knowing, as opposed to dialectical, which he views as too methodologically controlling. Dialogical knowing, according to Fowler, encourages others in the conversation to express their opinions freely and allow other perspectives to be explored without interrupting and imposing on the process.[14]

Stage Five persons, therefore, could be seen as open-minded and embracing of other religious views, perspectives, and pluralism. Truth for these persons is not one-dimensional but multifaceted, and they acknowledge partial truths in many belief systems that a closed-minded person would not see. Persons in this stage seem to also express tolerance for others whose beliefs may differ from their own, and they are less judgmental of others, which allow them to be seen as controversial figures. The intellectual capacity of these persons is well-developed and broad in scope. Their affection and moral system seem well informed and transcend mere right-or-wrong categories, thus holding together the notion of *both* right and wrong in a dialectic and more so dialogical tension. The sociopolitical and religious undertakings of these individuals are also broad. A person in this stage would have a well-developed knowledge-base that constantly informs his/her actions and faith.

The thoughts expressed about Stage Five can be applied to persons who claim to have had a born-again experience. Their spiritual journey and development would have gone through the metamorphoses of the previous

Chapter Six: Formation and Transformation

stages to arrive at this stage, in which individuals can relate to God and neighbor not, just in mature but in dialogical/dialectical ways. Understanding that God can be experienced in ways other than the faith tradition they embrace, they would also have a relativistic understanding of what it means to love God and neighbor in praxis. (Karl Rahner's theory of anonymous Christianity, which is discussed in an earlier chapter, would be plausible for persons in this and moreso Stage Six.)

Fowler refers to Stage Six as universalizing faith, and Erikson characterizes it as integrity versus despair. According to Fowler:

> Stage 6 is exceedingly rare. The persons best described by it have generated faith compositions in which their felt sense of an ultimate environment is inclusive of all being. They have become incarnators and actualizers of the spirit of an inclusive and fulfilled human community. They are "contagious" in the sense that they create zones of liberation from the social, political, economic and ideological shackles we place and endure on human futurity... Many persons in this stage die at the hands of those whom they hope to change. Universalizers are often more honored and revered after death than during their lives...Their community is universal in extent...Life is both loved and held to loosely. Such persons are ready for fellowship with persons at any of the other stages and from any other faith tradition.[15]

Fowler also cites examples of persons who arrived at this stage of faith—including Mahatma Gandhi, Martin Luther King, Jr., Mother Theresa, Dietrich Bonheoffer, etc.—who clearly were ahead of their time, and were extraordinary in character and strength. They demonstrated an ethic and praxis that included and sought for all of humanity to be liberated and transformed through their various causes. They were most embracing of diverse peoples, and deconstructed oppressive structures even in the face of death. The causes that they championed transcended them and their time, and gave them an inner peace and tranquility that overcame their fears of death. Those attributes they displayed further generated an enthusiasm, optimism, and hope that many uncontrollably shared. The intellectual, affective, moral, sociopolitical, and religious dynamics that ordered these persons' lives could be classified as superlative.

Two other persons that could be characterized as universalizers are Jesus and the Apostle Paul (not when he was Saul); their lives and ministries exemplified the traits of Stage Six candidates expressed above. Although this stage has very few candidates, as Fowler observed, reaching this stage should probably be the quest of every Christian and born-again believer, as we should strive for excellence.

B. Transformational Logic

Transformation, like formation, is an ongoing experience; however, transformation takes place prior to and during formation. It is that experience that moves a person from one stage of faith to another, which I call *macrotransformation*. There are also various transformations that take place in each stage of a person's faith and spiritual development that move the formation process along, which I refer to as *microtransformations*. Therefore, transformation occurs both on a micro and a macro level within the various stages, and from one stage to another.

James Loder describes transformation as, "…the major term, designating a change in form from lower to higher orders of life along a continuous line of intention or development. A typical case of transformation is the change in form that occurs when a caterpillar turns into a butterfly…"[16] A caveat Loder inserts is that transformation does not always effect a positive change, as is often implied.[17] Here Loder's *transformational logic* is engaged as a possible framework for transformation in Christian faith. Loder argues that it is within the human spirit that the transformational logic occurs—in other words, the human spirit guides and drives the transformation process,[18] which eventually transforms the whole person. Also, this transformational logic can be used to arrive at various forms of knowing: scientific, aesthetic, therapeutic, and other transpositions.[19]

Loder's transformational logic, or knowing event, demonstrates how transformation occurs. It has five steps: "conflict-in-context," "interlude for scanning," "constructive act of the imagination," "release and openness," and "interpretation." Conflict initiates the transformation process, as Loder,

Chapter Six: Formation and Transformation

explains: "The first step begins when there is an apparent rupture in the knowing context. *Conflict* initiates the knowing response, and the more one cares about the conflict the more powerful will be the knowing event."[20]

Following the conflict is a second process called "interlude for scanning," which involves the conscious or unconscious searching for possible solutions and meaning, delineating errors, holding parts together, and discarding others in an effort to address the conflict previously initiated.[21] In the third step, called constructive act of the imagination, "…an insight, intuition, or vision appears on the border between the conscious and unconscious, usually with convincing force, and conveys in a form readily available to consciousness the essence of the resolution."[22] The fourth step, "release and opening" involves two dynamics:

> A *release* of the energy bound up in sustaining the conflict and second by an *opening* of the knower to him- or herself and the contextual situation. The release of energy is a response of the unconscious to the resolution and the evidence that one's personal investment in the event has reached a conclusion; the conflict is over. The opening of the knower to his or her context is the response of consciousness to being freed *from* an engrossing conflict and *for* a measure of self-transcendence… Without the release of bound up energy and the liberation of the self-transcendence of consciousness, it must be assumed that the conflict has not been sufficiently resolved and the unconscious mind will continue to search for solutions… the release of tension that emerges with the "Aha!" is accompanied by an opening of one's mind; if the sense of self-transcendence is voiced, we say something like, "now that is off my mind…"[23]

Practically, the problem is solved in the fourth step, or at least, there is partial resolution to the urge felt, and the next step is for this solution to be accurately interpreted and verified.

The "interpretation and verification" of the fifth step "…is *interpretation* of the imaginative solution into the behavioral and/or symbolically constructed world of the original context. This interpretation works in two directions, both backward and forward, so to say." According to Loder, congruence "…makes explicit, congruent connections from the essential structures of the imaginative construct back into the original conditions of the puzzle," and correspondence "...makes the apparent congruence public and a matter of consensus."[24] In the fifth step, therefore, complete resolution takes place, whereby the conflict or urge in its original form is revisited and solved and verified afterward.

In sum, the transformation process on the micro and macro levels is initiated by some conflict that could be interpreted as a drive, desire, urge, or rupture prior to and/or during the formational and spiritual-developmental stage. The implicit growth and formation demand a radical and almost irresistible change in the individual's life, and this takes the person to the next level. This naturally leads the person to scan his/her life and relationships (horizontally and vertically) to delineate meaning and resolution for the existing urge, followed by intuition and/or options emerging to address the conflict. With all being equal, the person then has an "aha" experience, which signifies the urge to change radically, and leads to an acceptance of the need for such change. This best possible option is then carefully interpreted and tested in light of the existing urge, and consequently modification takes place in the faculties of the person's intellectual, emotional, moral, sociopolitical, and/or religious consciousness, fueled by a person's fundamental nature. At this point, one can testify of the micro and/or macro transformation that occurred in one's life.

Concluding Remarks

The faith community's formational and transformational praxis should be intentional, and designed to impact and provide meaning to the various stages of life and faith. A person's faith journey occurs throughout one's life, and the spiritual born-again experience could occur at any stage in a person's physiological and psychological development. Whenever it occurs, regardless of age and stage of development, the person would still be considered a "newborn babe in Christ," and would be expected to grow to maturity in the faith.

Clearly, transformation and formation are not the same experience, but they do not occur in isolation of one another. Transformation often takes place prior to or during formation, and it is that radical change that moves a person from one stage to another, and allows a person to progress in any given stage. The framework for transformation in this chapter is Loder's transformational logic, which involves conflict-in-context, interlude for scanning, constructive act of the imagination, release and openness, and interpretation and verification. The transformation is initiated by a conflict, drive, or urge in the formation process, and this occurs regardless of the stage a person is in. The individual responds to this urge by scanning for meaning and resolution, and then comes up with a solution that is not always productive. When the necessary option is deduced and selected, then an "aha" experience is generated, signifying that the problem or urge is resolved. Finally, before the solution to the conflict is fully applied, it is tested and verified, at which point complete transformation perhaps occurs.

Note, however, that transformation can happen during any stage, and produces changes sufficient for that stage, or simply moves a person from that stage to another. As mentioned above, transformation, like the other major elements of Christian faith, is both an event and a process. The conversion, formation, and transformation that occur in human nature eventually change a person's whole life and external environment. Also, significant to Christian faith formation are praxes, which we will engage in subsequent chapters: death and afterlife, spirituality and piety, gifts of the Spirit, communal worship and fellowship, and theological methodology.

Notes

[1] Grannell, Andrew, "The Paradox of Formation and Transformation," *Religious Education* 50.3(Summer 1985): 384–98, 397.

[2] Ibid., 397–98.

[3] Fowler, James W., *Stages of Faith: The Psychology of Human Development and the Quest for Meaning* (New York: Harper Collins Publishers, 1981), 106.

[4] Ibid., 121.

[5] Hill, *Faith & Theology*, 68.

[6] Fowler, *Stages of Faith*, 133.

[7] Ibid., 149.

[8] Ibid., 172.

[9] Ibid., 172–73.

[10] Ibid., 179.

[11] Ibid.

[12] Erikson, Erik, *Childhood and Society* (New York: W.W. Norton and Co. 1985), 263–66.

[13] Fowler, *Stages of Faith,* 185.

[14] Ibid

[15] Fowler, James, "Perspectives on the Family from the Standpoint of Faith Development Theory," *The Perkins Journal*, vol. 33.1 (Fall 1979): 13–14, cited in Fowler, *Stage of Faith,* 200–01.

[16] Loder, James, *The Transforming Moment* (Colorado Springs, Colorado: Helmers & Howard Publishers, 1989), 43.

[17] Ibid. 2–3.

[18] Ibid., 44–64.

[19] Ibid., 37.

[20] Ibid.

[21] Ibid., 38.

[22] Ibid., 38–39.

[23] Ibid., 39.

[24] Ibid.

CHAPTER SEVEN

Death and Afterlife

It is clear that the human body does not live forever, and that many find assurance in the notion of life after death. Humans live to a certain age and then die; the timetable and manner vary according to factors such as genetics, proper health care, natural causes, traumatic circumstances, and divine providence. After physical death, what happens to the soul of a person? Does it live on? Is there an afterlife? Death, however, does not diminish God's love for us; it could be seen as a gateway to God's everlasting life of love—which Christ exemplifies. Christ's death, at first, was seen as the end for many who watched Him die a painful death on the cross. Three days later, He was resurrected from the dead, later ascended, and is now exalted at the right hand of the Father in enduring *perichoretic* relationship. This *perichoretic* relationship is that inseparably loving relationship that the Trinity shares. This is a model for what the eternal soul in Christ shares with Christ in the afterlife. Death, therefore, is not the end for the believer, rather a passage to eternal love in Christ.

A. Mortality[1]

Qoheleth, the writer of Ecclesiastes, after surveying the meaning of life through various achievements—ranging from the outstanding work of building and planting (Ecc. 2:1–11; 17–25) to great wisdom (2:12–16)—concludes that death blurs and blots out all achievements.[2] Consequently, in Ecclesiastes, death is seen as the great equalizer that cancels all achievements, and it is inevitable.[3] Furthermore, Qoheleth uses the reality of death to equate humans with beasts. According to him, both humans and beasts were made from dust, and when both die, they return to the dust of the earth (Ecc. 3:18–20). Hence, death is not only the equalizer for humans rich and poor, but also humans and beasts. The fate that all people and animals undeniably share is death.

Gerhard Von Rad, in interpreting Qoheleth's statement, postulates that death diminishes any meaningful interpretation of life.[4] For Qoheleth, although death comes to everyone (9:3), and all hope is lost for the dead, the living has hope (9:5, 6).[5] It is clear that Qoheleth lived long, became wealthy and successful, and in his latter years vehemently refuted death and saw it as unfortunate.[6] Is it that Qoheleth is at a point in his life when he looks at being unable to overcome death, which is totally the opposite of what life means to him?

Hence, the Wisdom tradition and older Israelite tradition accept death as inevitable, and therefore emphasize the quality of life in the present.[7] When people die, they return to the dust of the earth (Gen. 2:7; Ps. 90:3) and gather by their ancestors (Jud. 2:10; Lk. 16:22). Long life on earth is seen as a blessing, and those who enjoy the blessings of longevity die "old and full of years" (Gen. 35:29; Job 42:17).

In the New Testament, the Pauline tradition, unlike the Synoptic tradition, has a fairly well-developed theology of death. Paul refers to death as the punishment for human sin (Rom. 6:23). It is, therefore, sin that brings about death (Jas. 1:15). Death came into the world through Adam's disobedience, and life came through Christ's obedience (Rom. 5). At Christ's Second *Parousia*, the dead in Christ shall be raised first (1 Thess. 4:13–18). In the Johannine tradition, believers in Christ have already passed from death to life (John 5:24), and they will live even after dying a physical death because they receive eternal life, which triumphs over death. In Revelation, we see two kinds of death—physical and eternal (2:11; 20:6; 21:8)—but in the end, God will finally destroy death (1 Cor. 15:26, 54, 57; Rev. 20:14; 21:4).

Jürgen Moltmann points out that to ignore the reality of death and pretend that it does not exist is a superficial and fraudulent way of thinking.[8] Moltmann posits that the awareness of death should not be suppressed, as Epicurus advocates, because in so doing, one is depriving oneself of life. The reality of

Chapter Seven: Death and Afterlife

death, when suppressed and lodged in the recesses of our subconscious, saps our energies.[9] Moltmann further argues that the reason death is so frightening and appears as the end of all events is because of the obsession that modern men and women have with the self (individualism). This, he argues, runs counter to how pre-modern or extra-modern people viewed death, as a natural progression from this life into the world of their ancestors. Hence, for extra-modern people, death is not seen as the finality or rupture of life, but that which ushers them into the realm of their ancestors, and life continues in their offspring.[10]

Death, therefore, is a reality that cannot be ignored or suppressed. According to Moltmann, "All human life advances towards its own death. That is something we cannot change."[11] Death is probably one of, if not the most, tragic things in life, yet it is the most inevitable thing that happens to people. From the day we were born, we are said to be dying. Aging is a sign of dying. Daily, we grow older. The various organs in our bodies only function effectively for a while. As we grow older, our vital organs are more prone to developing infections and becoming ill, which leads to death. The human body is constantly dying, regardless of how well we take care of it. Those who take good care of themselves and do all the right things relating to living healthy—such as eating right, exercising, and getting enough rest—will most likely have a healthier life than people who do not, but this does not make these persons immune to death. Regardless of race, class, creed, gender, wealth or poverty, physical death is a given for everyone.[12] The only exception to a physical death is what many in the Christian tradition call the Rapture. The understanding is that Christ will one day receive the believers unto Himself, in the heavens, and this could happen at any moment.[13]

Many people throughout their adult lives make plans for retirement, hoping that after retirement they will be able to enjoy their lives, which is a good principle, but there is no guarantee that one will live to retire. Some people believe in an afterlife—that is, life after death. Thus, some people live in preparation for the life to come, but what if the afterlife is only an illusion? The Christian tradition espouses the belief that one will receive merits for the life that they live on earth, and therefore those who live well and righteously on earth will inherit rewards accordingly after death. On the contrary, those who live wretchedly will receive punishment in the afterlife at the judgment seat of God.[14]

In Hinduism, Jainism, and Buddhism, there is the belief that people have to live out their *karma*. If one attains enlightenment and liberation while on earth, such a person will not have to continue in the cycle of births and deaths (reincarnation). According to these faiths, a good *karma* will yield good rewards after death, and bad karma will result in punishment.[15]

Those who believe in euthanasia, or mercy killing, see death as that which puts terminally ill people out of their misery. Those who are sick with terminal illnesses, suffering much pain and agony, could anticipate death as that which will relieve them completely of all their pain. Some people resort to suicide to avoid unbearable situations.[16] Many of the early Christians who were martyred for their faith anticipated death with joy for Christ's sake. The early Christians also believed that the death of the believer was not final; it was seen as a temporary state of rest because, in the fullness of time, the dead in Christ would be resurrected from the dead to be with Christ.

Death can be so horrific that one could easily question any merit in it. Is there any value in death? Is death anything to look forward to? Death often brings pain, not happiness, to loved ones. Those who survive the passing of a loved one, friend or even a neighbor, could attest to the hurt they feel. Death may well help to take a person out of pain and misery, but it leaves those loved ones behind with much grief and agony. People wish that they would never lose those who they love most to death, but that they would live forever in a peaceful and happy world. Even those who suffer wish for a better life, not necessarily death. Given the pain, separation, and sadness that death brings, it is hard to see how death could be anything but cruel, and therefore it is only through the lens of faith that death seems to make some sense.

Finally, death could be seen as a transition from mortality to immortality, and therefore this life is temporary, a shadow of the life to come. Consequently, we live this life to live the life to come. Many religious traditions speak of an afterlife, but in the Christian tradition, the afterlife is congruent with eternity. Living in the present, however, determines the quality of life people will sustain when they transition from mortality to immortality. Therefore, death could be seen as a transition from one life to another. Some believe that when one dies, one only sleeps and will one day wake up to meet one's ultimate fate. The Christian tradition holds that God will judge both the living and the dead on the Day of Judgment. Clearly death is not final.[17] Hallelujah!

B. Immortality

It is rather natural to ask what happens after death. Is there life after death? Some people, it appears, live in the present in preparation for the life to come. There is a great emphasis on the afterlife in many of the world's most prominent religions: Christianity, Islam, Buddhism, Hinduism, and Aboriginal traditions. Scholars argue that the ancient Israelite tradition did not affirm the afterlife. According to Jack Sanders:

> Ancient Israelite religion, of course, seemed to entertain no notion of what we call immortality; and in this it agreed with other ancient Near Eastern religions. Sheol was not Hades; it was the pit, *shahat*. A few lines in the Psalms may be taken as implying some kind of *hope* in a conscious existence beyond death [Ps. 16:10; 73:24], but those may be late—post-exilic in any case, at the earliest; and of course at least one post-exilic statement in Isaiah seems to speak of such an overcoming of mortality [Isa 26:19]. But, if those few texts *do* imply some kind of immortality, they are rare exceptions.[18]

Some of the few indications of an afterlife in Old Testament thought are seen in questions such as: "Does God work wonders for the dead?" (Psalm 88:10), "If a man dies, shall he live again?" (Job 14:14), and "Can these bones live again?"(Eze. 37). Elsewhere, Isaiah affirms that dead bodies shall indeed live again (Isaiah 24–26). This same sentiment is echoed in Daniel, but here the dead shall wake up to an impending judgment, and the result shall be everlasting life or everlasting shame and contempt, issued according to the deeds done in body and soul (Dan. 12:2).

Qoheleth, rejects the notion of an afterlife and recommends enjoying life in the present while we can, because life is unpredictable, unjust, and elusive.[19] Still Qoheleth hints at the possibility of immortality in his writings (Ecc. 3:20, 21).[20] Scholars believe that this implicit notion of the afterlife is not intrinsic to the Hebrew Wisdom tradition. Robert Gordis, along with some modern scholars, thinks that Qoheleth's notion of the afterlife flows out of the Israelite and Judaic traditions in which he lived.[21] The majority of modern scholars, such as M. Hengel and N. Lohfink, however, hold that Qoheleth's notion of the afterlife was influenced by foreign traditions. In general, scholars agree that Qoheleth was engaging the subject of the afterlife because it existed in his context.[22] Consequently, some critics accuse Qoheleth of contradicting his claim about the nonexistence of the afterlife (3:21) when he somewhat affirms it later (12:7). Gordis comes to Qoheleth's defense in pointing out that this is not a contradiction on Qoheleth's path, but that Qoheleth's apparent equivocation is an acknowledgment that life comes from God and goes back to God.[23]

Sanders argues that the Wisdom tradition gives little or no attention to the question of the afterlife because it emphasizes living the good life in the present life. The book of Proverbs, for example, relishes following wise instructions and the commandments therein because they lead to longevity and peace (Prov. 3:1–2). Except for one far-off allusion in Proverbs 15:24, scholars argue that it contains no reference to immortality.[24] Although Job raises the issue of immortality,[25] he rejects the notion of it actually happening (Job 14:12, 14).[26] N. Habel suggests that Job contemplates resurrection from *Sheol* in order to prove his innocence, because he thought that he would have died from his illness, which his friends claimed, was a result of his sins, and this therefore would prove his guiltlessness and vindicate him. This point, however, is refuted by some scholars on the grounds that it is too optimistic[27] for Job's line of thought.

For Ben Sira, who is believed to be the author of a noncanonical book called *Sirach* that fits in the category of the Wisdom tradition, the solution to the question of theodicy is "just wait." It appears that Sira both embraces and rejects immortality.[28] Sira raises questions about the apparent injustice seen in God, sometimes exalting the unrighteous and allowing the righteous to suffer, which contradicts the teaching of Proverbs, in which righteousness always leads to blessings and unrighteousness to suffering. Sira encourages his audience not to focus on the achievements of the wicked, however, because it is Yahweh who ultimately exalts the poor. Furthermore, Sira reasons that what is seen of a person during life may not be the same at the

Chapter Seven: Death and Afterlife 97

end of life, when God finally judges and rewards both the righteous and unrighteous. One's fate is not final until the end of the ages.[29]

Observing that a person's good name and reputation will outlive him/her, Sira uses this nominal immortality to engage the question of theodicy. This line of argument suggests that Sira is making a strong case for the immortality of one's good name, not of the soul.[30] In so doing, Sira accommodates immortality but still embraces the prevailing perspective in the Wisdom tradition that death is final, the end of human existence.[31] Unlike Sira, who merely accommodates the notion of an afterlife, the apocryphal book *Wisdom of Solomon* forthrightly affirms immortality.[32]

Therefore, as time unfolded, the Wisdom tradition slowly progressed into embracing future rewards of wisdom in the afterlife. For, while most of the authors in the tradition speak of immortality with scant regard, the author of the *Wisdom of Solomon* does so forthrightly. It is said that the Wisdom tradition ceased after the *Wisdom of Solomon* was written, but in essence it continued with resounding effects that got amplified in the apocalyptic book of Daniel, other Jewish works, Qumran documents, and the New Testament.[33] In the Qumran documents, the apocalyptic pattern of resurrection and judgment is united with the Wisdom tradition in contending that the wicked will be judged by God with punishment and the righteous with favor. Hence, the righteous will receive eternal life, and the wicked will be annihilated, and consequently the Qumran community is admonished not to exchange their souls for wealth.[34]

The New Testament presents a clearly defined theology that affirms immortality. In the gospels, Jesus made numerous references to the afterlife and eternity. Christ, in His teachings, promised that the one who cherishes his/her life will lose it, but the one who loses it for His sake will find it later.[35] Christ's resurrection is a model for the saints; He is the first of them that was dead and is eternally resurrected.[36] In the theology of Paul, we see an even more expanded version of the theology of immortality. For example, Paul encouraged the Thessalonians—who were grieving the loss of their loved ones—that the dead in Christ only sleep temporarily because one day they will be resurrected from the dead and dwell with Christ eternally.[37]

Two prominent views of immortality coexist in Western thought: one is about the immortality of the soul (that the soul of humankind never dies), and the other is about the resurrection of the dead and eternal life. The idea of the immortality of the soul is consistent with the beliefs of the ancient world, and this view is based on the "self transcendence" of humankind.[38] This notion originated with Plato, who taught that the soul of mankind never dies.[39] Three perspectives on the immortality of the soul, flowing out of Plato's school of thought, are worthy of highlighting: the soul as divine substance, transcendental subject, and the kernel of human existence.

As a divine substance, the soul produces life, and people are born from the dead; the soul is preexistent and, as a result, in life we gather that which the soul already knew; the soul anticipates death in order to be separated from the body so that it can exist by itself.[40] Kantian Johann Gottlieb Fichte, on the transcendental substance of the soul, proposes that in humanity there is the empirical "I" and the transcendental "I." The former should seek to be attuned with the latter, which is immortal.[41] The thought that the soul is the kernel of existence is perpetuated by Ernst Bloch, who articulates that what we now call life is a progression to our real existence, because our true identity is hidden in the kernel of our existence. Hence, our true reality is emerging as we progress throughout life, and death brings us into this reality because, when our shell is no more, our kernel emerges. Death does not affect the kernel of our existence because it cannot destroy that which is not yet a consummated reality.[42]

The second view of immortality in Western thought is the biblical teaching that the dead shall live again. This view is based on the self-transcendence of God, almighty, over death.[43] In general, the resurrection is the Christian hope, the core of the Easter message, and the crux of Christian eschatology. Resurrection theology reduces death to a temporary reality that will one day be swallowed up in victory when believers are transformed from corruptible to incorruptible (1 Cor. 15:54). Death will eventually cease to exist (Rev. 21:4). Death is the last enemy of God and His creation that will be permanently obliterated (1 Cor. 15:26). The life that we live on earth is indicative of the kind of resurrection that we will have (1 Cor. 15:42–44; John 12:25; Matt. 10:39; Lk. 17:33). The archetypical resurrection is Christ's own resurrection from the dead by the agency of God's Spirit. Christ is therefore the firstborn of the dead; the first of them who sleep to be resurrected from the dead (Acts 26:23). Also, Christ is seen as having resurrectional power and life (Jn. 11:25), and in the fullness of time, this same Christ will cause the believers to be changed from mortal to immortality (1 Cor. 15:54).

Concluding Remarks

Christ's love for us—demonstrated by His death on the cross—saved humanity from the doom of death by conquering the hopelessness that death brought prior to His resurrection. Christ assures us throughout His teachings that there is eternal life for those who believe in Him. Hence, death is no longer the finality of mankind. This satisfies the question of whether the soul of mankind lives after death. Our response to Christ's life-giving act must be love demonstrated to God and our neighbor. Christ conquered death and gave eternal life that we might live in loving relationship with God and neighbor both in the present, and not yet kingdom of God.

Notes

[1] In general, Christian thought, like Pauline theology, sees death as a consequence of the fall because prior to the fall, humankind was immortal.

[2] Branick, Vincent P., "Wisdom, Pessimism, and 'Mirth.'" *Journal of Religious Ethics* 34.1 (2006): 69–87, 79.

[3] Middlemas, Jill, "Ecclesiastes Gone 'Sideways,'" *The Expository Times* 118.5 (2007): 218; Ecc. 8:8a, 11:7–12:7.

[4] Rad, Gerhard Von, *Wisdom in Israel* (Nashville, TN: Abingdon, 1972), especially 226–37; Sanders, Jack T., "Wisdom, Theodicy, Death, and the Evolution of Intellectual Traditions," *Journal for the Study of Judaism* 36.3 (2005): 263–77, 268.

[5] Ibid., 268–69.

[6] Ibid., 269.

[7] Ibid.

[8] Moltmann, Jürgen, *The Coming of God*, trans. Margaret Kohl (Minneapolis: Fortress Press, 2004), 50.

[9] Ibid., 51.

[10] Ibid., 51–52.

[11] Ibid., 54; Psalm 90:10–12.

[12] With the exception of Enoch (Gen. 5:23–24, Heb. 11:5) and Elijah (2 Kings 2:11–13) who did not experience death, Christians who believe in Rapture theology maintain that the Rapture could occur at any time, and that it is the only thing that will cause them to escape death in this life.

[13] 1 Thess. 4:17.

[14] Rev. 22:11, 12.

[15] See Fisher, Mary Pat, *Living Religions,* 7th ed. (New Jersey: Pearson Prentice Hall, 2008); Fisher, Mary Pat and Lee W. Bailey, *An Anthology of Living Religions* (New Jersey: Prentice Hall, 2008).

[16] For arguments on euthanasia and physician-assisted suicide, which include historical overview, contemporary developments, state and federal laws/its constitutionality, relevant distinctions, moral reasoning, and case studies, *see* Devettere, Raymond J., *Practical Decision Making in Health Care Ethics,* 3rd ed. (Washington, DC: Georgetown University Press, 2010), chapter 13; *and* Degrazia, David, Thomas Mappes, and Jeffery Brand-Ballard, *Biomedical Ethics,* 7th ed. (New York: McGraw-Hill Higher Education, 2006), chapter 6.

[17] In Christian thought, the soul and human nature seem to be one and the same reality, and are often used interchangeably. There are occasions when the human heart (not the physical heart) is used interchangeably with the human soul and nature as well. In the Genesis account, God told the first people that in the day they eat of a certain tree they shall surely die (Gen. 2:17). The death that is seen in this text is both a soul and bodily death. The death of the soul is the separation of the soul from God, and physical death is when the soul leaves the body. There are some who subscribe to a third death, spiritual death, which is separation of the human spirit from God.

[18] Sanders, "Wisdom, Theodicy, Death ," 263–64.

[19] Ibid., 268.

[20] Ibid., 269.

[21] Gordis, Robert., *Koheleth—The Man and His World,* 3rd augmented edition, (New York: Schocken Books, 1968), 53–54; Burkes, Shannon, *Death in Qoheleth and Egyptian Biographies of the Late Period* (Atlanta: Society of Biblical Literature, 1999), 88–89, 115; Sanders, "Wisdom, Theodicy, Death," 269.

[22] Sanders, "Wisdom, Theodicy, Death," 269, 270.

[23] Ibid., 270.

[24] Ibid., 264.

[25] Ibid., 265.

[26] Ibid., 266, 267, 268.

[27] Ibid.

[28] bid., 271.

[29] Ibid.

[30] Ibid., 272.

[31] Ibid., 273.

[32] Ibid.; Winston, David., *The Wisdom of Solomon* (New York: Doubleday, 1979), 29–30.

[33] Sanders, "Wisdom, Theodicy, Death," 276.

[34] Ibid., 274, 275.

[35] Matt. 10:39.

[36] Acts 26:23.

Chapter Seven: Death and Afterlife

[37] 1 Thess. 4:13–18.

[38] Moltmann, *The Coming of God*, 58.

[39] Plato, *Phaedo*, trans. D. Gallop (New York: World's Classics, 1993), 72e ; Moltmann, *The Coming of God*, 58; Sanders, "Wisdom, Theodicy, Death," 273; Winston, *The Wisdom of Solomon* , 29–30.

[40] Plato, *Phaedo*, 72e, 75bff, 80e, 81a; Moltmann, *The Coming of God*, 58, 59.

[41] Moltmann, *The Coming of God*, 61–63.

[42] Ibid., 63–65.

[43] Ibid., 58.

CHAPTER EIGHT

Personal Spirituality and Piety

This chapter is not an extensive treatment of spirituality and piety; rather it highlights some of the elements significant to that end. Our task, therefore, is to point out the significant role of the fruit of the Spirit, sanctification, and the universal priesthood of all believers in one's personal spirituality.

A. Fruit of the Spirit

The fruit of the Spirit seen in the Pauline corpus (Galatians 5:16–26) is the result of a life that lives out love of God and neighbor through the agency of God, the Spirit. Therefore, the "fruit" of the Spirit, which consists of many graces and virtues, is an inward experience of the working of the Spirit that manifests outwardly in a person's lifestyle and praxis. It is Christ's nature and character that the Spirit imprints on the believer and seeks to perfect in the person.

R. Hollis Gause points out two issues significant to a Pauline understanding of the fruit of the Spirit. Gause articulates that Paul "emphasizes that this fruit is the expected product of being born of the Spirit."[1] He also explains that the fruit that is born is a result of the indwelling of the Spirit.[2] Gause refers to the "fruit" of the Spirit as "graces." The implication here is that these graces are virtues of the Spirit that are necessary for a holy and morally correct life. These graces and virtues or fruit of the Spirit are love, joy, peace, long-suffering, goodness, faith, meekness, gentleness, and temperance.

According to Gause, "...the graces which are listed here [Galatians 5:22–23] deal with all of man relationships: to God, to society, and to himself...all of these graces contribute to the wholeness of man in all his relationships."[3] These virtues cannot be prescribed by a legal code or a set of rules and regulations. Paul echoes this sentiment in the statement, "Concerning such things as these [virtues] there is no law" (Gal. 6:23). According to Gause:

> The one who is cultivating and practicing these things by the indwelling presence of the Holy Spirit is not under the law. He is not subject to its condemnation and yet he is in harmony with the holiness and purposes of the law.[4]

The Apostle Paul acknowledges that there is a constant struggle between the Spirit and the flesh. While the Spirit persists to perfect virtues and graces in us, the flesh works against it: "...the Spirit works to implant these spiritual qualities in the experience of the new birth."[5] It is the Spirit's work to free us from the laws of sin and death (Rom: 8:2), and insulate the "fruit" of the Spirit in us from being encumbered by our Adamic nature. The baptism of the Holy Spirit, Gause claims, gives added growth and fruitfulness to the Spirit. Given that one continues to walk in the Spirit (5:16), one will not fulfill the lust of the flesh, which works contrary to the virtues and graces. Hence, walking in the Spirit means walking in the character and ways of the Spirit, in harmony with the Spirit's nature, and by the Spirit's graces and power.

The Spirit bears fruit(s)[6] in the believers' lives, and this is consistent with Jesus' ethics, and counters the vices or works of the flesh.[7] These fruits are virtues that address a person's multiple relations with God, neighbor, society, and self.[8] The fruit of the Spirit encompasses cardinal virtues, such as temperance, courage, prudence, and justice, and theological virtues, such as faith, hope and love.[9] Christian virtue and morality should be lived out in a sanctified life.[10] John Wesley held that the believer should live not only a sanctified life, but an entirely sanctified life, which is perfect love.[11]

Furthermore, walking in the Spirit is walking in love, as God is love, and therefore the Spirit of God is love. The essence of the Trinitarian community is love. How much more tangibly can one walk in the Spirit than through one's demonstration of love of God and neighbor in everyday life?

B. Works of the Flesh

The works of the flesh serve as vices to the virtues and graces of the Spirit. Here the term "flesh" is not used in reference to human anatomy but to the aspect of human nature that is deemed carnal and is susceptible to sinful desires and ambitions.[12] The human "carnal nature" is analogous to Augustine's notion of "nature's corruption" discussed earlier. Paul gives a list of what he deems works of the flesh in the book of Galatians, which Gause classifies into three general groups. The first group is called "sins of bodily appetites," which are satisfied outside of the law of God: fornication, moral (sexual) filth, and indecency (of language, bodily movements, and bodily contact). The second kinds he claims are perversions of worship, idolatry, and witchcraft. The third types are sins of excess and perversions of human emotions, including hatred, variance (i.e. contention, strife, wrangling), emulations (rivalry, jealousy, quarreling), wrath (rage, fury, and anger), strife, sedition (division into parties based on individualistic opinion), envy, drunkenness, and revelry. Paul's list of vices, like the virtues of the Spirit, is not meant to be exhaustive, merely representative.[13] In addition, the works of the flesh are not derivatives of the Spirit, rather the result of sin, the consequences of Adam's fall. The vices are embedded in nature's corruption, and consequently manifested in human action when it is not guided by the double-love command.

In contrast, the virtues of the Spirit are consistent with the fundamental goodness in human nature. The Spirit of God not only impresses virtues and graces, but also resurrects them as they were placed in us from the beginning by God, who made us in God's likeness and image. The more we exercise these virtues/graces, the more prevalent they are in our lives. One cannot deny our ongoing personal struggle in which nature's corruption wars against the fundamental goodness in us. This is exemplified in Paul's own story, when he says that every time he tries to do good, evil presents itself.[14] This battle can only be won through the application of the double-love command that militates against nature's corruption and perfects nature's innate goodness. Humans should strive volitionally to do good and avoid the evil that presents itself, and this can be attained through application of the love imperative.

C. Sanctification

Sanctification is often used interchangeably with holiness; this phenomenon cleanses and makes a person live purely. Sanctification, therefore, prevents a person from being engulfed in sin and evil. A sanctified life negates the "works of the flesh" that lead to sin and immorality, and it inclines someone to emulate God. John Wesley expands the dialogue by insisting that believers should be entirely sanctified. He maintains that believers often achieve "entire sanctification" at the point of death, because death is the final trial and challenge of faith. This does not mean, however, that entire sanctification cannot be achieved earlier in one's life. According to Wesley, it is possible for one to be sanctified completely at any stage of one's life. It seems as though Wesley's theology anticipates entire sanctification as the ultimate goal and standard of Christian living. Wesley does not restrict the goal of entire sanctification to a few, but demands it of everyone. In his view, all persons can realize this goal: "Be perfect, therefore, as your heavenly Father is perfect" (Matt. 5:48 NIV), because if this was unattainable, God would not require it of us all.

Wesley believes that the goal of entire sanctification is perfect love. The attainment of entire sanctification, perfect love, is a divine work of grace, which seeks to mend the broken human condition. It is also what makes a person wholly free and victorious over sin, through the redemptive work of the Spirit. Entire sanctification means loving with one's whole being. As a result, inward sins are removed. Entire sanctification is both instantaneous and gradual, as it is a past, present, and future action. For Wesley, entire sanctification is not an alternate path for the believers; it is the way and destiny of everyone in Christ. This can only be achieved through the Spirit's working because human effort alone cannot forestall the pervasiveness of sin and evil; therefore the Spirit's help is also needed to make entire sanctification possible.[15]

The Apostle Paul's declarations to the believers indicate that entire sanctification is possible in this life. He admonishes that it is Christ who sanctifies the church in order that Christ might present it to Himself without spot, wrinkle, or blemish (Eph 5:26, 27). Also, he calls the Christians in Corinth, "those sanctified in Christ Jesus" (1 Cor 1:2) and tells them, "you were sanctified" (6:11). Paul also says to the Corinthians, "Let us cleanse ourselves from all defilement of flesh and spirit, perfecting holiness [literally, 'completing sanctification'] in the fear of God" (2 Cor 7:1 ASV). Similarly, he instructs the Christians in Rome to present their "members to righteousness for sanctification" (Rom 6:19, 22).

In the Old Testament, the dominant theme of sanctification is that God (Himself) is holy and is the source of all holiness. God sanctifies His people, who in turn sanctify God's name by living according to God's standard of holiness.[16] Both the Old and New Testaments agree that God's people are to be holy. The Old differs from the New Testament, however, in that one particular people from a particular ethnicity were chosen to be holy. In the New Testament, all people (from every nation and ethnic origin) in Christ are to be holy. Holiness in the Old Testament is ritualistic, whereas in the New Testament it focuses on ethical purity.[17]

The New Testament's emphasis on sanctification primarily points to a personal relationship with God. Thus, Christians are set apart in Christ unto a new relationship with God.[18] It is clear in the New Testament that the Father, Son, and the Holy Spirit are the agents of sanctification.[19] Sanctification is also past, present, and futuristic in essence (as mentioned earlier).[20] It occurs yesterday, today, and tomorrow, and it is therefore relevant in retrospect, contemporary times, and the future. Perfect love makes authentic spirituality and piety possible and connects and sustains a person in his/her multiple relations with God, self, neighbor, and creation.

D. Believers' Function: Prophet, Priest, and King

All believers share Christ's offices as prophet, priest, and king,[21] and are endowed with gifts of the Spirit, or charisms, to serve the community of faith. First, all believers share in Christ's priesthood in that each and every believer has direct access to God through Jesus Christ. Consequently, a believer is able to draw near to God through prayer and personal worship (Heb. 4:14–16; 10:19–21; Matt. 27:51), and intercede on the behalf of others. The priesthood of all believers also allows a person to confess his/her sins directly to God, and Christ's death on the cross atones for the sins of all believers, thus making the forgiveness and redemption of all possible (Col. 2:13–15; 1 Jn. 1:9). All believers can offer sacrifice to God, not in the form of Old Testament rituals, but rather in the form of praise, worship, contrition, thanksgiving, and service to God and neighbor (Rom. 15:16; Phil. 2:17; Heb. 13; 1 Peter 2:9–10). Second, all believers share in Christ's "prophethood" in that they are called to proclaim God's truth and Word.[22] Third, all believers share in Christ's kingship, in that Christ has given them authority and dominance on earth to do good. Christ said, "I will give you the keys of the kingdom of heaven; and whatever you bind (declare to be improper and unlawful) on earth must be what is already bound in heaven; and whatever you loose (declare lawful) on earth must be what is already loosed in heaven" (Matt. 16:19; 18:18 AB).

The Christian, then, is given the same authority that God gave the first Adam, which Christ (the new Adam) fully appropriated and made possible to all believers—that is, to have dominion over the elements of the sea, earth, and firmament (Gen. 1:26, 27). This, however, does not mean that the Christian is not vulnerable to suffering, and in fact, the Christian should triumph in and through suffering. As a result, "those who suffer with Him [Christ] will also reign with Him" in the eschatological kingdom. The three offices of Christ make all believers members of the royal priesthood and ambassadors of Christ. In addition, Michael Downey argues that, "All ministers, ordained and nonordained, are first and finally members of God's Holy People, who are consecrated for mission and whose mission is consecration of the world through Christ in the gift of the Spirit to the glory of God the Father."[23]

In relation to Pauline ecclesial structure, all believers are given charisms, or gifts of the Spirit, to carry out specific functions in the community of faith and world, and the Spirit endows these various gifts upon the believing community as the Spirit deems necessary. It is through these charisms that the whole community of believers should serve. Paul clearly enumerates in his ecclesiology a number of gifts that are given to the believers, according to the measure of the Spirit. Not all believers are given the same gifts, but each is expected to serve the community with his/her gift(s) for its edification, growth, unification, and glorification of God.

The charism of love is the most excellent gift, yet the most common, because all believers should possess love, regardless of the gifts that each person has. It is expected that love for God and neighbor is exemplified in, and is the goal of, the believer's personal spirituality and piety. No charism, therefore, is more important than the other. Each has its function and purpose.[24]

The Pastoral epistles clearly emphasize an ecclesial structure that is more bureaucratic[25] than an earlier free-flowing charismatic ecclesial structure. There is an understanding that the ecclesial structure, as seen in the Pastoral epistles, was a later development than the Pauline charismatic structure. This ecclesial structure in the Pastorals empowered some of the believers to be bishops, elders, and deacons. What was the role of the other believers? Obviously not everyone can lead in certain roles, but the core leadership comes from all the believers, and before one can serve in church offices, one has to be a part of the believing community. The leadership charism is not given to all the believers.

Problems arise in an ecclesial structure when factors other than charisms, such as race, ethnicity, and gender, are the determining criteria for serving in church offices. Also, not all believers are experts in the manner of teaching and preaching that is necessary to guide the whole flock. They do not all embody the charisms of leadership, teaching, and preaching as a unit, which bishops and elders should embody. Therefore, not all believers are bishops, but all bishops are believers. There is a way in which all believers share in the leadership of the church in and through their specific gifts and callings, while bishops, elders, and deacons perform the general leadership of the church via the teaching and leadership charisms dispensed to them. A problem emerges, however, when leadership in the community of faith is reduced to an ecclesiastical hierarchy, because everyone should lead in and through the charisms given to them. No charism should be elevated over the other, as some who embrace the Pastoral epistles' bureaucratic leadership model advocate, oftentimes, in exclusion of Pauline charismatic leadership structure.

Concluding Remarks

The fruit(s) of the Spirit can be seen as spiritual virtues that enrich a believer's life. The works of the flesh are the spiritual vices to avoid, as they annihilate a believer from loving relation with Christ. Sanctification keeps the believer from dangling in the vices, and allows the virtues to be present by constantly purifying one's life. The sanctified believer shares in Christ's priesthood, prophethood, and kingship. (A sanctified life is further endowed by the Spirit with gifts of the Spirit that enable a believer effectively to serve in the body of Christ; this we will explore in the subsequent chapter).

Notes

[1] Gause, R. Hollis, *Living in the Spirit: The Way of Salvation* (Cleveland, Tennessee: Pathway Press, 1980), 100.

[2] Ibid.

[3] Ibid.

[4] Ibid., 103.

[5] Ibid., 98.

[6] Gal. 5:22–23.

[7] Gal. 5:19–21.

[8] Curran, Charles E., *The Catholic Moral Tradition Today* (Washington, DC: Georgetown University Press, 1999), 73; Gause, *Living in the Spirit*, 100.

[9] Lovin, Robin W., *Christian Ethics* (Nashville, Tennessee: Abingdon Press, 2000), 68–79; 1 Cor. 13:13.

[10] Exod. 15:11, 31:13; Lev. 21:8, 15; Ps. 60:6; Ezek. 28:22; Amos 4:2; Matt. 6.9; 1 Pet. 1:1–16.

[11] Oden, Thomas C., *John Wesley's Scriptural Christianity: A Plain Exposition of His Teaching on Christian Doctrine* (Grand Rapids, Michigan: Zondervan Publishing House, 1994), 327–33; Carver, "Biblical Foundations", 8–13.

[12] Gause, *Living in the Spirit*, 99.

[13] Gal. 5:19–21.

[14] Rom. 7:18–21.

[15] Oden, *John Wesley's Scriptural Christianity*, 327–33. *See also*, Carver, "Biblical Foundations," 8–13.

[16] Mills, *Mercer Dictionary of the Bible*, 794.

[17] Ibid.; see also Carver, "Biblical Foundations," 13–19.

[18] Mills, *Mercer Dictionary of the Bible*, 794.

[19] Ibid.

Chapter Eight: Personal Spirituality and Piety

[20] Ibid.

[21] Breshears, Gerry, "The Body of Christ: Prophet, Priest, or King?" *Journal of the Evangelical Theological Society* 37.01 (March 1994): 3–26. *See* Powers, David N, "Priesthood Revisited: Mission and Ministries in the Royal Priesthood," in *Ordering the Baptismal Priesthood: Theologies of Lay and Ordained Ministry*, ed. Susan K. Woods (Collegeville, Minnesota: Liturgical Press, 2003), 92–97. *See also* Dockery, David. "King, Christ As," in *Holman Illustrated Bible Dictionary*, ed. Chad Brand, Charles Draper, and Archie England (Nashville, Tennessee: Holman Bible Publishers, 2003), 984–85.

[22] Breshears, "The Body of Christ," 16–19.

[23] See Downey, Michael, "Ministerial Identity: A Question of Common Foundations," in *Ordering the Baptismal Priesthood*, ed. Susan K. Wood (Collegeville, Minnesota: Liturgical Press, 2003), 6.

[24] For further readings on the charismatic structure of the church, see Rahner, Karl, *The Spirit in the Church* (New York: The Seabury Press, 1979), 37–38; O'Meara, Thomas, *Theology of Ministry* (New York: Paulist Press, 1983), 65–79; *and* Küng, Hans, "The Charismatic Structure of the Church: From the Church and Ecumenism," *Concilium* 4 (1965): 60–61; McDonnell, Kilian, *Christian Initiation and Baptism in the Holy Spirit: Evidence from First Eight Centuries* (Collegeville, Minnesota: Liturgical Press, 1994), 79.

[25] For information on structured church leadership, see Fitzmyer, Joseph A., "The Structured Ministry of the Church in the Pastoral Epistles," *Catholic Biblical Quarterly* 66.4 (October 2004): 582–96; Balcer, J. M., "Athenian Episkopos and the Achaemenid 'King's Eye,'" *AJP* 98 (1977): 252–63. *See also* Porter, L., "The Word *episkopos* in Pre-Christian Usage," *ATR* 21 (1939): 103–42; Borsch, F. H., "Apt Teachers: Bishops as Teachers and Theologians," *ATR* 79 (1997): 102–44; *and* Meier, J. P., "*Presbyteros* in the Pastoral Epistles," *CBQ* 35 (1973): 326–27. *See also* Keller, B. R., "1 Timothy 5:17—Did All Presbyteroi Proclaim God's Word?" *Wisconsin Lutheran Quarterly* 96 (1999): 43–69.

CHAPTER NINE

Gifts of the Spirit

There are various charisms (gifts of the Spirit) that are given to believers to serve one another, in love, in the body of Christ. There are diverse gifts that the Spirit distributes as the Spirit wills. Some of these gifts are deemed ordinary and others extraordinary, but all are for the building-up and edification of the body of Christ. Our lives are the primary context in and through which the charisms' operations and workings are manifested.

A. Definition

The Greek words *charisma* (singular) and *charismata* (plural) are used almost exclusively by the Apostle Paul. The term *charisma* appears seventeen times in the New Testament; sixteen of these occurrences are in Paul's writings, and one is in the First Epistle of Peter (1 Peter 4:10).[1] The word *charisma* has no Hebrew equivalent,[2] but has several meanings. In general, *charisma* is used in reference to the gift of salvation. Paul says, "For the wages of sin is death, but the gift [*charisma*] of God is eternal life through Christ Jesus our Lord" (Rom. 6:23; cf. 5:15ff. KJV). *Charisma* is also used in reference to blessings bestowed on Jews. Paul states that, "For the gifts [*charismata*] and the calling of God are irrevocable" (Rom. 11:29 NKJV). It is through the charisms that Paul was delivered from suffering and death; he believes that *charisma* was granted to him and his travelling companions through the prayers of many (2 Cor. 1:11). Furthermore, *charisma* is a special spiritual gift bestowed upon believers by the Holy Spirit for service to the community of faith.[3] According to Paul, *charismata* "are endowments of the Holy Spirit" (1 Cor. 12:11). *Charisma* in itself does not mean "spiritual gift," as it is commonly used today. It is only in Romans 1:11 that Paul uses *charisma* (gift) and *pneumatikon* (spiritual) together, in a precise way indicating that *charisma* means "grace-gift."[4]

The Greek term *pneumatika* literally means "spiritual things," but the context of 1 Corinthians 12–14 suggests that Paul meant "spiritual gifts." Furthermore, Paul used the terms *charismata* and *pneumatika* interchangeably (1 Cor. 12:31).[5] *Pneumatika* (spiritual gifts) indicate the Spirit's close relationship with the gifts, while *charismata* highlight the gracious character of the gifts.[6] *Charisma* is not merit-based, and is not given upon condition of human effort. The Holy Spirit is the source, giver, and distributor of these grace-gifts (1 Cor. 12:11). In 1 Corinthians 12:4–6, Paul uses three terms (*charismata, diakonai,* and *energemata*) in reference to spiritual gifts. According to Paul, "...now there are varieties of gifts [*charismata*], but the same Spirit. And there are varieties of ministries [*diakonai,* services], and the same Lord. And there are varieties of effects [*energemata,* operations], but the same God who works all things in all persons." French Arrington presents the meaning and function of these terms, as seen in 1 Cor. 12:4–6, in an interesting way. According to him, *charismata* suggest that divine grace is the source of spiritual gifts. The term *diakonai* (service) highlights the practical appropriation of spiritual gifts. *Energemata* means "effects" or "workings," and draws attention to God the Father as the ultimate source of all spiritual gifts.[7] Spiritual gifts are also called *doma*. The term *doma* seems to be equivalent to *charisma*.[8] "Christ gave gifts [*doma*] to men" (Eph. 4:8). Finally, *charismata* are gifts the Spirit gives through grace to the believers to perform the services/functions of the local church. *Charismata* are spiritual gifts because they flow from the Spirit, the source of all charisms.

B. Variety of Gifts

Paul states that there are various kinds of charisms (Rom. 12:6–8; 1 Cor.

12:28–31; Eph. 4:11) that produce manifold operations and functions. Hans Küng categorizes these various charisms into four general classifications: *Charismata* that are connected with *glossolalia* (tongues, miraculous activities or cures, and exorcism), *preaching* (apostles, prophets/prophetesses, teachers, evangelists, and exhorters), *practical aid* (deacons/deaconesses, alms givers, attendants of the sick, and devoted widows), and *leadership* (administrators, *episkopoi*/presbyters, and pastors). There are other charisms not included in the above classification, such as the charism of suffering (Col. 1:24), married and unmarried (1 Cor. 7:7), circumcised and uncircumcised (1 Cor. 7:18–20), and bond and free (1 Cor. 7:21–24).

The list of charisms is innumerable. Paul specifies that charisms are given to meet the needs of the church. Therefore, the Spirit unfolds charisms as the Spirit wills. Every ministry seems to be born out of the charisms. In other words, the charisms produce the various ministries. One could see every ministry as *charisma* and every *charisma* as ministry, or that every *charisma* has the potential to be developed into a ministry. These lists of charisms were not intended to be exhaustive. Therefore, these gifts should be viewed from an open-ended perspective.[9] Paul was likely just highlighting some of the gifts that were present and operative among the believers.

C. Ordinary and Extraordinary Gifts

Charismata can be ordinary as well as extraordinary. They are ordinary in that all the believers are expected to manifest gifts of the Spirit. Also, it is expected that charismatic expression is a normal way of life for the believers. These gifts should be manifested in the day-to-day affairs of persons' lives. For example, love is a charism that everyone should practice daily in relation to both God and neighbor. Persons who possess this charism in extraordinary ways will demonstrate acts of love in more exceptional, yet ordinary ways, if that is possible, because love is always ordinary, as anyone who chooses to love can love. In another example, the charism of healing should not only be manifested in a healing service or in a formal liturgical setting, but it should be applied wherever it is needed.

On the other hand, gifts of the Spirit are extraordinary in that they are given by the Spirit to carry out special functions. These charisms are workings of the Spirit manifested in and through the believers' lives as extraordinary results like signs and wonders. Furthermore, charisms are extraordinary because they are grace-gifts; they are not earned and are given through divine rather than human effort. It is through these gifts that God expresses divine grace and unfolds His will for each of us. Thus, charisms are given for the building-up of the body of Christ (Eph. 4:12). Charisms enhance the common good and welfare of the community of faith (1 Cor. 12:7) and unite the local church (Rom. 12:3–8; Eph. 4:1–16) in carrying out its mission around the world.

Gifts of the Spirit promote unity in diversity in the local church, and should cause people to function in relation to each other because of their dependence on each other's gifts and callings. Just as the body of Christ has many members, the gifts are many. Through the various members of the church, the gifts operate to achieve the overall purpose of the body of Christ. The body of Christ is not confined to the four walls of a church building. The believers also undertake numerous activities outside of the walls of the local church for the church. The gifts are not just to be used inside the structure of the physical church, but for the purpose of the church everywhere. Oftentimes, persons perform tasks within the structures of the church, not for the benefit of the church. The primary emphasis of the church must be love of God and neighbor, and the charisms given to each person should achieve this end whenever and wherever they are used.

A Pauline theology of the workings of the Spirit should not be confined to extraordinary activities, except for those charisms that are associated with *glossolalia,* speaking in tongues, exorcism, faith healing, and miraculous workings or power (1 Cor. 12:10, 14:15; Acts 10:46; 19:6; Mk. 16:17). All the other charisms are ordinary, and are associated with reaching people consciously and responsibly in service (Rom. 12:7); teaching (Rom. 12:7, 1 Cor. 12:28); utterance of wisdom/knowledge (1 Cor. 12:8); faith (1 Cor. 12:9); discernment (1 Cor. 12:10); administration/help (1 Cor. 12:28); and the greatest gift, love, "the most excellent way" (1 Cor. 12:31).

D. Manifestation of Gifts

The local church, the "people of God," and their openness to the Spirit are contexts for the manifestation of the Spirit.[10] The charisms are birthed within the context of the church to meet the needs of God's people everywhere. It is through the "people of God" that the charisms operate, for charisms do not manifest in isolation from the "people of God." Also, the Spirit has to be given liberty to operate as the Spirit wills (1 Cor. 12:6, 7, 11). Consequently, out of the Spirit's operations come forth the gifts of the Spirit necessary for the transformation of such contexts. Charisms are seen as the vehicle through which the Spirit is manifested in the community of faith.[11] The Spirit is present in the community in and through the charisms. A suggested model for the manifestation of the Spirit and function of the gifts of the Spirit in the church is implicit in 1 Corinthians 14:26. In the Post-Apostolic age (70 CE–110), charisms were seen as ministries, gifts coming from the Lord through the Spirit.[12] Consequently, persons would spontaneously minister through the charisms given to them by the Spirit. The charism in the believer was the ministry given to the believer by the Spirit to serve (minister) within the church and community.

E. Source of Charisms

Christ and the Spirit are the two sources of charisms, but the two are intimately connected. Edward Hahnenberg points out that ministry is discussed through two lenses of two 'missions' of the trinity: "…the incarnation of the word in Jesus of Nazareth and the continuing presence of the Holy Spirit in the church and in the world."[13] There are two extremes, however, of these sources of ministry seen in the contemporary church. One view has to do with the high theologies of ministry (seen in Roman Catholic tradition), which holds that priests and pope are like Christ on earth. Hence, "…ministerial structures, such as papacy or priesthood, [is seen] as established in exact detail by the historical Jesus and described the ordained priest as a spiritualized "other Christ" (*alter Christus*)."[14] The other view, low theologies of ministry (seen in some Protestant traditions) articulates that gifts of the

Spirit are bestowed upon persons to serve in ministry: "Charisms freely bestowed directly on the individual by the Holy Spirit make ministerial structures unnecessary."[15]

Neglect of either of these sources of ministry, Christ and the Spirit, threatens a theology of charisms that is fully Trinitarian. Due to the Pentecostal/Charismatic movement's strong emphasis on the Spirit, one could easily think it sees the Holy Spirit as the only source of charism. This, however, causes Benny C. Aker to caution Pentecostals against the practice of "Spirit-monism."[16] As Aker argues, "…all Spirit activity must in some way be Christological and soteriological in nature."[17]

Concluding Remarks

The Spirit of God gives various charisms to the believers for Christian service, thus advancing the kingdom of God on earth. Regardless of the charism a person possesses, each person should use it in accomplishing the principal goal of Christian faith: love of God and neighbor. When the believer uses his/her gift to undertake service to another, such person is demonstrating love for God as well. For example, when a believer through his/her gift imparts healing to a sick person, this is an act of love. The Apostle Paul emphasizes the importance of all the charisms, but he highlights love as "the most excellent pathway." The charism of love can and should be attained by everyone, because if one carries out one's service, even sacrificially, and does not do so for love's sake, one's effort is vain. Paul emphasizes that prophesying or giving one's body to be burnt sacrificially profits nothing if done without love (1 Cor. 13). Therefore, regardless of the charisms that a person has, that person should also possess love.

Notes

1. Arrington, French, *Encountering the Holy Spirit* (Cleveland, Tennessee: Pathway Press, 2003), 233.
2. Küng, "The Charismatic Structure of the Church," 58–59.
3. Arrington, *Encountering the Holy Spirit*, 234.
4. Ibid.
5. Ibid., 236.
6. Ibid.
7. Ibid., 240.
8. Ibid., 239.
9. Ibid., 242–43.
10. Ibid., 238.
11. McDonnell and Montague, *Christian Initiation and Baptism in the Holy Spirit*, 66–75.
12. Bernier, Paul, *Ministry in the Church: A Historical and Pastoral Approach* (Mystic, Connecticut: Twenty-Third Publications, 2003), 49. See also Aker, Benny C, "Charismata: Gifts, Enablements, or Ministries?" *Journal for Pentecostal Theology* 11.1 (2002): 53–69. Aker's thesis is that the gifts of the Spirit should more appropriately be thought of as ministries that flow out of a believer's being a part of the temple of God. See also Berding, Kenneth, "Confusing Word and Concept in 'Spiritual Gifts'; Have We Forgotten James Barr's Exhortations?" *JETS* 43.1 (March 2000): 37–51. To eliminate the confusing different viewpoints that emerge from the use of the term *charismata*, Berding proposes that the term be interpreted exclusively as ministries, instead of Spiritual gifts or as Spirit-given abilities/enablements to do ministry.
13. Hahnenberg, P. Edward, *Ministries: A Relational Approach* (New York: A Herder & Herder Book, The Crossroad Publishing Company, 2003), 39.
14. Ibid.
15. Ibid., 40.
16. Aker, "Charismata," 53.
17. Ibid.

CHAPTER TEN

Communal Worship

It is imperative that believers gather in love to worship God who is love. In this setting, worshippers call upon God with many voices, yet one voice in prayer, declaration, singing, and through various modes and sensibilities. In the Pentecostal/Charismatic context, public worship is perhaps the most visible intimate display of the believers' corporate love for God, which is amplified in ritual sight, sound, and gesture of worshippers. The Pentecostal/Charismatic assembly or communal worship setting, therefore, could be seen as a context for the display and outpouring of love for God.

A. Theological Overview of Assembly

The word assembly is a translation of the Greek term *ekklesia*, used in the Septuagint, which is analogous to the Hebrew word *qahal*.[1] The term *qahal* has both civic and spiritual implications. It refers to the assembly that the king called together, and to the people who gathered under the covenant of God to celebrate and relate with God. Fundamentally, the *qahal* of Yahweh resembles the church gathering to encounter God. According to Mark Francis:

> *Qahal* signifies both the call that convokes the gathering and those who respond to the call and constitute the assembly. Thus the term evokes both the gathered people and the event of gathering as well. In Israel the *qahal* was convoked to hear the words of the king and to give an "official" communal response to these words. In the case of

a *qahal Yahweh*, of course, this solemn assembly assumed more than civic importance—it directly dealt with the relationship between God and Israel. The *qahal Yahweh* was the privileged place and time for the people of Israel to celebrate their identity as God's chosen people. This choice was acknowledged and the covenant with God ratified by the people in *qahal* after hearing God's word. It is for this reason that the Greek ἐκκλησία, with its connotation of a duly summoned assembly, was such an appropriate rendering of *qahal*.[2]

Francis further argues that the solemn *qahal* experienced much evolution over the centuries, yet maintains certain distinctive features. These distinctive features are:

> 1) A gathering of the people convoked by God; 2) an event during which God is present in a special way to the people; 3) a moment of solemn proclamation of God's word that is in turn received and acknowledged by those gathered; 4) a solemn ratification of the relationship (covenant) between God and the people, usually by means of sacrifice.[3]

There are several examples of solemn *qahal* in the Old Testament. The *qahal* in Exodus 19 is seen as the primary and first assembly of Israel after its liberation from Egypt. In this text, the Lord told Moses to summon the ancient Israelites to the foot of Mount Sinai so that the Lord could meet with them. In the assembly, Moses functioned as mediator between God and the people. There are other examples of solemn assemblies in the Old Testament, but they are all related to the first assembly in Exodus 19. In Deuteronomy 5, we see a solemn *qahal*. In this assembly, Israel renewed its covenant with Yahweh before taking possession of the Promised Land. Another example of solemn *qahal* is the assembly that King Josiah convoked to renew the Mosaic covenant and purify the temple (2 Kings 23). A solemn *qahal* is also seen in Ezra calling the people together. In this gathering, the sacred scroll was read and interpreted, and the people were instructed in the Word of the Lord (Nehemiah 8–10).

The preferred New Testament word for the gathered assembly or Christian community is *ekklesia*, or church. This is so because of its association with the Old Testament term *qahal*. There are several other terms, however, such as *crowd* and *synagogue* that are used to represent assembly in the New

Testament.[4] In Acts of the Apostles, the term *ekklesia* was first used in reference to the Christian assembly in Jerusalem, the same as the Jerusalem church. Later, the usage of the term was broadened to refer not only to the local assemblies of believers in Jerusalem, Antioch, Judea, Galilee, and Samaria, but also to Christian assemblies throughout the entire world, the church universal.[5] On two occasions, the Synoptic gospels use the term *ekklesia* in reference to the disciples of Christ, the immediate core group of followers that Jesus formed (Matt. 16:18; 18:18). Jesus states that His presence is evident wherever His disciples are assembled (Matt. 18:20).[6]

The Apostle Paul seems to use the term *ekklesia* more frequently than any other New Testament author. *Ekklesia* is used 65 times in Pauline epistles, and Paul is said to be the first to use this term in the New Testament. He primarily uses the term in relation to the local communities of believers to whom he was writing. There are other ways in which Paul uses the term *ekklesia*, such as to characterize the action shaping the assembly (1 Cor. 11:18), the eucharistic communion (1 Cor. 10:17), the newness and equality among those who form the assembly (2 Cor. 5:17; Gal. 3:28), and Christ as head of the assembly (Col. 1:18, 24). The local assemblies make up the church universal and the body of Christ in general. The writer of Hebrews underscores the importance of the gathered assembly in the admonition not to neglect the assembling of the brethren, and also draws out the eschatological implication of such gatherings (Heb. 10:24–25).[7]

The assembly maintained its significance and proper function, especially after the death of the Apostles, and was an integral part of the incipient church's life and praxis. The *Didache* (a first-century Christian document) summons Christians to come together, confess sins, break bread, and give thanks on the Lord's Day.[8] The Lord's Day was when the early church gathered for worship and to celebrate the paschal mystery. The Day of the Lord is "…a designation for the first day of the week (Rev. 1:10), celebrated by Christians as the day of resurrection of Jesus Christ and thus the day of worship—Sunday,"[9] and not the Sabbath day. Justin Martyr (around 150 AD) points out that the early Christians assembled on Sundays for the liturgy of the Word, prayer, Eucharist, and attending to the needs of the poor and marginalized. According to Martyr:

> On the day which is called Sunday we have a common assembly of all who live in the cities or in the outlying districts, and the memoirs of the Apostles or the writings of the Prophets are read, as long as there is time. Then, when the reader has finished, the president of the assembly verbally admonishes and invites all to imitate such examples of virtue. Then we all stand up together and offer our prayers.... [Later] bread and wine and water are presented... [Then a freewill offering is collected from the wealthy that the president of the assembly uses to care for all those in need].[10]

In the Didascalia of the Apostles, believers are admonished to be faithful to the assembly of the church, because the one who isolates oneself from the assembly is isolating oneself from Christ, and depriving the body of Christ of one of its members.[11] Later, John Chrysostom makes a strong case for people to attend the assembly on a regular basis. In Chrysostom's assembly, corporate prayer seems to have more power and impact than individual prayer. According to Chrysostom:

> Do not say, 'can I not pray at my own home?' Of course you can pray at home, but your prayer has more power when you are united to other members, when the whole body of the church raises its prayer to heaven with a single heart, the priests being there to offer the vows of the gathered multitude.[12]

Yet this insistence on the assembly did not continue. Francis states, "Despite the emphasis placed on the importance of the assembly in the patristic Church, the period just after the sixth century and continuing into the High Middle Ages witnessed its gradual eclipse in the West."[13] The church in the West gradually grew away from the practice of assembling on Sundays for worship because more people resorted to personal spirituality and piety.

B. Pentecostal/Charismatic Assembly

Pentecostals usually have their formal corporate worship or assembling[14] on Sundays, as practiced in the church throughout the centuries. A typical Pentecostal gathering features music, declaration, prayer, testimonies, altar call, and other symbolic acts. Music is an integral part of Pentecostal worship, which is derivative of its Wesleyan origins. Pentecostals usually begin their formal service with "praise and worship,"[15] which primarily involves singing and music. Here people sing, clap, and dance unto the Lord in the Spirit. At times, people will lift their hands in the air, waving them or making gestures unto the Lord. This liturgy of "praise and worship" serves to usher people into the presence of God and prepare them for the whole service.

Pentecostal singing and music are consistent with that seen in the Old Testament, which recounts that the ancient Israelites often sang and made melodies unto God. When they were liberated from Egyptian bondage and passed through the Red Sea, they sang unto God (Exod. 15:1–18). The pages of the Psalms are filled with songs of praise and worship. As the Psalmist declares:

> Praise the Lord. Sing to the Lord a new song, His praise in the assembly of His faithful people. Let Israel rejoice in their maker; let the people of Zion be glad in their king. Let them praise His name with dancing and make music to Him with timbrel and harp. For the Lord takes delight in His people; He crowns the humble with victory.[16]

The Psalmist used, and encouraged the use of, various kinds of instruments in worship, such as the trumpet, harp, lyre, tambourine, strings, flute, and cymbals (Ps. 150: 3–5). This practice among the ancient Hebrews continued into the New Testament and early church (Matt. 26:30; 1 Cor. 14:26; Eph. 5:19).[17]

Music reflects both the cognitive and non-cognitive aspects of life. It affects our manner of thinking and perception, emotions, and moods. Through music we can express our hope, fear, sorrow, joy, and reverence. Music connects us with God and neighbor, and as a result, many broken hearts are healed and people are delivered, restored, and revived through music. Finally, music and singing tend to usher the Pentecostal/Charismatic assembly into the presence of God, and function as a mean through which the Spirit moves and manifests in the gathered assembly and dispenses charisms. Oftentimes, people testify of being Spirit-filled, transformed, delivered, and strengthened from just sharing in the music and singing.

Stanley Grenz contends that declaration of the Word was given more prominence than music in early churches' worship. According to him, "Although in its experience of worship the Old Testament community focused on music, center stage in Christian worship is reserved for declaration. The gathered community comes together to speak and to listen."[18] Declaration played an important role both in the ancient Hebrew tradition and the early church:

> Declaration includes telling each about the greatness and goodness of God. It also means corporately extolling God for who He is and what He has done. In corporate worship, however, declaration entails as well the proclamation of God's word. In ancient communities, such declarations often took the form of prophetic utterances (1 Cor. 14:1–5, 26–32). But a central place was also given to the reading and explication of the Torah (Neh. 8:1–9) or of the Scriptures (1 Tim. 4:13). This biblical tradition forms the foundation for the contemporary sermon.[19]

In Protestant Christian tradition, the Word is the primal liturgy of the gathered assembly. Everything that takes place prior to the sermon builds up to the message, which may come in the form of preaching, teaching or exhorting and brings the service to a climax.

In general, prayer is fundamentally an aspect of declaration—specifically, declaration directed to God. According to Grenz, "…in prayer the community turns the focus of its address away from humans to the God who is the foundation of its existence."[20] Prayer consists of adoration, confession, thanksgiving, and supplication, and these elements are consistent with Jesus' model prayer (Matt. 6). In adoration, the Spirit prompts us to revere God. Acknowledging that God is awesome, majestic, and splendid, is a fitting way of approaching the "throne room" of God. The act of adoration allows us to see ourselves and our weaknesses in light of who God is. Isaiah, after seeing God's splendor, realized that he was filthy and wretched, and needed forgiveness and pardon (Isa. 6:1–6). The Spirit often convicts our hearts or conscience of our wrong deeds. In response, we confess our sins to God, repenting and asking for forgiveness. God forgives the one who confesses sins from a penitent heart. Confession is also a way of ushering us into the presence and promise of God (Dan. 9:20–23). As we recognize our sins, forgive those who sin against us, and seek and receive God's forgiveness, we progress in gratitude for God's past, present, and future actions in our lives (1 Thess. 5:18). Prayer also involves the element of supplication. In supplication,

Chapter Ten: Communal Worship

we should present to God personal needs, and the needs of people both local and universal (1 Thess. 5:25; Phil. 4:6; 1 Tim. 2:1–4).

Testimony is another liturgy in Pentecostal/Charismatic assembly. This is an act of storytelling, a person narrating his/her experience in light of God's present and/or past action in his/her life and context. Oftentimes, parishioners, clergy, and those leading various aspects of the liturgy will share their stories of God's actions in their lives. The people may talk about personal defeat and failure, success, victory, deliverance, prosperity, revelation, warnings, correction, and instructions received. Each oral narrative reveals the action and presence of God in the believer's *sitz-im-leben* (life settings), serving to strengthen those listening and further empower the storyteller. The writer of Revelation alludes to believers overcoming by the words of their testimonies (Rev. 12:11). Some testimonies are about the goodness, greatness, and love God bestowed upon God's children—powerful reminders that God will never leave or forsake God's children and will be with them always, even to the end of the ages (Matt. 28:20). Testimonies affirm that God answers prayer, does powerful things in our lives, and rewards those who diligently seek Him (Heb. 11:6).

After the Word is proclaimed in the context of Pentecostal/Charismatic communal worship, people are often invited to an altar of prayer for salvation, deliverance, healing, and Spirit empowerment. Altar call is an invitation that a preacher, pastor, or leader in the church often extends to individuals to come to the altar to pray and be prayed for in order to encounter God. Through the Spirit's prompting, some persons may yield to the altar call, while others may ignore it. At times, people receive immediate results at the altar. The altar is a place where people bring their offerings and sacrifices, and petitions for an encounter with God. This rite comes at the end of most services, but it may happen at the beginning or during the service. Usually, one goes to the altar voluntarily out of one's conviction in response to the propulsion of the Holy Spirit.

Various symbolic acts are carried out in Pentecostal/Charismatic worship. These acts include sacraments,[21] "laying-on-of-hands," and handshakes. Through these acts, the Spirit makes Christ present and puts humans in communion with the Trinity and fellow humans. Water baptism usually happens after a person is at least initially converted. The person being baptized is usually immersed in water, which symbolizes dying to sin and being resurrected in Christ, but there are times when a person may be rebaptized if deemed necessary by the church and the one being baptized. This usually happens when a person backslides and subsequently returns to Christ. The rebaptism formula in the Pentecostal/Charismatic context can be interpreted in two ways. On the one hand, rebaptism reaffirms the first; on the other hand, rebaptism replaces the first. In the second instance, a candidate is considered so far removed from the faith, backslid altogether, and as a result the person is no longer considered a Christian. Hence a second baptism is ensued, which some churches would consider unorthodox. Water baptism is usually reserved for adults, but children may also partake of the sacrament (in some circles) if it is deemed that they comprehend the rite.

The Eucharistic celebration or the Lord's Supper is practiced in *anamnesis* of the paschal mystery, the reign of God, and in anticipation of Christ's Second *Parousia*. In Roman Catholic circles, the Eucharist is celebrated very frequently; it is the focal point of their mass. Foot-washing in Pentecostal circles serves to foster fellowship, servitude, and perpetual cleansing among the saints. This rite is usually done around the same time as the Lord's Supper, usually in the same setting and may precede or follow the Lord's Supper. Water is usually poured in a basin from which participants wash one another's feet, thus reenacting Christ washing the disciples' feet. In most cases, men wash men's feet and women wash women's feet. This rite signifies the ongoing cleansing that goes on in those who are in Christ, and a person washing another's feet signals humility and unconditional acceptance of each other.[22]

Anointing and the "laying-on-of-hands" are common practices in the church, often employed during healing rituals,[23] spiritual endowments and blessings,[24] and ordination and commissioning rituals.[25] In general, anointing and "laying on of hands" in their various forms are coupled with prayer, initiating healing, deliverance from demon possession, supernatural encounters with God, and power for service. Additionally, it is customary for an usher standing at the door of the sanctuary to shake the hands of those entering the sanctuary. A handshake can be a way of expressing and experiencing Christian love, warmth, and acceptance among the believers as well. It may also break down various barriers and prejudices, and puts persons at ease and peace with each other. Sometimes the handshake is accompanied by hugs, kisses, and warm embraces.

C. Pentecostal/Charismatic Modes and Sensibilities

Pentecostal/Charismatic worship generates pneumacentric celebrative energy. The broadest range of characteristically Pentecostal/Charismatic expressions probably occurs within the mode of celebration.[26] This celebratory attitude can be seen throughout the entire worship service, but is more obvious during "praise and worship." In a typical worship service, people will sing, dance, and sway their bodies to the festive music, clap their hands, and raise their hands in praise, while others will lift a hand or both hands heavenward with smiles (and at times, tears of joy).

Daniel Albrecht contends that the celebrative mode of worship in the Pentecostal/Charismatic context is more playful. He further observes that this playful celebration is not exclusive to the praise and worship aspect of the service, but rather it is essential to all Pentecostal/Charismatic rituals.[27] According to Albrecht, "…the celebrative mode of Pentecostal ritual is characterized by a sensibility that is playful, expressive, spontaneous, and free, the ritual service on a whole is normally balanced by a mode of "transcendental efficacy."[28] Transcendental efficacy:

> Refers to an attitude that participates in "pragmatic ritual work" particularly, as it is related to a transcendental reality (i.e. God) and to the power of that transcendental reality to produce an effect... Among Pentecostals, rites performed in the transcendental efficacious mode strike a note of expectancy. When Pentecostals pray in this mode they expect an answer. Unlike the sensibilities of celebration which may freely play, enjoying and experiencing the meaning of symbols, the mode of efficacy employs the symbols, declaring how things work by working them... Rites of and prayers for healing, miracles, and Spirit baptism are examples of this pragmatic mode within Pentecostal service, rites and spirituality....The pragmatic dimension of Pentecostal spirituality is clearly demonstrated in the rite of altar/response…. Transcendental efficacy is an attitude, a ritual sensibility, that vitalizes Pentecostal actions, especially those

acts seen as empowered ministry.[29]

The mode of transcendental efficacy, therefore, emphasizes the practical faith dimension of Pentecostalism. A sense of immediacy when praying is embedded in the psyche of many believers. People often expect things to happen when praying, as they are used to seeing things happen when the community of faith or someone in the community prays. People have seen the mighty wonders of God through the manifestation and application of extraordinary charisms. A person who is endowed with the gift of healing applies oil, lays his/her hand, and prays for the sick in the assembly, then instant and sometimes progressive healing takes place. Many signs and wonders are also seen in gatherings, which are predicated upon faith and prayer. The early Pentecostals used to tarry for the outpouring of the Spirit. People would gather at the altar with the anticipation that God would fill them with the Spirit and that they would manifest visible signs of the Spirit's outpouring, such as speaking in other tongues and discovering powers to do extraordinary things.

Contemplation, the third mode of Pentecostal/Charismatic worship, brings out the more reflective and contemplative notion of the worshipper in the Pentecostal/Charismatic experience. According to Albrecht:

> The Contemplative ritual mode is characterized by a sense of openness to God, a deep receptivity. The Pentecostal ethos is shaped by this mode...The mode of contemplation itself approaches the divine in a reverent interrogative mood. While the mode of celebration actively plays and mode of transcendental efficacy engages in ritual work toward its pragmatic goal, the contemplative mode attentively waits.[30]

Believers often speak of waiting on the Spirit of the Lord to fill and empower them and give discernment and clear directions to their lives. Persons at times leave the assembly feeling that the Lord has spoken to them. People operate in the contemplative mode even when they are functioning in other modes. They frequently ask, "What is God saying to me or to us?" Or they might say, "Speak, Holy Spirit!" They not only operate inside this mode in a ritual context, but also outside the context of communal rituality. Before one makes a significant moral or ethical decision, one seeks the will of God

Chapter Ten: Communal Worship

or knowledge of God in relation to that particular situation.

Finally, the Pentecostal/Charismatic worship experience has various ritual sensibilities, such as sounds, sights, and kinesthetics. The sounds that one would normally hear in a Pentecostal/Charismatic assembly include the exclamations "Hallelujah!" "Glory!" "Praise the Lord!" and "Amen". Whooping, groaning, and sobbing often are signs of someone's grief, brokenness, deliverance, and sometimes breakthrough. Laughter may vocalize someone's joy and cheerfulness in God. Pentecostals/Charismatics sometimes clap or cheer when they are in strong agreement with something that is said by the preacher or moderator. In corporate prayer, when the whole assembly prays together, this body generates a kind of sound that spurs one to pray and participate in the movement of God that is breaking forth. At times, when the Spirit is felt through a prayer or through other liturgies, the congregation often makes sounds that represent that move of the Spirit. These sounds are often spontaneous yet appropriate. Albrecht succinctly summarizes the ritual sounds of Pentecostal/Charismatic worship:

> Walking into a Pentecostal service for the first time one might well be struck by a cacophony of sounds. However, what is sonic dissonance to the outsider, is to the Pentecostal a symphony of holy sounds...Among the Pentecostal ritual sounds, music especially functions as an auditory icon....The Pentecostal world of worship is shaped by the sounds that surround the worshipper. As part of the ritual field, these ritual sounds are one of the elements that help to produce the matrix within which Pentecostals encounter their God and each other.[31]

The second sensibility is ritual sight. The Pentecostal/Charismatic worship context resembles traditional Protestant ritual symbols, but as Albrecht points out, the most powerful visual symbols in the Pentecostal/Charismatic assembly are the fellow worshippers. The sight of another person worshipping spurs one to worship, even though fellow worshippers are not the center or focus of worship. In a typical Pentecostal/Charismatic assembly, you will not see icons fashioned out of wood or stone; the thing that draws people to worship is the act of worship itself.[32] The ritual sights of Pentecostal/Charismatic worship, however, could be strengthened by Pentecostals/

Charismatics employing and demonstrating a deeper appreciation for the aesthetics of worship. Pentecostals/Charismatics could learn this from churches with more formal liturgies.[33] As it relates to the kinesthetic dimension of Pentecostal/Charismatic worship, Albrecht states that:

> The human body and its movement has another important iconic role in Pentecostal ritual: the kinesthetic (and tactile) dimensions of Pentecostal worship. Enthusiastic Pentecostal ritualists have been labeled "holy rollers"....The faithful may sway or even dance as they sing. They clap to the music and use applause as a "praise offering." They raise their hands enacting celebration; join hands in prayer, extend hands in prayer toward those in need but distanced. At times they "fall under the power." They bow, kneel, stand and sit all as part of their kinesthetic worship experience...the Kinesthetic dimension of worship is closely linked to the experience of God....Experiencing God is the fundamental goal of the Pentecostal service. This experiencing or encountering God is often symbolized as felt presence of the divine... As we look closely at the created corporate context in which Pentecostals experience their God, it is clear that they experience their God in a very social context. The Pentecostal ritual experience is not a solo affair, each worshipper is greatly impacted and facilitated by fellow worshippers. Sounds, sights and movements, primarily produced by other ritualists, are not incidental to the (corporate) spirituality.[34]

Closing Remarks

Pentecostals/Charismatics are not hesitant to respond to the experience of God and the impressions of the Spirit during the worship exercise. To the onlooker, it might seem strange to see someone "slain under the power of the Spirit," but to the Pentecostal/Charismatic believer, this is always anticipated. This further reveals that the Spirit is at work in the Pentecostal/Charismatic assembly, as the different movements and actions in the assembly are often symbolic of the Spirit's leadership and presence. A person cannot assume, however, that everything people do in worship is of the Spirit. Sometimes, persons are driven by their own passion and zeal, but this does not discredit the authentic move of the Spirit in other worshippers.

Chapter Ten: Communal Worship

Notes

[1] Francis, Mark, "Liturgy and Assembly," in *Handbook for Liturgical Studies*, ed. Anscar J. Chupungco (Collegeville, Minnesota: The Liturgical Press, 1998), 131.

[2] Ibid.

[3] Ibid., 132.

[4] Ibid.

[5] Ibid., 133.

[6] Ibid.

[7] Ibid., 133–34.

[8] The Didache 14:1–3. *See also,* Aaron Milavec, *The Didache: Text, Translation, Analysis, and Commentary,* (Collegeville, Minnesota: Liturgical Press, 2003), 35; *and* Deiss, Lucien, *Springtime of the Liturgy: Liturgical Texts of the First Four Centuries,* trans. by Matthew J. O' Connell (Collegeville, MN: The Liturgical Press, 1979), 77.

[9] McKim, *Westminster Dictionary of Theological Terms.*

[10] Apologia 1: 67; Martyr, Justin, St., *Writings of Justin Martyr,* Hermigild Dressler, Robert Russell, Thomas Halton, William Tongue, and Josephine Brennan, eds., (Washington D.C: The Catholic University of America Press, 1965), 106–107.

[11] Deiss, Lucien, *Springtime of the Liturgy,* 176–77.

[12] Francis, "Liturgy and Assembly," 135.

[13] Ibid., 136.

[14] Cheryl Johns points out that the Pentecostal worship context has pedagogical implications for its participants. According to her, "The context of worship becomes a primary context for formation. As a drama of God's unfolding actions, the setting of worship and the liturgies contained within the act of worship, serve to instruct, exhort and to model the life of faith." See Johns, *Pentecostal Formation,* 124.

[15] Seamone, Donna Lynne, "Body as Ritual Actor and Instrument of Praise: Verna Maynard's Experience as Praise Leader in the Kitchener Church of God," *Journal of Ritual Studies* 12.1 (Summer 1998): 17–26. In this article Seamone addresses the segment of Pentecostal worship service that is called "Praise and Worship." Seamone does this study via scrutinizing Verna Maynard's praise leadership at the Kitchener Church of God in Kitchener, Ontario, Canada. *See also* Percy, Martyn, "Sweet Rapture: Subliminal Eroticism in Contemporary Charismatic Worship," *Theology & Sexuality* 6 (1997): 71–106. In this article, Percy attempts to show how worship songs about God, packed with images and analogies of intimacy, immediacy, power and eroticism, lead to the forms of embodiment and somatic experience that are peculiar to aspects of contemporary Charismatic Renewal.

[16] Psalm 149:1–4.

[17] Grenz, *Theology for the Community of God,* 492.

[18] Ibid., 493.

[19] Ibid.

[20] Ibid., 494.

[21] Baptism and Eucharist are the two sacraments that are primarily observed in most Protestant circles, but Pentecostals employ Foot-washing as a third ordinance. For further understanding of the theology and historical development of the doctrine of sacraments, *see* Gonzalez, Justo L., *A History of Christian Thought: From the Protestant Reformation to the Twentieth Century* vol. iii (Nashville, Tennessee: Abingdon Press, 1987), 64–68, 82–85. For further thoughts on the sacraments as they

relate to the Anglican/Methodist tradition, *see* Jackson, Thomas, ed., *The Works of John Wesley* (Grand Rapids: Baker Book House, 1979); Outler, Albert C., ed., *John Wesley*, vol. v (New York: Oxford University Press, 1964); Osborn, George, *The Poetical Works of John and Charles Wesley* (London: Wesleyan-Methodist Conference Office, 1869); Baker, Frank, *John Wesley and the Church of England* (Nashville, Tennessee: Abingdon Press, 1970); and Harper, Steve, *Devotional Life in the Wesleyan Tradition* (Nashville Tennessee: Upper Room, 1983). The Roman Catholic tradition observes seven sacraments (Baptism, Conformation, Eucharist, Penance, Anointing of the Sick, Orders, and Marriage). For Catholic sacraments, *see* Bouley, Allan, ed., *Catholic Rites Today* (Collegeville, Minnesota: The Liturgical Press, 1992); *and* Vorgrimler, Herbert, *Sacramental Theology* (Collegeville, Minnesota: The Liturgical Press, 1992).

[22] Foot-washing is a rite/sacrament that many Pentecostals observe. This is said to have legitimacy and a place among the sacramental rites. See Thomas, John Christopher, *Foot-washing in John 13 and the Johannine Community* (Sheffield: Sheffield Academic Press, 1991). See also Thomas, John Christopher, *Ministry & Theology* (Cleveland, Tennessee: Pathway Press, 1996), 39–48, 169–73.

[23] In general, Pentecostal healing rituals seek to achieve holistic healing and wholeness in body, mind, and Spirit.

[24] In various ceremonies, such as weddings, couples are often asked to kneel at the altar while the pastor lays his/her hand on them and prays as an act of sealing and blessing the marriage covenant and the couple together.

[25] When one is being ordained or commissioned to Christian service (such as Presbyterate and Episcopate), the "laying on of hands" formula is usually employed. This gesture symbolizes the succession or handing down of ministerial authority. This act, in the Pentecostal/Charismatic context, does not explicitly mean "Apostolic succession," as seen in other traditions. This practice, however, is consistent with Apostolic leadership and the leadership of the church in general throughout the centuries (see 1 Tim. 4:14, 5:22; Acts 6:6).

[26] Albrecht, Daniel E., "Pentecostal Spirituality: Looking Through the Lens of Ritual," *Pneuma* 14.2 (1992): 107–25, 116.

[27] Ibid., 116–17.

[28] Ibid., 117.

[29] Ibid., 117–18.

[30] Ibid., 118–19.

[31] Ibid., 111–12.

[32] Ibid., 113.

[33] For a treatment of aesthetic in liturgy, *see* Maggiani, Silvano, "Liturgy and Aesthetic," in *Handbook for Liturgical Studies*, ed. Anscar J. Chupungco (Collegeville, Minnesota: The Liturgical Press, 1998), 263–80.

[34] Albrecht, "Pentecostal Spirituality," 113–14.

CHAPTER ELEVEN

Communal Fellowship

Fellowship is a very important aspect of the Christian faith in that it binds people together in love. This chapter sets out to explore models of *koinonia*. It shows that the Spirit is the agent and sustainer of true fellowship, and that the Spirit uses various instruments to accomplish this end. There are various factors that hinder fellowship, as well as factors that foster fellowship.

Definition of Fellowship

Bradley Chance traces the etymology:

> "Fellowship" is the English translation of words from the Hebrew stem *Chabar* and the Greek stem *Koin*. The Hebrew *Chabar* was used to express ideas such as common or shared house (Prov. 21.9), "binding" or "joining" (Exod. 26.6; Eccles. 9.4), companion (Eccles. 4.10), and even a wife as a companion (Mal. 2.14). *Chabar* was used for a member of a Pharisaic society. Pharisees tended to form very close associations with one another in social, religious, and even business affairs. A most important dimension in the life of these *Cheberim* was a sharing together in the study of Scripture and law and table fellowship.[1]

Chance's argument indicates that *koinonia* (fellowship) is rooted in corporate sharing and togetherness, and it implies communality among people on religious, social, and economic levels. The *Westminster Dictionary of Theological Terms* uses this term interchangably with fellowship, participation, and communion, and therefore defines it as "...the relationships experienced by Christians with God, Jesus Christ, the Holy Spirit, and among themselves in the early church (Acts 2.42–47; 1 Cor. 1.9; 2 Cor. 13.14 [13.13, NRSV]; 1 Jn. 1.3, 6)."[2]

Paul uses *koinonia* in many ways. First, and most frequently, Paul employs this word in light of the believers' relationship with the risen Christ and the salvific benefits that come through Christ.[3] This fellowship of the believers is with the Son (1 Cor. 1:9), Holy Spirit (2 Cor. 13:14), and in the gospel (1 Cor. 9:23; Phil. 1:5). Second, Paul uses the term in describing the Lord's Supper. It is believed that the Christians' reference to the Lord's Supper goes back to this Pauline usage. Paul's rhetorical questions about the cup and bread in 1 Cor. 10:16–17 shed light on the Christians' communion and sharing in both Christ's blood and body. Paul further charges that a person cannot participate in both the communion of the Lord's blood and body, and idol rituals. A believer should avoid contrary religious practices if he/she intends to share in the Lord's Supper (1 Cor. 10:19–21). Here Paul is echoing the words of Christ that a person cannot have allegiance to two masters at the same time (Matt. 6:24, Lk. 16:13). Those who partake of Christ's supper are doing so in *anamnesis* (remembrance) of His passion, resurrection and pending Second *Parousia* (coming), which is in conflict with the practice of idol feasting. Also, fellowship with Christ in the Lord's Supper facilitates fellowship between believers. Consequently, those who partake of the Lord's Supper should not ignore the needs of their fellow brothers and sisters and create divisions and factions, as some of the Corinthian believers were criticized for doing (1 Cor. 11:17–18, 21).[4]

Paul's third use of *koinonia* is in reference to Christians sharing their lives with each other. Paul charges that the one who receives the gospel should share it with others (Gal. 6:6). Financial contributions to the poor and needy were one of the ways in which this fellowship was realized, as seen when Paul collected funds from the non-Jewish Christians for the poor Jewish Christians in Jerusalem (Rom. 15:26; 2 Cor. 8:4; 9:13). Also, Paul maintains that the Jewish Christians were entitled to material blessings from non-Jewish believers, as they shared in their Spiritual blessings (Rom. 15:27). Hence, Chance concludes, "Such mutual sharing of one's blessing is a clear

Chapter Eleven: Communal Fellowship

and profound expression of Christian fellowship."[5]

A fourth reference by Paul relates *koinonia* to the believers' sharing in Christ's suffering (Phil. 3:10; Col. 1:24). Believers should exemplify Christ in suffering for the sake of the "people of God" (2 Cor. 4:7–12; Col. 1:24). The followers of Christ will also share the same end as Christ—that is, glorification after suffering (Phil. 2:9–11). Those who suffer for the sake of Christ will share with Him in His glory (Rom. 8:17; Phil. 3:10–11).[6] Finally, Paul uses *koinonia* in the context of the "…unity and bonding that exists between Christians by virtue of the fact that they share together in the grace of the Gospel."[7]

Koinonia also has a special and important place in the Johannine tradition, as illuminated in D. Edmond Hiebert's summary of the meaning of *koinonia* in John 1:1–4. According to Hiebert:

> The noun "fellowship" (κοινωνίαν), based on the Greek adjective meaning "common" (κοινός), denotes the active participation or sharing in what one has in common with others. The nature of what is mutually shared molds the nature of the group. Here, as in Acts 2.42, the intimate bond of fellowship that unites the group is their common faith in Christ, based on the apostolic message. By its very nature the new life in Christ creates and stimulates the desire for such fellowship. The Christian life is a call not for isolation but for active participation with other believers in this new life. Desiring to preserve and promote this horizontal fellowship, John declared the vital vertical aspect of Christian fellowship: "and indeed our fellowship is with the Father, and with His Son Jesus Christ"…This vertical fellowship is vital for true fellowship horizontally. Each reflects and influences the other.[8]

Hiebert's statement indicates that fellowship in the Johannine tradition means active participation among Christian brethren. When believers come to Christ, they are called to fellowship with God and other believers.

Pheme Perkins articulates that the Johannine letters imply that the Johannine community is divided into three groups. The first group is loyal to the author of the epistles, and 1 John and 2 John are addressed to this group. 3 John reveals the presbyter's attempt to form a new house church or missionary outpost in the house of Gaius. Obviously Gaius' household was loyal to the presbyter. The second group opposes and separates itself from the presbyter of these epistles; as a result, the author in these epistles castigates this group. The third group, led by Diotrophes, seems to be in conformity with the presbyter.[9] The presbyter's message indicates that a believer abiding in Christian fellowship is also abiding in the body of Christ, because fellowship is one of the hallmarks of Christianity. Scholars recognize that *koinonia* has the dual functions of symbolization and social reality in both the Johannine and Pauline traditions.[10] Perkins further explains, "The Johannine community has invested *koinōnia* with the symbolic language by which it understands the relationship between Christians and Christ."[11]

Therefore, the presbyter of the Johannine epistles argues that *koinonia* is intricately connected with the preaching of the gospel "from the beginning" (1 Jn. 1:1–3). Consequently, his audience is expected to be mindful of the gospel that is preached to them. Obviously, it is this gospel that brought them into Christian fellowship, and deviation from the gospel means separation from true fellowship with the saints and God and Christ. Christian *koinonia* is associated with both Jesus and God. Consequently, God calls people to enter into this *koinonia* unendingly, and when people drift from the fellowship of God, they have an advocate who is with the Father, Christ the Lord, who intercedes on their behalf and restores them to fellowship. Professing that a person has no sin is contrary to the presbyter's claim, which denies the atoning death and work of Jesus as the source of the forgiveness of sin and restoration of Christian *koinonia* (1 Jn. 1:9). Remaining in authentic *koinonia* will guarantee the believers' cleansing through the blood of the paschal lamb (1 Jn. 1:7).[12]

The presbyter of the Johannine epistles maintains that those who walk in authentic fellowship are children of the light who do not associate with those who walk in evil ways. The presbyter charges his loyal audience not to intermingle, associate, and pray with his opponents and their followers, who are separated from true fellowship. The message of the presbyter's opponents was erroneous and obviously did not represent true gospel and *koinonia* (1 John 5:16; 2 John 11). Consequently, the presbyter's line of thought is that good and evil do not dwell together, and that those in true *koinonia* should share a singleness of mind and purpose.[13]

B. Models of Koinonia

Models of *Koinonia* in the early church can be gleaned from the arguments of Klaus Schafer, Elizabeth Schussler Fiorenza, and Karl Olav Sandnes. Schafer argues that the bond of Christian brotherhood and sisterhood among believers in the early church was different from that of the household and family structure, because the former was egalitarian fellowship, whereas the latter was patriarchal in essence. According to Schafer:

> A dichotomy [exists] between the fellowship as a brotherhood, and real family life, such that brotherhood becomes a theological symbol for an egalitarian fellowship. He considers household and brotherhood as contrasting models in Pauline ecclesiology: the household represents the patriarchal model, while brotherhood represents the egalitarian and participatory.[14]

The incipient church, even though it was operating within a household, was not governed by the household or family structure, rather by egalitarian fellowship. This egalitarian paradigm, however, gradually waned as it was replaced with the patriarchal structure. According to Fiorenza:

> In the beginning the early church was an egalitarian community with no patriarchal elements in it. This is witnessed in texts like Mark 3:31–35; par. Matt 23:8–10 and the baptismal confession in Gal. 3:28. The egalitarian character of the Christian counter-cultural groups was destroyed as the church gradually replaced the egalitarian forms of community by patriarchal structures. This can be seen in the letters of the New Testament in general, and in particular in the adoption of the household codes and in the Pastoral Epistles. A decline into household structures took place in early Christianity. The family terms are here interpreted within a framework of a specific reconstruction of the history of the early Church.[15]

Sandnes highlights that the dichotomy between brotherhood and household fellowship both Schafer and Fiorenza perceive is questionable. Sandnes argues that brotherhood and household structures converged in the early churches. Moreover, Sandnes contends that it appears neither of the structures replaced the other, rather a model of Christian fellowship emerged from an integration of both structures. For Sandnes, both the brotherhood and household structures existed together and not as different entities. The household was the context in which the egalitarian community existed. According to Sandnes:

> Two factors were decisive in shaping the structure of primitive Christianity as family-like: the churches originated when households embraced the faith, and conversion of individuals often caused a family crisis.... Christians gathered in private homes (1 Cor. 11:34; 14:35). In some texts Paul names the head of the household where the believers came together: 1 Cor. 1:16; 16:15–16, 19; Rom. 16:5 (cf. Col. 4:5).[16]

Clearly, the church evolved in a household that was converted to Christianity, and the converted family then became the newly formed church. When just one of the family members was converted, particularly a subordinate, conflict in the home often ensued. Invading differences in faith and praxis cut against the prevailing family tradition.

Therefore, the early local Christian fellowships or churches usually began with the conversion of the head of a household (*paterfamilias*), because the members of the household would follow such person's lead (Acts 10:24; 11:14; 16:15). Sandnes states that:

> The starting point of the churches was normally the conversion of the *paterfamilias*, who embraced the Christian faith together with his whole household. Conversion of households fixes the character of the Christian fellowship; the embryo of the community was a family and the household is turned into a congregation. The social matrix of early Christianity was *oikos* and kinship.[17]

When someone other than the head of the household was first to convert to the Christian faith, such person typically was ostracized by family members. As Sandnes recounts, "...the crisis within households is usually witnessed when a subordinate embraced the faith."[18]

C. Spirit and Koinonia

Albert Curry Winn illuminates the role of the Spirit as life-giving (Eze. 37:1–14; 2 Cor. 3:6; John 6:63), and this function of the Spirit is crucial for sustenance of the community of faith. The Spirit gives life both to individuals (e.g. Judg. 6:34; 1 Sam. 11:5–7; 1 Kings 18:12; Deut. 34:9; Exod. 31:3; 35:31; Num. 11:17) and to the community. Yahweh promises to pour out His Spirit upon the house of Israel and its descendants (Num. 11:29; Eze. 39:28–29). The prophecy of Joel highlights Yahweh's promise and the outpouring of the Spirit upon all flesh. The prophet Joel states:

> And it shall come to pass afterward, that I will pour out my Spirit upon all flesh; and your sons and your daughters shall prophesy, your old men shall dream dreams, your young men shall see visions: And also upon the servants and upon the handmaids in those days I will pour out my Spirit.[19]

This passage shows a corporate bestowal of the Spirit, which is fulfilled on the notable day of Pentecost and has implications for the contemporary church. Peter affirms this bestowal of the Spirit in his sermon (Acts 2:16–18). The Evangelist recounts the events of Pentecost as follows:

> And when the day of Pentecost was fully come, they were all with one accord in one place. And suddenly there came a sound from heaven as of a rushing mighty wind, and it filled all house where they were sitting. And there appeared unto them cloven tongues like as of fire, and it sat upon each of them. And they were all filled with the Holy Ghost, and began to speak with other tongues, as the Spirit gave them utterance.[20]

This corporate outpouring of the Spirit continues in the early churches, including the Johannine community (John 20:22), Samaria (Acts 8:14–17), Ephesus (Acts 19:1–6), and elsewhere (Acts 10:44–48). The Spirit not only gives life, but also functions as the agent of *koinonia* in the Christian community, fostering fellowship in the early churches and among believers. The Evangelist summarizes:

> And they [the early believers] continued steadfastly in the apostles' doctrine and fellowship, and in breaking of bread, and in prayers.

And fear came upon every soul: and many wonders and signs were done by the apostles. And all that believed were together, and had all things in common; and sold their possessions and goods, and parted them to all men, as every man had need. And they, continuing daily with one accord in the temple, and breaking bread from house to house, did eat their meat with gladness and singleness of heart. Praising God, and having favor with all the people. And the Lord added to the church daily such as should be saved.[21]

The early churches flourished due to the ongoing presence of *koinonia* via the agency of the Holy Spirit. This further resulted in the ongoing prayers, signs and wonders, sharing, oneness, gladness, praising of God, breaking of bread, and tremendous church growth.

Winn further describes the Holy Spirit's mission as to initiate, sustain, renew, and shape the shared life of the community, so the bestowal of life upon believers is instrumental to that end.[22] According to Winn, "…the primary work of the Holy Spirit is to bestow koinonia, shared life, on the people of God—provides a fruitful criterion for evaluating various theologies and movements as they relate to the Holy Spirit."[23] Winn's argument seems consistent with both Scripture and tradition in that the Nicene Creed states, "And in the Holy Ghost, Lord and Giver of life; who proceeds from the Father, who with the Father and the Son together is worshipped and glorified; who spake by the Prophets."[24]

In Winn's account, John Calvin, one of the most prominent Reformers, highlights "the Holy Spirit as the *interior magister,* the inward teacher who alone enables us to understand Scripture by opening our blind eyes and unstopping our deaf ears."[25] Winn adds that Friedrich Schleiermacher, in his discussion of the *ordo salutis* in the life of the individual, "…scarcely mentions the Holy Spirit. But in his discussion of the church, which he defines as the fellowship of believers, the Holy Spirit appears with great prominence, and precisely as the bestower of shared life on the people of God."[26] Winn sees this as an indication that Schleiermacher "…takes seriously what we have defined as the principal work of the Holy Spirit: the bestowal of koinonia, shared life, on the people of God."[27]

Barth, in Volume IV of the *Church Dogmatic*, talks about the Holy Spirit in connection with the gathering, building up, and witness of the Christian

Chapter Eleven: Communal Fellowship

community, Winn observes.[28] He also cites Part Four of Paul Tillich's *Systematic Theology*, in which "…it is very clear that the work of the Spirit has to do with life in all its dimensions, not just with the understanding; and that the life the Spirit gives to the individual is instrumental to corporate life he gives to the community."[29]

Finally, "…it is precisely in the discussion of *glossolalia* and other gifts that it is made crystal clear that the primary work of the Holy Spirit is to bestow koinonia, shared life, on the people of God,"[30] as Winn articulates. Therefore, the Spirit is the agent of *koinonia* and the source from which it comes, and the evidence of *koinonia* in a community shows that the Spirit is present in that community.

D. Instruments of Koinonia

The early churches helped to bolster *koinonia* in the faith community with what can be referred to as instruments of ecclesial communion. These instruments include faith in Christ, circulation of letters, ecclesial authority, symbols of faith (declaration of faith), and episcopal assemblies or councils. Celsius (at around the second half of the second century) highlights many differences in Christianity, hence various Christian communities had their unique praxes of faith. These differences reveal that Christianity at that time was diverse and that despite the various differences among the various Christian groups, their common faith in Jesus Christ united them and distinguished the Christian from other faith traditions. Therefore, writing and receiving letters from the various Christian communities kept the early church united. Members from one community of faith would travel with a letter from that community to gain acceptance into another community. Angelo Di Berardino affirms that, "…the laity, too, traveled with 'letters of communion' so that they would be welcomed in other communities…"[31] Letters helped to define and clarify Christian doctrine and theology among the various communities and preserve Christian *koinonia*. Di Berardino highlights "…a frequent exchange of letters between the various communities, so that 'the church which is in Rome' felt that it was not only united but was a unity with 'the church which is in Corinth.'"[32] Some of these letters later formed the authorized New Testament canon. Di Berardino states:

> The frequent contacts between the churches were necessary not only in order to compare the doctrines received, to reject those which were erroneous and to strengthen one another in the same faith. Relations were maintained by Christians traveling from one community to another and by the exchange of letters. Ecclesiastical communion was not identified with universal uniformity, but was that of individual churches with the main churches.[33]

Clearly, circulation of letters helped to keep the believers in the one faith, and facilitated ongoing dialogue and fellowship with the various churches.

There are numerous ways in which people refer to symbols of faith: "rule of faith," "rule of truth," "rule of piety," "declaration of faith," and so on. Di Berardino contends that two types, or forms, of profession of faith developed in the early churches: one that was structured with questions and answers, and the other in the form of a declaration. Catechumens were expected to repeat the profession of faith prior to their baptism and to memorize and recite this formula or creedal statement as deemed necessary.[34] Basil of Caesarea illustrates that:

> As for the profession of faith which we set down on our first entry (to the community) when we put away idols and drew near to the living God, whoever does not guard it on every occasion and adhere to it throughout his life as to a sure safeguard, puts himself outside the promises of God, going against what he wrote with his own hand and set down as a profession of his (own) faith.[35]

Basil's argument reveals that strict adherence to the profession of faith was required of the believers, and commitment to the creed was paramount and expected to last a lifetime.

Just as the various Christian communities were diverse, so too were their creedal formulations, yet consistent with the central doctrine of Christianity. Di Berardino maintains, "Although the doctrinal formula differed in detail from church to church, it also became a proof of the perfect and right faith."[36] Hence, the church councils sought to craft a document that could serve all the churches:

The various councils of the fourth century simply developed formulations as a sign of their own doctrinal identity, pre-occupied in finding a formula on which all could agree. To a degree, the creed of the council of 381 was established when it was accepted by the Council of Chalcedon in 451: on the one hand it was the instrument of communion, and on the other it also became a reason for conflict with the introduction of the *filioque* in the West.[37]

These churches believed in one baptism, one faith, one Lord, and Father of all (Eph. 4:5, 6). Diversity of creeds did not necessarily mean major doctrinal differences. Still, the attempt by the councils to formulate and generate a central creed was a step in the right direction. Having one central creed would serve to hinder the possibility of varying belief systems.

Furthermore, the various councils or ecumenical assemblies, for the most part, united the local churches in the one holy Catholic (universal) Church. Various doctrinal issues and controversies were worked out in these gatherings. For example, "…the Acts of the Apostles (ch. 15) relates a meeting of apostles and Christians from various cities to resolve the very sensitive problem of the conditions for admitting Gentiles to Christianity."[38] Later, various other councils were held, such as the First Council of Nicaea 325, First Council of Constantinople 381, and Chalcedon 451. These councils had a lasting impact on the preservation of Christianity. Di Berardino states, "The ecumenical councils of the first millennium, all celebrated in the East, guaranteed the communion of the *orbis christianus,* the Christian world."[39]

E. Factors that Hinder Koinonia

Few of the many factors that work against communal *koinonia* are: warring factions, heresies, individualism, exclusivism, and extreme uniformity. Factions have existed throughout the history of the church. Divisions are sometimes caused through rebellion against leadership, doctrine, power struggle, etc., as illustrated in the New Testament when, for example, Paul had to address the divisions that existed in the Corinthian church. The writer of the Johannine literature shows that factions were evident in his community, and he warns his faithful followers not to associate with those causing factions. Later in the history of the church, the East and the West split, resulting in Roman Catholicism and Eastern Orthodoxy, and later Protestantism emerged from protest against Roman Catholicism. Within Protestantism, there have been numerous splits, resulting in multiplicities of denominations and independent church groups. At times, factions emerged out of heresies and doctrinal differences, seen since the inception of Christianity, and these have usually been detrimental to the unity and fellowship of the Church universal. Those who are a part of the body of Christ should reconcile their differences in love; hence the fellowship that is so essential to the survival of the church (local and universal), and empowerment of the believers will be preserved and most powerful.

Individualism is another factor that militates against the grain of fellowship. Oftentimes, individual members of the body of Christ think that they can survive in exclusion from the rest of the body (or other members). There is the notion that individual salvation, prayer, and personal relationships can suffice for the communal reality of the church. While one needs to accept Christ as personal Lord and Savior, one also needs to take note of the Scripture's strong emphasis on communality. Scripture proclaims, "For where two or three are gathered together in my name, there I am in the midst of them,"[40] and admonishes believers not to neglect the assembling of the brethren together.[41] True *koinonia* cannot be attained via mere individual efforts, but rather must come through corporate effort. In fact, the local church is a community of believers that connects and communes with other believers across the world, thus making up the global church. *Koinonia* is not circumscribed by denominational, cultural, racial, and demographic peculiarities, or any form of exclusivist tendencies, but rather transcends all those categories. The Trinitarian community is a model for the whole church's communion as the body of Christ: our manner of fellowship and relationship with each other should be a true reflection of the Trinity.

Fellowship in the body of Christ does not mean uniformity, but unity in diversity. The various parts (members) of Christ's body neither look the same nor carry out the same function, yet they complement the whole body and accomplish the same goal, love of God and neighbor. The church in general

Chapter Eleven: Communal Fellowship

should strive to embrace unity in diversity, which is intrinsic to the true *koinonia* of the church. Clearly, *koinonia* is ruptured when uniformity is chosen over diversity. No doubt the instruments and elements of *koinonia* articulated in this chapter can protect the church against these factors.

The chief founder of the Pentecostal movement, Seymour, attempted to restore human equality in the "body of Christ." Ithiel Clemmons notes,

> [Douglas J.] Nelson has convincingly argued that William J. Seymour's Azusa Mission represented the restoration of human equality in the body of Christ for the first time since the first Christian Pentecost and early Christianity. Seymour's leadership gave something to western European civilization, something that was missing—and since was rejected and remains lost. Seymour brought together the apostolic vision of no barriers or walls with the early practices of glossolalia creating the "beloved community" of human equality.[42]

Though Seymour, Charles H. Mason and others constructed the Pentecostal movement and the all-inclusive egalitarian fellowship it entails, which defines and emboldens the movement from its inception, their work is often overlooked by some theologians and historians. According to Clemmons:

> Even more than Seymour, Charles Harrison Mason has been heretofore shamefully neglected and underestimated; despite his importance in the origin, rise and spread of the Pentecostal Movement. It was C. H. Mason, not C.F. Parham, who grasped and stood with Seymour in the revival that united glossolalia with Pauline vision of an all-inclusive egalitarian fellowship in which there is "...neither Jew nor Greek, bond nor free...male nor female" (Gal. 3.28, Col. 3.11).[43]

This shows that early Pentecostalism was built upon a vision that embraces all people and transcends all social classes and barriers. Clemmons further points out that, "... a community of the Spirit transcending class and caste was the original driving vision of Pentecostalism..."[44] He contends, "The fact that Seymour and Mason were both Black Americans caused them to be shamefully neglected. But their vision of a Glossolaliac-Inclusive New Testament Koinonia still remains a challenge to the modern church."[45]

Therefore, it is incumbent upon the Pentecostal/Charismatic church today to recapture and incorporate the all-inclusive egalitarian fellowship that Seymour promoted along with other elements of *koinonia*, such as sharing, participation, and hospitality infused with a renewed theology of the cross. These dynamics will combat destructive factors, such as exclusivism (including racism, classism, sexism, and casteism), individualism, factions, heresies, and extreme uniformity that rupture and continue to destroy any true Christian fellowship.

F. Elements of Koinonia

Some visible elements of *koinonia* in the early churches were hospitality, participation, egalitarianism, and a strong theology of the cross. Michael Poellet argues that hospitality is both "guesting" and "hosting."[46] By guesting, Poellet means being received and welcomed by another. Guesting, then, is being on the receiving end of the continuum of hospitality. Consequently, believers should be both guests and hosts. Poellet contends that the church needs to invite itself into the lives of its neighbors, such as their homes, businesses, schools, city halls, and community meetings. Poellet maintains that Jesus always acted as the guest, except on two occasions in which He functioned as host, when he was feeding the 5,000-plus people and at the Last Supper meal with His twelve disciples.

There are, however, other occasions when Jesus was host. After His resurrection, Christ was seen on several occasions preparing meals for His disciples. The multitudes of people who followed Jesus during His ministry often put Him on the giving end rather than on the receiving end, because He had to teach the word, heal their sick, raise their dead, exorcise their demons, etc. Jesus, however, was the guest of many people: Martha, Zacchaeus, Simon the leper, and various tax collectors, to name a few.[47] The Apocalypse represents Christ, saying, "Here I am! I stand at the door and knock. If anyone hears my voice and opens the door, I will come in and eat with that person, and they with me."[48] In Luke 10, Jesus sent out seventy people into the towns of Galilee to appropriate His mission, and the people in those towns were to treat them like guests. In Matthew 10, we see a similar pattern wherein Christ

Chapter Eleven: Communal Fellowship

sent out His twelve disciples to the "lost sheep of Israel." In both accounts, the people were to treat Christ's servants as guests, supplying their needs and welcoming and extending kindness to them. Those who received the workers of Christ obtained the peace of God in their houses, while those who rejected the servants of Christ, not treating them as guests, would receive severe punishment in the future.

Hospitality is also hosting. Welcoming and giving to neighbors are means of hosting. As pointed out earlier, Jesus did much hosting throughout his ministry. Jesus said that the second-greatest commandment is to "love your neighbor as yourself" (Matt. 22:39), implying that those around you should be treated as you would yourself. Church leaders and all believers should assume the responsibility of hosting, since they are called to be the salt and light of the world (Matt. 5:13, 14).[49] An adequate model of hospitality seems to be one that integrates both guesting and hosting. This allows hospitality to accomplish a dual role, as each reciprocates the other, meaning that the host is a guest and the guest is a host.

Poellet argues that the Apostle Paul frequently uses the imagery of the "body of Christ" in his references to participation and sharing in *koinonia*. Believers then share with one another in the local body of Christ. The one body consists of many members; if one member suffers, the whole body suffers, and when one member rejoices, all rejoice together (1 Cor. 12:25–26). As it relates to worship, eucharistic celebration, prayer, foot-washing, feastings, oral liturgy, etc., the whole body should participate together. Poellet makes the case that in many churches, the whole body of Christ does not participate in the various liturgies because most people in the assembly seem to be mere attendees and spectators watching a few key actors and players entertaining everybody else. Also, people seem to think that once the pastor, praise team, and other key participants are present in the service, everything is fine. What about the others? Everyone in the body of Christ, therefore, should participate in the whole life of the body of Christ. Poellet reasons that *koinonia* involves both "being there" and "being-with;"[50] and that "with-ness" means to live with, suffer with, crucify with, die with, bury with, raise with, and be glorified with.[51]

Another element of *koinonia* is egalitarianism. The letter to Philemon serves as a model of egalitarianism because of its emphasis on equality and inclusiveness. Here I will draw upon Sandnes' treatment of the letter Paul wrote to Philemon:

> There is, however, hardly any doubt that the letter is concerned with Christian brother- and sisterhood; the master-slave relationship between Philemon and Onesimus was changed into a brotherhood relationship in all respects. This change is due to the conversion Onesimus experienced while visiting Paul in custody…The change is spelled out in verse 16: 'no longer as a slave but more than a slave, a beloved brother—especially to me but how much more to you, both in the flesh and in the Lord.'[52]

Philemon was the leader of the church in his home, but he still kept Onesimus as his slave. He was converted prior to Onesimus, yet it was Onesimus' conversion that changed the dynamics of their relationship, because Christian brotherhood became superior to the master-slave relationship. Philemon could no longer see Onesimus as a slave but as a brother, because that is what the Christian message articulates. This, however, does not imply that it is fine for a Christian to enslave a non-Christian. In reality, Philemon should have liberated Onesimus immediately after his own conversion, not after Onesimus' conversion to Christianity, because slavery in whatever form has no place in Christ's teachings. Slavery was acceptable in the Greco-Roman world, but Christ in no way affirms slavery.

Therefore, all believers are one in Christ. In Christ, we are all answerable to the one and same Lord, who is Christ. Not only is Christ our Lord, He is also our elder brother, father, and God. Consequently, everyone in the body of Christ shares the same status as liberated children of God. Furthermore, equality in the body of Christ cuts against contemporary social stratification, discrimination, segregation, and exclusivist tendencies. The Christian church is still one of, if not the most, segregated institutions on earth. Everyone in the body of Christ should be included and afforded equal opportunities and privileges. Although there are diverse functions in the body of Christ, everyone shares the same status as children of God.

In caring for neighbors, one realizes that many people who are marginalized, victimized, and oppressed do not feel welcome in society and, sadly, in the church as well. Like Christ, the Church should mingle with and care for those within and outside its fellowship. Those outside looking in at the caring among believers will be drawn into such fellowship, although this cannot suffice for tangible outreach beyond the walls of the church. It is the church's responsibility to take its fellowship to people wherever they are located. Christ, in His words and deeds, expressed an option for the poor and those most hurting among mankind. Consequently, He insists, "It is not the will of your Father who is in heaven that one of these little ones should perish" (Matt. 18:14 NKJV). Christ promises to issue rewards and punishments respectively to those who care for and those who exploit the weak and vulnerable (Matt. 25:31–46).

The world's system lauds self-preservation over altruism. Conversely, Christ teaches that we have to lose ourselves for His sake to find our true identity and destiny. This further implies that we should give of ourselves and service to one another for the advancement of fellowship in the kingdom of God, which is breaking forth in this present age.

Concluding Remarks

Human beings are social beings, and we desire the fellowship of others. The fellowship articulated above is both Christocentric and pneumacentric, yet interpersonal and horizontal. Our fellowship is both with God and people. It is paramount that we militate against things that destroy true Christian fellowship: warring factions, heresies, individualism, exclusivism, and extreme uniformity. We must seek to employ the elements that foster real fellowship, such as togetherness, sharing with one another, participating in activities and rites that bond us together, fostering inclusiveness and diversity, and espousing an authentic theology of the cross. We must not forget the role of the Spirit in all of this, as the Spirit is the breath and life of authentic fellowship.

Notes

[1] Chance, Bradley, "Fellowship," in *Holman Illustrated Bible Dictionary*, ed. Chad Brand, Charles Draper, and Archie England (Nashville, Tennessee: Holman Bible Publishers, 2003), 563–64.

[2] McKim, *Westminster Dictionary of Theological Terms*, 154

[3] Chance, "Fellowship," 564.

[4] Ibid.

[5] Ibid., 564–65.

[6] Ibid., 564.

[7] Ibid., 565.

[8] Hiebert, D. Edmond, "An Exposition of 1 John 1.1–4," *Bibliotheca Sacra* 145.0578 (April–June 1988): 197–210, 208.

[9] Perkins, Pheme, "Koinonia in 1 John 1.3–7: The Social Context of Division in the Johannine Letters," *Catholic Biblical Quarterly* 45.04 (1983): 631–41, 631, 632.

[10] Ibid., 632–33.

[11] Ibid., 634.

[12] Ibid., 635–36.

[13] Ibid., 636.

[14] Sandnes, Karl Olav, "Equality within Patriarchal Structures: Some New Testament perspectives on the Christian fellowship as a brother- or sisterhood and a family," in *Constructing Early Christian Families*, ed. Halvor Moxnes (New York: Routledge, 1997), 150.

[15] Ibid., 150–51.

[16] Ibid., 151.

[17] Ibid., 153.

[18] Ibid., 154. Jesus predicted that His followers would suffer persecution, even from family members, as a result of following Him (Matt. 10:34–36).

[19] Joel 2:28–29.

[20] Acts 2:1–4.

[21] Acts 2:42–47.

[22] Winn, Albert, "The Holy Spirit and the Christian Life," *Interpretation* 33.01 (January 1979): 47–57, 50.

[23] Ibid., 51.

[24] Ibid.

[25] Ibid., 52.

[26] Ibid., 53.

[27] Ibid., 54.

[28] Ibid.

[29] Ibid., 55.

[30] Ibid., 57.

[31] Di Berardino, Angelo, "Patterns of *Koinonia* in the First Christian Centuries," in *The Ecumenical Constitution of Churches*, ed. Jose Oscar Beozzo and Giuseppe Ruggieri (London: SCM Press, 2001), 47.

[32] Ibid., 48.

Chapter Eleven: Communal Fellowship 155

33 Ibid.

34 Ibid., 49.

35 Ibid., 49–50.

36 Ibid., 50.

37 Ibid.

38 Ibid.

39 Ibid., 51.

40 Matt. 18:20.

41 Heb. 10:25.

42 Clemmons, Ithiel, "True Koinonia: Pentecostal Hopes and Historical Realities," presented at the Eleventh Annual Meeting of the Society for Pentecostal Studies—on the campus of East Coast Bible College, Charlotte, NC. *Pneuma* 4.01 (1982), 51.

43 Ibid., 53.

44 Ibid., 55.

45 Ibid., 56.

46 Poellet's point indicates that *koinonia* as hospitality—guesting and hosting—holds much promise for love of God and neighbor to be concretely expressed both within the church and society. Poellet, Michael, "Ecclesial Darwinism and the Collapse of Koinonia," *Consensus* 15.1 (1989): 47–62, 56.

47 Ibid., 54.

48 Rev. 3:20.

49 Poellet, "Ecclesial Darwinism," 56.

50 Ibid., 58.

51 Ibid.

52 Sandnes, "Equality Within Patriarchal Structures," 156.

CHAPTER TWELVE

Method

This chapter explores three theological methods: the Pentecostal fivefold gospel, Curran's stance, and Wesley's quadrilateral. These can be seen as three basic models of practical theological decision-making. Each of these systems is different, but they do share similarities. They can be used either individually or integratively to inform our practical theological undertakings.

A. Fivefold Gospel

Pentecostals often understand morality in light of spirituality, and their emphasis on right living is seen through spiritual lenses. Thus, they emphasize spirituality over morality and interpret morality in light of spirituality. A spiritual person is moral, but a moral person is not necessarily spiritual. Consequently, their primary emphasis is on spiritual development rather than moral character development.[1] Therefore, Pentecostal theology and praxis are better understood through the lens of spirituality.[2]

The Pentecostal movement had as its pillars, at least in its formative years, what it calls the "full gospel" or "fivefold gospel:" 1) justification by faith in Jesus Christ, 2) sanctification by faith as a second definite work of grace, 3) healing of the physical body as provided for all in the atonement, 4) the premillennial return of Jesus Christ, and 5) baptism in the Holy Spirit, evidenced in speaking in unknown tongues. The Pentecostal "full gospel" could be seen as the cardinal doctrine of Pentecostal spirituality. The full gospel flows out of the early Pentecostals' desire for the restoration of apostolic doctrine. Therefore, this fivefold/full gospel serves as a restoration of the apostolic faith and power for the end time.[3]

The doctrine of justification by faith was restored to the church by Martin Luther, the German reformer, and the doctrine of sanctification was restored by John Wesley. Healing was restored through various nineteenth-century holiness preachers. The premillennial return of Christ was restored through the various prophecy conferences toward the end of the nineteenth century. Last, Spirit baptism was restored to the church primarily by William Seymour, through the Azusa Street revivals. Spirit baptism empowers the believers to do the final work of Christ in the last days. Because of its restoration, the world could experience the full gospel, which would result in the transformation of humanity for Christ's Second Coming. Christ is coming back for a spotless church, and therefore everyone who desires to reign with Him should be immersed in the full gospel of the kingdom. The full gospel acts as a theological and moral guide for the Pentecostal believer, and it is by this guide that the Pentecostal believer supposedly lives in right standing with God and neighbor, avoids evil, and does good.

Therefore, *justification* by faith means that "…a person is pardoned from committed sins by believing in Christ's work on the cross. A person cannot merit salvation through good works, but only through faith in Christ's atoning death."[4] *Sanctification* subsequent to Justification cleanses the believer of innate sins. This doctrine teaches that one's sinful nature can be removed through Christ's atoning work.[5] Sanctification makes it possible for the believer to live without sinning, or to live contrary to God's nature and character. *Healing* is available through the atoning work of Christ. William Faupel points out that the Pentecostal doctrine of healing ultimately hinges on a literal interpretation of Scriptures, such as: "And He Himself bore our sins in His body on the cross, so that we might die to sin and live to righteousness; for by His wounds you were healed" (1 Peter 2:24 NASB). Faupel further points out that this doctrine of healing leads to the conclusion that a person having sufficient faith to be both justified and sanctified also has sufficient faith to be healed. As a result, proponents of this doctrine were averse to medicine and consulting a physician on the premise that doing so shows lack of faith in the atoning work of Christ. Proponents of this doctrine contend that divine healing comes through faith in Christ's all-sufficient work. This doctrine was propagated by many nineteenth-century holiness preachers, including A. J. Gordon and A. B. Simpson.[6]

The *Second Coming* of Christ is another significant pillar of the fivefold gospel. The early Pentecostals' doctrine of the millennial return of Christ is generally consistent with the wider Christian tradition. Faupel argues that the early Pentecostals' doctrine on the Second Coming was particularly influenced by the teachings of John Nelson Darby, founder of Plymouth Brethren. Darby's view was based on a literalistic understanding of the Scripture. Darby's translation of 1 Thessalonians 4:16–17 reads:

> For the Lord himself, with an assembling shout, with archangel's voice and with trump of God, shall descend from heaven; and the dead in Christ shall rise first; then *we*, the living who remain, shall be caught up together with them in [the] clouds, to meet the Lord in [the] air; and thus we shall be always with [the] Lord.[7]

Darby draws out several sequential eschatological themes from Scripture to support his claim. The Church will be raptured (caught up in the air) prior to a seven-year tribulation period on earth: during such time, the Antichrist will be revealed. Upon the completion of the seven years, Christ will return with the saints. At this point, there will be a great battle of Armageddon, and Christ will triumph over Satan and his angels. Christ will then reign on earth with the saints for 1,000 years. Satan will then be released for a season. Then, the great white throne judgment will determine the fate of everyone. The righteous will go to heaven, and the unrighteous to hell.[8] Faupel charges that, "The second coming of Jesus was the central concern of the initial Pentecostal message."[9] This statement implies that formative Pentecostalism was primarily eschatological in nature.

Spirit-baptism is the sole Pentecostal contribution to the fivefold gospel,[10] because the other pillars are inherited from various Christian traditions over the centuries. At the birth of the Pentecostal movement, these doctrines, except Spirit-baptism, were already well developed and in practice. Pentecostals teach that Spirit baptism, with initial evidence being speaking in other tongues, is subsequent to sanctification. They witness that the Spirit indwells a righteous and sanctified life. Hence, the early Pentecostals emphasized justification, sanctification, and Spirit-baptism as prerequisites for miracles (divine healing) and anticipation of Christ's Second Advent. Sanctification and Spirit-baptism are necessary realities for living a morally sound life in the "already," and usher in the "not yet" kingdom. When Christ returns, he will only take those who are pure; the Spirit-filled believers have a moral responsibility to bring the message of His coming to the ends of the earth so that all can be reached and be ready for His coming.

B. Curran's Fivefold Stance

Curran's fivefold formula involves creation, sin, incarnation, redemption, and resurrection-destiny. First, Charles Curran points out that the *creation* is fundamentally good. According to him, everything that God made is good, and therefore "…the world and everything in it, although finite and limited, is not fundamentally evil but basically good."[11] Curran's understanding is consistent with the teachings of the Roman Catholic tradition. Curran reasons, "…the Roman Catholic tradition recognizes the fundamental and basic goodness of the human world, human reason, and all that God has created."[12] The early Pentecostals did not see the world as good, but as fundamentally evil and corrupt, and unregenerated human nature and reason as extensively tarnished due to sin. The early Pentecostals avoided the world and separated themselves from it. They taught that "One should be in the world but not of the world." Consequently, there was an urgent quest on the part of the early Pentecostal believers to get out of this world. The imminent rapture that accompanies the Second Coming of the Lord will be the primal exit route from this evil world. This belief allows some people to accuse the early Pentecostals of practicing an *overrealized* eschatology and escapism. The quick appearance of the Lord places a sense of urgency on Pentecostals to preach the gospel in the entire world. The empowerment of the Spirit was for the witnessing of Jesus in the entire world, and they saw the Christian moral life primarily as preparation for the Second Coming of Christ, and secondarily for living in this world.

Curran's second point is that *sin* and evil are products of humanity, and human beings are the cause of sin in this world. He argues that the account of Genesis primarily emphasizes sin and evil, not creation, and Curran further notes however that the Roman Catholic tradition acknowledges the existence of sin in the world.[13] Curran points out that Thomas Aquinas' teaching affirms that sin does not take away our basic humanity, but instead wounds it to some extent. Many Protestant groups as well as Pentecostals teach that sin completely destroys the fundamental goodness of creation and tarnishes human nature. Hence, justification by faith is the process by which God forgives people of Original Sin, which puts humans in right standing with God. Justification renews the image of God in humans, restores our lost humanity, and puts us in right relation with God. Through sanctification, believers strive for perfection, the fullness of our state prior to the fall, and when Christ returns, the whole order will be restored to its former perfect state.

Curran's third point is that the *incarnation* unites the human and the divine in Christ, and supports and strengthens the fundamental goodness in every human being. He further argues that the divine and the human in Christ are not in conflict, and therefore the incarnation is intricately connected with the redemption.[14] The incarnation does not merely strengthen the fundamental goodness in humanity, but restores such goodness in humanity that was lost in the fall.

For Curran, *redemption* is the triumph of Christ over the powers of sin and evil. The reality of the redemption is amplified in the cross and the resurrection, making salvation available through the redemptive work of the incarnated Christ. Redemption is the "already" of the reign of God. In part, through the redemption, believers are experiencing the fullness of the reign of God.[15] Pentecostalism and the wider Protestant tradition share Curran's theology of redemption. This leads us to Curran's final pillar, *resurrection destiny*. Curran sees the resurrection as destiny. It is the "not yet" of the reign of God or the fullness of the reign of God. The resurrection destiny will not happen in this world, in this history. The Christian's ultimate destiny lies outside of the realm of this present world system, and this is the hope of the Christian believer. The challenge is to live in the tension of the "already" and "not yet" of the reign of God.

For the most part, both the Pentecostals' and Curran's formulas are consistent with the double-love command, but do not necessarily elevate it as the central goal of Christian faith and praxis. For the early Pentecostals, it seems like the *Second Parousia* (Christ's Second Advent) is the goal of the Christian life, and thus justification, sanctification, Spirit-baptism, and healing are preparation for the eschatological reality that will be consummated in the anticipated premillennial return of Christ.

Proponents of Pentecostalism could argue that by living the dictates of the fivefold gospel, they are demonstrating love for God and neighbor, for they adhere to and spread this gospel because of their love for God, and their love of neighbor is the reason they impart this gospel to neighbor. Pentecostalism started among the marginalized and flourished in the margins, but over the decades the movement has become powerful in many parts of the world, and now attracts people from all walks of life. Still, there is a need for the contemporary Pentecostal/Charismatic movement to advocate for the marginalized and oppressed across the world in more tangible ways. A starting point for Pentecostals in achieving this end would be the explicit insertion of the double-love command at the helm of their theology, which would mean making love of God and neighbor the fundamental goal of their faith and praxis. Hence, the Spirit's work and gifts in the believer would be to fulfill the double-love command. The theology that follows would be more than an ontological dynamic, rather an existential reality that is evident in Pentecostal/Charismatic holistic concern and action toward the poor and hurting around the globe, because love of God and neighbor always demand those actions.

C. Wesley's Quadrilateral

John Wesley's Quadrilateral implies that Christian faith should be informed by Scripture, tradition, reason, and experience—thus grounding it in orthodoxy (right belief), orthopathy (right affection), and orthopraxy (right action). This quadrilateral bears witness to the centrality of the double-love command in the Christian tradition, and the manner of affection and conduct that find fulfillment and purpose when they attain the love imperative. For what is the merit of Christian Scripture, or tradition, or reason, or experience if not the love imperative?

As mentioned above, for Wesley, Christianity is a way of life, and this lifestyle is an *entirely sanctified one*, and exemplifies perfect love. Christian living should be consistent with orthodoxy (right beliefs), orthokardia (right affection/heart), and orthopraxy (right action)[16] that is steeped in Scripture, tradition, reason, and experience.[17] The life of faith is not just internal, but should be lived out in the contexts of the home and family, *kerygmatic* and *didactic* settings, society and culture, through reflections, meditations, and communal rituals.[18]

Wesley describes himself as *homo unius libri,* a man of one book, the Bible, and this book was to be read in its *sensus literalis,* the plain, literal and historical sense. He maintains that Scripture is authoritative and inspired, but continually needs both exegetical aid and supernatural assistance for its proper interpretation. Human rationale and science alone cannot be used to understand Scripture, because the interpretation of any text also requires the aid of other Scriptures and the Holy Spirit. Wesley argues that Scripture should interpret Scripture (as one passage of Scripture validates another) in its literary and grammatical sense. The context in which Scripture was written should not be ignored as we seek to apply it to contemporary settings and situations. Scripture, therefore, should transcend and transform any context in which it is read and appropriated, but not to the exclusion of its grammatical-historical particularities.[19] Like Wesley, the Pentecostal tradition[20] gives primacy of place and prominence to Scripture—over tradition, reason, and experience—as the primary frame of reference for its theology, spirituality, and morality.

Wesley reveres and embraces the tradition paved and preserved by the fathers and mothers of the church. Wesley does not equate the church tradition with Scripture, but he sees it as next to Scripture. He regards the exegesis and commentary of the church pioneers as of great assistance to our understanding of church dogmas.[21]

Reason is the third prong of Wesley's quadrilateral. Wesley argues that reason is important in religious pursuit, and that an irrational religion is a false one. For Wesley, human reason works hand-in-hand with the divine in the course of learning, and Scripture and reason are not foes, for together they help us to find the plain Scriptural meaning. Wesley further points out that reason may not give us faith, hope, love, real virtue, or happiness,[22] but it can help to reveal the Scriptures. Finally, Wesley endorses the experiential side of the faith, emphasizing that one is assured of salvation by way of experiencing it; this thought flows out of his conversion experience on Aldersgate Street, but he cautions that experience is not the source of Scriptural authority, so one should be careful of excessive reliance on it for guidance.[23]

Concluding Remarks

At the core of early Pentecostal practical theological decision-making is justification by faith in Jesus Christ, sanctification by faith as a second definite work of grace, healing of the physical body as provided for all in the atonement, the premillennial return of Jesus Christ, and baptism in the Holy Spirit. Curran's fivefold Stance is concerned with creation, sin, incarnation, redemption, and resurrection destiny. Wesley's quadrilateral, the most comprehensive of the systems, consists of Scripture, tradition, reason and experience. It takes in the previous two systems. According to Wesley's system, when making a practical theological decision, one should first consult Scripture: What does Scripture say about this matter? And then, how consistent is this matter with tradition? Reason? And experience? The fundamental question, however, that any theological methodology must answer is: Does this system lead to love of God and neighbor? The rule of thumb and/or the depth and scope of any theological methodology should be its consistency with the double love command, nothing else.

Notes

[1] Wan, Yee Tham, "Bridging the Gap Between Pentecostal Holiness and Morality," *AJJS* 4.2 (2001): 153–80, 163.

Chapter Twelve: Practical Theological Methodology 165

[2] Land, *Pentecostal Spirituality*, 47. The term spirituality "indicates the work of the Holy Spirit in Christian experience." Also spirituality is the quality of being spiritual. There are various dimensions of Christian spirituality, which are expressed through rituals and practices that advance the realization of God's presence and existence. See Mckim, *Westminster Dictionary of Theological Terms*, 268.

[3] Land, *Pentecostal Spirituality*, 18.

[4] Faupel, D. William, *Everlasting Gospel: The Significance of Eschatology in the Development of Pentecostal Thought* (Sheffield: Sheffield Academic Press, 1996), 28; Bloch-Hoell, N., *The Pentecostal Movement: Its Origin, Development, and Distinctive Character* (Oslo: Universitetsforlaget, 1964), 122–41.

[5] Faupel, *Everlasting Gospel*, 29.

[6] Ibid.

[7] 1Thess. 4:16–17.

[8] Faupel, *Everlasting Gospel*, 29–30.

[9] Ibid., 20.

[10] Ibid., 30.

[11] Curran, *The Catholic Moral Tradition Today*, 33.

[12] Ibid., 34–35. Also, Roman Catholic tradition maintains that Original Sin contaminated creation in general, and in particular has left a blemish on human character. For the official view, *see* www.vatican.va/archive/catechism/p1s2c1p7.htm.

[13] Curran, *The Catholic Moral Tradition Today*, 33.

[14] Ibid., 33–34.

[15] Ibid., 34.

[16] Clapper, Gregory S., "From the 'Works of the Flesh' to the 'Fruit of the Spirit': Conversion and Spiritual Formation in the Wesleyan Tradition," in *Conversion in the Wesleyan Tradition*, ed. Kenneth J. Collins and John Tyson (Nashville, TN: Abingdon Press, 2001), 216. See also Clapper, *John Wesley on Religious Affections: His Views on Experience and Emotion and their Role in the Christian Life and Theology* (Metuchen, NJ: Scarecrow Press, 1989); and Clapper, "Orthokardia: The Practical Theology of John Wesley's Heart Religion," *Quarterly Review* 10.1 (Spring 1990): 49–66.

[17] Ibid. For thoughts on Wesley's Quadrilateral, *see* Oden, *John Wesley's Scriptural Christianity*.

[18] For further treatment on faith formation in antiquity, *see* Wilken, Robert Louis, "Christian Formation in the Early Church," in *Educating People of Faith*, ed. John H. Van Engen (Grand Rapids, MI: Eerdmans, 2004), 48–62. *Also see* Matthaei, Sondra Higgins, "Rethinking Faith Formation," *Religious Education* 99.1 (Winter 2004): 56–70. In this article, Higgins argues that "an intentional, effective, and life-giving ecology of faith formation within the communion of a faith community is necessary. Elements of an effective ecology including relationships, structures, and practices…"

[19] Oden, *John Wesley's Scriptural Christianity*, 55–64.

[20] John Wesley is revered by some scholars as the grandfather of the Pentecostal/Charismatic movement, because the movement has grown out of the eighteenth-century and nineteenth-century Wesleyan Holiness movements. Land, *Pentecostal Spirituality*, 48, 49.

[21] Oden, *John Wesley's Scriptural Christianity*, 65–69.

[22] Ibid., 71–84.

[23] Ibid., 84–90.

CHAPTER THIRTEEN

Source and Goal

This chapter briefly points out that Christ and the Spirit in God are the sources of Christian theology and faith praxis. Hence the various practices of the Christian faith should flow out of Christ and the Spirit. Regardless of how dynamic or sincere one's faith praxis may seem, if it is not about love, it is seriously lacking.

New Testament Spirit Christology reveals interconnectedness between Christ and the Spirit. This amplifies the inseparable loving relationship that the triune God shares. Gordon Fee points out that the core of Paul's theology is God's salvation to the world through Christ in the Spirit.[1] Fee maintains that the Spirit is the personal presence of both God and Christ, recognizing the Spirit as both the Spirit of God and Christ, but distinct; the Spirit is the renewed presence of God and the risen Christ.[2] The Synoptic gospels[3] and the Johannine tradition[4] affirm this inseparability between Christ and the Spirit. This understanding is in harmony with the Councils of Nicea and Chalcedon[5] and is consistent with theological themes, such as trinity,[6] incarnation,[7] paschal mystery,[8] and salvation,[9] significant to Christian teaching and praxis.

A theology of the intimate connection between Christ and the Spirit can be dubbed *Spirit Christology*. This Christological approach is considered more adequate than classical Christological approaches such as *pneuma-sarx* and *logos*. *Pneuma-sarx* Christology is said to have been among the first attempts at expressing the relationship between Christ and the Spirit of Yahweh.[10] Jewish monarchianists or adoptionists, such as the Ebionites, proponents of *Pneuma-sarx* Christology, taught that "Yahweh is the "sole source" (*monarchia*) of all reality; [they] tried to link Jesus to the God of the Old Testament by means of his impersonal adoption by the Spirit of Yahweh during his lifetime, and thus to skirt entirely the question of the pre-existence of Jesus."[11] The Ebionites argued that the same Spirit that was upon Adam, Moses, and the prophets was transferred upon Jesus, in whom this divine Spirit became incarnate and found complete realization.[12] Spirit Christology is far more comprehensive than a *Pneuma-sarx* Christology; it does not see Christ as just a man possessed by the Spirit, but as both God and human who was intimately connected and enmeshed in the Spirit of God.

Logos refers to "…the second person of the Trinity, Jesus Christ (John 1:1), who as the creative power of God embodied truth and was God incarnate," and *Logos* Christology is thus defined as the "…understanding of Jesus that begins with the divine, eternal Logos and sees Jesus as its concrete, historical expression."[13] *Logos* Christology, David Coffey argues, does not do justice to the humanity of Jesus because it renders it deficient.[14] Second, *Logos* Christology does not recognize and incorporate the Holy Spirit in Christ, because it makes no appeal to the Holy Spirit and the Spirit's work in Christ.[15] A third point is that *Logos* Christology is built on the theology of the immanent Trinity almost in exclusion of the economic Trinity.[16] A Christology that does not integrate both the immanent and economic Trinity is lacking, because both models hold a Trinitarian-theology in balance. Spirit Christology, however, integrates both the immanent and economic trinity.

David Coffey argues that a *Logos* Christology is even more adequate when it is employed and incorporated in a Spirit Christology, and therefore, while Spirit Christology can incorporate a *Logos* Christology, a *Logos* Christology cannot employ a Spirit Christology.[17] Coffey maintains that *Logos* Christology is inadequate, and that many contemporary forms of Spirit Christology are proposed as alternatives to *Logos* Christology.[18] Spirit Christology, therefore, does more justice to the humanity of Jesus and the Scriptures than *Logos* Christology does.

The goal, therefore, of any Christian theology and praxis must be the double-love imperative—love of God and neighbor—which is the summary of Scripture and the goal of Christian theology and praxis.[19] Major theological themes such as trinity, incarnation, paschal mystery, and salvation, exemplify the double love command through-and-through. Christian service and practice, however dynamic, is purposeless if its goal is not love. The Apostle Paul in First Corinthians 13 affirms love as the most excellent way, and regardless of the other charisms that a believer may possess, they mean nothing if they are not about love. Our work in the church, community, society and world largely is our utilization of the gifts and abilities naturally given to us, and those we acquire through studies and training. These gifts and abilities are to attend to the needs of one another in the spirit of love. Love allows us to forgive and reconcile with each other regardless of differences, and therefore it is only through love, and for love, that forgiveness and reconciliation are possible, especially when someone has wronged you. The starting point and goal of Christian theology, morality, and faith praxes should be love, nothing else.

Concluding Remarks

Faith praxes, such as conversion, formation and transformation, death and afterlife, spirituality and piety, gifts of the Spirit, communal worship and fellowship, and practical theological decision-making, must flow out of Christ and the Spirit in God, for love's sake. For example, the aspect of our faith praxis called worship and its various sacraments or elements are mere rituals if not ultimately about love. The ancient Israelites often mistakenly thought that it was about their sacrifice, moral codes, and rituals, when it was about love of God. Also, the laws, codes, and rules governing our lives are often merely legalistic and oppressive when not about the double-love command. It is impossible to ignore the pain and suffering of neighbor, like that of the Good Samaritan, when transformed by love.

Notes

[1] Fee, Gordon, "Paul and the Trinity: The Experience of Christ and the Spirit for Paul's Understanding of God," in *The Trinity: An Interdisciplinary Symposium on the Trinity*, eds. Steven Davis, Daniel Kendal, and Gerald O'Collins (Oxford: Oxford University Press, 1999), 52.

[2] Ibid., 62–63.

[3] Mansfield, Robert, *Spirit and Gospel in Mark* (Peabody, MA: Hendrickson Publishers, 1987), 164, 165; Charette, Blaine, *Restoring Presence: The Spirit in Matthew's Gospel* (Sheffield: Sheffield Academic Press, 2000), 22–23; Menzies, Robert P., *Empowered for Witness: The Spirit in Luke-Acts* (Sheffield: Sheffield Academic Press, 1994), 104–89.

[4] Gilbert, Marvin, *The Holy Spirit and Counseling* (Peabody, MA: Hendrickson Publishers, 1985), 25, 29.

[5] Haight, Roger, "The Case for Spirit Christology," *Theological Studies* 53.2 (1992): 257–87, 274.

[6] Ibid., 285; Coffey, David, "Spirit Christology and the Trinity," in *Advents of the Spirit : An Introduction to the Current Study of Pneumatology*, eds. Bradford Hinze, D. Lyle Dabney (Milwaukee, WI: Marquette University Press, 2001), 325, 326, 328; Coffey, David, "The Incarnation of the Holy Spirit in Christ," *Theological Studies* 45.3S (1984): 466–80, 475.

[7] Haight, "The Case for Spirit Christology," 276.

[8] Rosato, Phillip, "Spirit Christology: Ambiguity and Promise," *Theological Studies* 38.3S (1977): 423–49, 444, 446, 447; Ratzinger, Joseph [Pope Benedict XVI], *Introduction to Christianity*, trans. by J. R. Foster (New York: Herder and Herder, 1970), 256.

[9] Haight, "The Case for Spirit Christology," 278, 280.

[10] Rosato, "Spirit Christology," 430.

[11] Ibid; Pannenberg, Wolfhart, *Jesus, God and Man* (Philadelphia: Westminster Press, 1968), 116–20.

[12] Ibid., 434; Schoeps, H. J., *Jewish Christianity: Factional Disputes in the Early Church* (Philadelphia: Fortress Press, 1969), 68–73.

[13] McKim, *Westminster Dictionary of Theological Terms*, 164.

[14] Coffey, "Spirit Christology and the Trinity," 317.

[15] Ibid., 317–18.

[16] Ibid., 324. Economic Trinity is "…a view of the trinity, propounded by Hippolytus and Tertullian, that stressed the functions ("economies") or work of the Father, Son, and Holy Spirit rather than their eternal being in relation to each other" and immanent Trinity is "…the relationships among the three members of the Trinity—Father, Son, and Holy Spirit—in and with themselves." *See*, McKim, *Westminster Dictionary of Theological Terms*, 86, 138.

[17] Coffey, "Spirit Christology and the Trinity, 317–18.

[18] Ibid., 316–17.

[19] Mark 12:29–31. This text goes back to Deut. 6:5; Lev. 19:18; St. Augustine, *Teaching Christianity*, 123, 124–25. *See also* Rom. 13:8; 1 Tim. 1:5.

PART IV
SOCIAL ACTION

Sociopolitical action when not about love results in injustice and oppression

As someone who was brought up in a developing country, over the years I became deeply concerned about people living in abject poverty, and the social injustices seen worldwide that are so prevalent among the voiceless, marginalized, vulnerable, and oppressed peoples of diverse race, religion, age, gender, and geographical localities. Consequently, in my prayers, I asked why life is so difficult for so many people.

The sociopolitical context, therefore when not guided by the love imperative is often oppressive, particularly to the weak and most vulnerable of society. Socioeconomic injustice, for example, seen in the form of extreme poverty and human-rights abuses—including human trafficking, Dalit oppression, and gender discrimination—devastates millions of people around the world daily. Through nonviolent and peacemaking initiatives, the conflicts and violence seen around the world should be resolved, since acts of violence and war only spark more conflict. The church and state, or the religious and political, should forge a relationship to help secure peace and prosperity for all people, as these are, perhaps, the world's most powerful institutions. Throughout the centuries, there has not been a worldview that is sympathetic to the needs of the most vulnerable of society, because the world's systems often empower some and disenfranchise others. Hence the fittest of the fittest survive and the poor and weak are trampled on and continue to suffer. The love imperative, however, advocates for a society and worldview in which each person demonstrates love for each other, and doing to each other what you wish done to you. The selfishness and greed seen in our world are contrary to the love imperative. It is, therefore, in humanity's best interest to employ the love imperative at the helm of its structures, as it is our greatest prospect.

CHAPTER FOURTEEN

Global Poverty

This chapter defines and outlines key elements of global poverty, and therefore articulates that education, hunger, health, human rights, and peacemaking should be the focus of any serious effort to reduce global poverty. One cannot adequately and comprehensively engage the double love imperative without addressing global poverty; it marginalizes scores of people around the globe.

Poverty Measurement

There are various ways in which poverty is measured: monetarily, using deprivations, and demographically, just to name a few. First, monetary poverty is measured using income or consumption.[1] According to this measurement, those who live on US$1 per day would be considered below the poverty line—approximately 1.2 billion people, one-quarter of the world's population, meet this definition.[2] More people live below the poverty line in Asia and Sub-Saharan Africa than anywhere else in the world. The number of people in recent years living below the poverty line in both Asia and Sub-Saharan Africa is about 40%, in the Middle East and North Africa 2%, and 5% in Latin America and the Caribbean. A caveat is that these numbers do fluctuate, and in percentage they may appear much smaller than they actually are. For example, a 2008 World Bank regional briefing revealed that 47 million people, more than 8% of Latin America and the Caribbean were living on less than a dollar per day.

Questions are raised about the integrity of the monetary scale used to measure poverty. Critics argue that this concept violates the standard definition of poverty, which categorizes the poor as those who do not meet minimum acceptable living standards. Another criticism is that the US$1 per day measurement is based on someone's ability to purchase a basket of basic items, but it does not hold up when the average income per capita changes, or even when there is economic growth in a country.[3] Furthermore, critics argue that the poverty incidence measured with a country's national parameter can be either higher or lower than the internationally acclaimed US$1 per day scale.[4] In addition, using the monetary data exclusively to determine poverty tends not to represent fully all those who live in poor conditions, and lack basic necessities, such as food and water. Consequently, some research confirms that the monetary instrument often excludes some people, and does not accurately represent the total number of people living in poverty. According to Shailen Nandy:

> Work on poverty and deprivation in South Africa…which used both income and deprivation indicators, found that income-based indicators missed a considerable number of people (around 3.7m) who were classified as poor by the deprivation indicators. The studies found female-headed households were over-represented among the poor, especially in rural areas, and there were clear differences between ethnic groups—an enduring legacy of the policies of Apartheid… Anti-poverty policies that predominantly focus on income poverty are unlikely to solve the deprivations (of food, education, housing, etc.) that affect the lives of millions.[5]

Another point is that economic growth in a country does not necessarily reduce poverty, because economic growth could have an adverse effect. For example, during economic boom periods around the globe in recent decades, the poverty level increased in many poor countries. According to Alberto Minujin:

> Excluding East Asia, poverty has increased at a rate of 12 million persons per year since 1987. This has occurred despite substantial growth in most regions and the strong growth of the international market of capital flows during the 1990s. For example, the increase in income per capita in Latin America was around 15 percent between

1990 and 1998... Nonetheless, the number of people below the poverty line increased by 6 percent during that period.... Similar results can be seen in southern Asia, where per capita income grew by one-third between 1990 and 1998, but the number of poor people grew as well and with little reduction in the incidence of poverty.[6]

Minujin concludes that the US$1 per day formula does not accurately represent the state of poverty, and therefore proposes that emphasis be put on social equity as the missing link that can bridge the divide between economic growth and poverty reduction.[7] By social equity, Minujin means access to education, public health, social participation, and inclusion of all, because when these services are not readily available, people are considered to be in poverty, even if they experience some economic growth and have more than a dollar a day.[8]

Another criticism is that the line used to measure poverty in poor countries is not the same as for rich countries, which amplifies the striking disparity between poor and rich countries. For example, the US is the wealthiest nation on earth, and is therefore considered a high-income nation. According to the US Census Bureau, in 2009, the US poverty line is set at an income of $17,098 for a household of three, and it estimates that 43.6 million people live below the US poverty line.[9] Although poverty in the US is different from what exists in developing countries, it must be taken seriously. The poor in the US, however, could be considered wealthy when compared with the approximately 1.2 billion extreme poor living elsewhere on less than US$1 per day. Most children in the US have access to education, water, and basic health care, compared to many children in poor countries, who are not just denied basic necessities, but have no access to them.

The second form of poverty is based on certain deprivations, and this involves the absolute and chronic poor. Here absolute poverty is defined as, "...a condition characterized by severe deprivation of basic human needs, including food, safe drinking water, sanitation facilities, health, shelter, education and information. It depends not only on income but also on access to social services."[10] Those living with one or more of these severe deprivations are not necessarily considered to be in absolute poverty, because it is possible for someone to experience a deprivation that is not related to poverty.[11] The absolute poor are those experiencing two or more of the severe deprivations above, and the chronic poor are those who have been absolutely poor for five or more years.[12]

Further classifications are the always poor, usually poor, fluctuating poor, occasionally poor, and the never poor. These five divisions are merged into three smaller groups: 1) chronic poor encompasses the always poor and the usually poor; 2) the transitory poor includes the fluctuating and occasionally poor; and 3) the never poor includes those who are at times wealthy and who could not be considered poor.[13] Further distinctions can also be made between chronic poverty and transient poverty. The chronic poor are the households whose predicted and existing consumption level is below the poverty line, while the transient poor's current household income consumption is below the poverty line, but predicted income is above it.[14]

The third form of poverty is specifically related to children, because they are most affected by and vulnerable to poverty. Using the international poverty line—US$1 per day—half of the world's poor would be made up of children. Child poverty is also measured by the lack of freedom to choose, capabilities, and entitlements.[15] Another way child poverty is measured is in terms of the violation of the universal rights of every child and adolescent. These rights were codified by the International Convention on the Rights of the Child (ICRC), which the General Assembly of United Nations adopted in 1989 as part of the Universal Declaration of Human Rights. The rights of children universally are summarized in four basic principles: each child and adolescent should be seen as an individual with social, civil, and political rights; a child's best interests should be taken into consideration; each child should have a right to life, survival, growth and development; and a child should not be discriminated against based on race, gender, nationality, or ethnicity.[16] The Convention on the Rights of the Child has been ratified by all the countries of the world except the United States and Somalia.[17] Despite acknowledgement of these universal rights, 11 million children under the age of five die annually from preventable and easily treatable diseases,[18] and 15 million under the age of five die each year from both malnutrition and infection in poorer countries.[19]

Many of the children in extremely poor countries who live beyond age 5 are condemned to perpetual poverty.[20] Children should never have to go through the atrocities that poverty brings. It is not just the humane thing to do to take care of all our children, but it is also the economically sound thing to do. Studies show that when children have access to healthcare and education, they can stimulate economic growth and reduce poverty significantly.[21] Early childhood education is also crucial to success in adult years, and lack of universal basic services impedes the progress from which the whole world could benefit. Rima Shores reveals that: "Human development hinges on the interplay between nature and nurture," and therefore, "...early care and nurture have a decisive and long-lasting impact on how people develop, their ability to learn, and their capacity to regulate their own emotions."[22] This argument for early childhood advancement is amplified in Minujin's point, "...cerebral mass grows rapidly in the first three years and, at this point, a series of tools indispensable for adult life are acquired."[23] Factors such as poor healthcare and economic hardship can indefinitely retard a child's ability to develop and function effectively in adult years. A child's basic need for survival can be met, even where economic growth is not vibrant. Studies show that it costs much less and yields much more to invest in children than to employ "second opportunity" intervention.[24] Consequently, any public policy geared toward reducing poverty should make eradicating child poverty its primary goal.[25]

B. Views of Poverty

Biblical Outlook:
When it comes to the subject of poverty, some are quick to point out that Christ said "the poor we will have with us always" (Matt. 26:11). Some people interpret this Scripture to mean that God intends for some people to always be poor. This Scripture is a quotation of Deut. 15:11, and its context encourages people to forgive debts so that none would be poor. A preceding verse states, "But there will be no poor among you" (Deut. 15:4). Christ always expresses preferential options for the poor: "...for I was hungry and you gave Me no food; I was thirsty and you gave Me no drink; I was a

stranger and you did not take Me in, naked and you did not clothe Me, sick and in prison and you did not visit Me." "Then they also will answer Him, saying, 'Lord, when did we see You hungry or thirsty or a stranger or naked or sick or in prison, and did not minister to You?' Then He will answer them, saying, 'Assuredly, I say to you, inasmuch as you did not do *it* to one of the least of these, you did not do *it* to Me'" (Matt 25:42–45; cf. Lk. 3:11NKJV). Hence, taking care of the poor is likened to attending to the needs of Christ. Central to Christ's mission on earth has always been the liberation of the poor (Lk. 4:18). According to the author of the Johannine epistles, "But whoever has the world's goods, and sees his brother in need and closes his heart against him, how does the love of God abide in him?"(1 Jn. 3:17 NASB). The Proverbs state, "One who is gracious to a poor man lends to the LORD, And He will repay him for his good deed" (Prov. 19:17 NASB). People's response to the poor reflect their relationship with their God (Prov. 14:21, 31; 17:5; 21:13; 28:27; 31:20).

Scripture opposes anyone profiteering at the expense of the poor (Prov. 22:16, 22–23). In Micah 2:1–5, God vows to severely punish those who oppress the poor. Micah responds, "He has told you, O man, what is good; And what does the LORD require of you But to do justice, to love kindness, And to walk humbly with your God?" (Micah 6:8 NASB). Attending to the poor and not cheating them is consistent with Micah's demands for people to live justly. The Mosaic Law that was in place before the prophets went as far as forbidding people from charging interest on loans given to the poor (Ex. 22:25; Lev. 25:35–37). God not only honors, but repays, generous deeds (Prov. 28:8). The Old Testament made provisions for the poor to be taken care of in the Hebrew society: farmers were not to reap all their produce; some would be left in the fields for the poor to glean (Lev. 19:9–10; 23:22; Deut. 24:19–20). A portion of church offerings was to help the poor and needy (Deut. 14:28–29; Rom. 15:25–27; 1 Cor. 16:1–2). In the Mosaic Law, provisions were also made to protect and help the poor by outlawing usury against them (Lev. 25:36–37), and the institutions of the Jubilee and Sabbath years were to free the poor of all their debts (Lev. 25; Deut.15).[26]

Ethical Perspectives:

Peter Singer charges that the wealthy ignoring those in absolute poverty is tantamount to murder, and he contends that the facts show that people in rich countries are allowing people in poorer countries to live in extreme poverty. Absolute poverty results in malnutrition, ill health, and ultimately death. Two arguments that respond to the challenge of poverty and who is directly responsible for its existence are consequential and nonconsequential.[27] The former argument states:

> On the one hand, we feel ourselves to be under a greater obligation to help those whose misfortunes we have caused. (It is for this reason that advocates of overseas aid often argue that Western nations have created the poverty of Third World nations through forms of economic exploitation which go back to the colonial system). On the other hand, any consequentialist would insist that we are responsible for all the consequences of our action, and if a consequence of my spending money on a luxury item is that someone dies, I am responsible for that death.[28]

Therefore, people who are on the consequentalist's side of the continuum would agree that those whose actions have caused poverty directly or indirectly should do what is necessary to alleviate the perpetual poverty their actions have systematically caused.

The nonconsequentialist's position basically objects to taking responsibility for the misfortune of the poor. John Locke and Robert Nozick position is that:

> If anyone has a right to life, and this right is a right against others who might threaten my life but not a right to assistance from others when my life is in danger, then we can understand the feeling that we are responsible for acting to kill but not for omitting to save. The former violates the right of others, the latter does not.[29]

Singer maintains, however, that if it is in our power to help others to promote good, we should do so, particularly, when doing so does not impede our well-being. In this case, even though a person might not be directly responsible for poverty in developing countries, if one can help to reduce it, why not? It would be the good and proper thing to do. According to Singer:

If it is in our power to prevent something very bad happening without thereby sacrificing anything of comparable moral significance, we ought to do it. This principle seems uncontroversial. It will obviously win the assent of consequentialists; but nonconsequentialists should accept it too, because the injunction to prevent what is bad applies only when nothing comparably significant is at stake.[30]

Furthermore, some arguments flowing out of the nonconsequentalist school of thought object to assisting people in abject poverty for various reasons. The first objection is on the grounds that people should first take care of people in their circle, family members, fellow citizens, then think about others in distant locations.[31] Yet, this argument does not hold up when we compare the more dire state of poverty in developing countries to what we see in developed countries. The second objection is on the grounds of property rights. Proponents of this argument, like Nozick, argue: "… provided one has acquired one's property without the use of unjust means like force and fraud, one may be entitled to enormous wealth while others starve."[32] Aquinas' argument contradicts that of Nozick: "Since property exists for the satisfaction of human needs, 'whatever a man has in superabundance is owed, of natural right, to the poor for their sustenance.'"[33] Singer, like Aquinas, rejects the theory of individualistic ethics of property rights.

The third objection articulates that overpopulation is the chief cause of extreme poverty, and helping those in poverty will only encourage more people to be born into poverty. Therefore, proponents of this view believe that rich countries and people should ignore those in extreme poverty and allow them to die until the population reaches a sustainable number of people that poorer countries can afford to feed. These proponents argue that if the rich help the poor, they are eventually helping them to hurt themselves and others, thus making life ultimately worse for all. In other words, they reason the rich should not help the poor, because in doing so they are encouraging overpopulation, which eventually makes everybody poor.[34] Clearly, this view is grossly fallacious and inhumane because it encourages that people stand by and watch others die of poverty without giving a helping hand.

C. Why Poverty Persists

Biblical Perspective:

The book of Judges points to examples of people being poor due to sins against God, and foreign oppressors being emboldened by God as punishment against His people (Judg. 6:1–10). Naomi became impoverished due to famine (Ruth 1:1), and then both she and her daughters-in-law were later impoverished due to the death of their husbands (Ruth 1:3, 5). Nehemiah struggled with poverty as a result of oppression caused by war (Neh. 1:1–3), intimidation by enemy nations (Neh. 4, 6), and oppression of the masses by the wealthy and powerful through debt and taxes (Neh. 5). Job, who was seen as the richest man in the east of the then-world, became poor because God allowed Satan to test him (Job 1). The book of Proverbs gives a number of reasons for a person being poor, such as laziness (Prov. 6:6–11), failure to accept correction (Prov. 13:18), seeking fantasies (Prov. 28:19), cosigning notes (22:26–27), pleasure and alcoholism (Prov. 21:17), corrupt justice system (Prov. 22:22), and oppression in general (Prov. 13:23).

The prophets also have much to say about the reasons people are poor. Many of the prophets preached that the courts and justice systems were bankrupt toward the poor and did not treat the poor fairly (Amos 2:7; 5:7, 10, 12; Mic. 3:1, 9, 11; 7:3; Zech. 5:3–4; 7:8; 8:16; Hab. 2:6–8; Hos. 10:3–4). The property and possessions of the poor were taken away illegally (Amos 5:11; Hab. 2:6–8) to provide luxury for the rich and powerful (Amos 2:7; 6:1–7; 8:4). Merchants robbed and took advantage of the impoverished (Amos 8:5; Mic. 6:10–11; Hab. 2:9–11; Hos. 12:7). Workers were cheated out of their wages (Mal. 3:5). Finally, the common laws that govern the fair treatment of humanity were disregarded (Amos 1:6, 11; Obad. 10–14).[35]

Socioeconomic and Political Factors:

Many factors contribute to contemporary poverty in developing countries. Due to the brevity of this chapter, however, I will primarily highlight the contributions of colonialism and neocolonialism to contemporary forms of extreme poverty in the developing world. Mai Palmberg points out that, "…

most African nations gained political independence during the 1960s, yet their economies are still shaped in part by their past experience as European colonies."[36] Therefore, Africa still struggles under the grip of colonialism that persists in the post-colonial era or neocolonialism. Palmberg further points out that, "…under colonialism, the country which owned the colony exported its raw materials to Europe where the raw materials were made into manufactured goods. Some of the goods were then shipped back to the colonies for sale."[37] In the neocolonial era, the same practice continues in slightly different form, because they are not officially colonies anymore.

Palmberg argues that during the 1960s, when Europe and the US realized that the political winds were changing, they developed new ways to maintain imperial reign,[38] by making the developing world economically dependent on them and by forging unequal trade policies that resulted in unequal exchange of goods and services. This economic dependence, in Palmberg's view, is based on two principles: "…a continued division of labor and foreign control of key sectors of the economy." These can be further fleshed out in three areas: A) "…a large part of production is sold for export…" B) "…most of the goods exported are a few unprocessed raw materials. These raw materials constituted more than half of the exports from Africa in 1968: oil, copper, cotton, cocoa, and ground nuts. In 1969, less than 10% of all exports from Africa were manufactured goods…" and C) "…more than four-fifths of Africa's export is directed to imperialist states. Three-fourths of Africa's imports originate there. Western Europe still dominates, but the United States, and to a lesser extent Japan, are also important trade partners. There is almost no trade between the African states themselves."[39]

With these principles in motion, the big foreign companies continue to export Africa's raw materials for "little or nothing," to the demise of the indigenous people. According to Palmberg, many foreign companies' "…annual turnover is far larger than the total state budget of the countries where they invest their capital."[40] Clearly, most of the profits from Africa's raw materials go to foreign companies, while only a pittance remains in and returns to independent Africa. These foreign companies usually hold a dominant position in Africa because of their weak economy and the fragility of domestic production. Some do have assembly plants in Africa, but again it increases their profitability because they do not pay much in taxes and very little to Africa's workers.[41]

Economic dependence also appears in the form of "development aid." Palmberg argues that development aid is not necessarily designed for the development of the developing world and for humanitarian reasons, but more to bolster and secure foreign interest in developing countries. Much of the aid goes to infrastructure development (in areas such as telecommunications, airports, harbors, energy supply, and irrigation projects) and to a lesser extent schools, hospitals, and administrative buildings. Development aid is also used to manipulate and control the receiving country's economy and to attract other foreign investors to further existing investors' economic agenda.[42] Oftentimes, poorer countries that are not very accommodating of these developed countries receive little or no development aid.

Unequal exchange is another factor that devastates developing countries because they are paid very little for their raw materials, while their neocolonial counterparts make a fortune. According to Palmberg, "…most raw materials which as we have seen make up the major share of the exports from underdeveloped countries, have decreasing prices on the world market, whereas the prices of manufactured goods which the underdeveloped countries import steadily rise…."[43] Another tragedy for developing countries is that they do not have much control over the sale of their raw materials; the price is determined by the developed countries with whom they trade. To illustrate this point, Palmberg points out that, "…between 1970 and 1975 the prices of foodstuffs that the developed countries exported to the developing countries rose by 138%. But the prices of foodstuffs exported by the developing countries themselves rose by only 98% during the same period."[44]

Hence, "African underdevelopment was not a lack of development, but distorted development, created by colonialism. Underdevelopment would last as long as this system of dependence would last."[45] As mentioned above, cheap labor is another injustice that the developed countries have used to exploit the African continent, and foreign corporations only pay a pittance for labor and taxes in developing countries, but make huge profits from the goods in the global marketplace.[46] Hence, Palmberg concludes, "As long as the majority of the third world countries believe that changes can be made in co-operation with those industrialized countries which have created and maintained the third world's underdevelopment, the neo-colonial policies have not completely lost the day..."[47]

Why are the African people starving and unable to feed themselves amid their vast natural resources? Kevin Danaher points out that the real reasons for famine in Africa are not drought, overpopulation, and local government, as the media often portrays. Rather, these are the result of several hundred years of colonial impoverishment. Danaher concludes that the widespread hunger in Africa is a direct result of the famine long created by unsophisticated colonial farming practices that deplete the soil and disrupt Africa's ecological system. According to Danaher:

> As European countries colonized Africa, they disrupted African farming and herding systems that for centuries Africans had adopted to changing environmental conditions. Ecologically balanced food systems were undermined; the best agricultural lands were seized for growing coffee, sugar cane, cocoa and other export crops that would benefit Europe. Private and government investment went into developing these cash crops, while food production for the poor majority was neglected.[48]

Danaher further points out that depletion of the soil by colonial cash-cropping eventually turned large areas of once-fertile land into desert and semidesert. In the process of carrying out this farming practice, acres of brush and trees were removed that once added nutrients and organically replenished the soil.[49]

Throughout the centuries, the systematic forces that have perpetuated poverty and hunger in Africa have done so for profiteering. Danaher states, "The forces that have institutionalized hunger in Africa are made up of African elites, multinational corporations, Western governments and international agencies. Together they form an "antifarmer coalition" whose lifestyle and interests are very different from those of Africa's rural majority."[50] Therefore, "...over the years this antifarmer coalition implemented policies that undermined food crops. Prices paid to farmers for food crops were kept artificially low..."[51]

The unfair prices that African countries receive for their exports on the world-trade stage are devastating to their local economy, and help to keep them in perpetual debt. As Danaher articulates, "The prices of manufactured imports tend to ratchet upward. By 1982 a full year's worth of African exports could pay only 27 day's worth of the continent's imports," and furthermore, "...the deterioration of Africa's terms of trade means that most African governments are forced to spend more in the world market than they earn. They have filled the gap by borrowing."[52] When developing countries find themselves in a situation where their debt is out of control, they can have trouble borrowing more money. Hence, they have to follow the dictates of their creditors and take actions that sometimes further deteriorate their economies. According to Danaher:

> The International Monetary Fund is forcing many governments to implement austerity measures (e.g., eliminating food subsidiaries and social services) in order to get new loans.... The world financial system is a greater cause of hunger in Africa than is the drought. If African governments were not so deeply in debt, they could buy food on the world market. They would not be forced to wait for unreliable shipments of donated food while millions go hungry.[53]

One should note also that the food aid that is given to some poor countries does not necessarily make their economies better, but at times can make them worse. Since, "...food aid can undermine local food production by flooding local markets and depressing food prices. It can also create dependencies on foreign aid or be used by recipient governments to manipulate the poor."[54] Developed nations can wield foreign aid as a political tool to further manipulate and control underdeveloped countries.

P. T. Bauer defines colonialism as "...simply one country controlling another country's political system," and as a result he concludes that, "...colonialism in Africa ended in the 1960s and cannot be held responsible for Africa's current problems."[55] Bauer contends that the West should not feel any guilt or responsibility toward the developing regions' (i.e. Asia, Africa, and Latin America and the Caribbean) economic retardation. Bauer's position is that those countries in the developing regions that are in direct contact with Europe and North America are doing well economically, whereas those countries that are more detached from the West—in the Soviet bloc, aborigines, pygmies, and desert peoples—are the ones most economically devastated.[56]

Bauer's argument is not necessarily accurate, because a long-standing pro-US country like Haiti battles with abject poverty beyond proportion, for decades, while pro-communist Venezuela—flourishes. Also, Bauer maintains that Africa should be grateful for Western introduction of certain plants and crops that became critical to Africa's raw-material exports and for the positive changes Western development brought to local government revenues, literacy rate, school attendance, public health, life expectancy, infant mortality, etc. What Bauer fails to point out, however, is that the colonizers brought plants to Africa for their own "profiteering," not to benefit Africans, and that many people in Africa still do not have access to those services that he highlighted. The very ways in which Bauer claims that the colonizers helped Africa are some of the very ways in which they systematically marginalized and oppressed Africa.[57]

Furthermore, Bauer sees Europe ending the Atlantic slave trade as a credit to European goodwill, forgetting that Europe started it and did everything in its power to maintain this system. In addition, the notion that Africa, as late as in the second half of the nineteenth century, was still uncivilized because it lacked wheel traffic, mechanical transportation, proper infrastructure, basic healthcare, formal education, advancements in science and technology, and had failed to eliminate hunger and famine and provide better living conditions, in some ways contradicts all of the advancements in Africa prior to colonialism.[58] Bauer fails to mention that prior to European colonization of Africa, the continent experienced much development and progress that were even greater, and to a lesser extent, comparable to that of Europe during the same period. In his book, *How Europe Underdeveloped Africa*, Walter Rodney highlights the advancements and developments that were occurring in precolonial Africa in places like Ethiopia, Nubia, the Maghreb, Western Sudan, Zimbabwe, and Egypt.[59]

Another charge Bauer makes is that the West does not manipulate international trade and markets, and has nothing to do with developing nations' indebtedness, which he blames on the governments' irresponsible actions, wasteful spending, and bad policies.[60] While there might be bits of plausibility to this argument, one cannot ignore that Western entities continue to benefit the most from Africa's resources and continue to pay insignificant wages to the African workforce.

Approach

Any poverty-reduction strategy that will have a significant and lasting impact must be concerned with issues such as education, food and water, health care, and social justice. There are many proposed poverty-reduction strategies, but I will only briefly discuss and engage two: the United Nations (UN) Millennium Goals (MDGs) and Nandy's recommendations for reducing poverty, which I find workable, measurable, and practical.

UN MDGs:

In 2000, the UN drafted its Millennium Development Goals: to eradicate extreme global poverty and hunger; achieve universal primary education; promote gender equality and empower women; reduce mortality; improve maternal health; combat HIV/AIDS, malaria and other diseases; ensure environmental sustainability; and develop global partnerships for economic development. The UN aims to reduce by half the number of the extremely poor, those who live on less than US$1 per day, suffer hunger, and are unable to access safe drinking water, by 2015. By the same date, the UN hopes that children everywhere, boys and girls alike, will have access to universal primary education. Another UN target is to reduce the mortality rate among pregnant women and children under the age of five by 3/4 and 2/3, respectively, by 2015. By the same date, the UN seeks to halt and begin to reverse the spread of HIV/AIDS, the scourge of malaria, and other diseases so prevalent among the poor. By 2020, the UN plans to significantly improve the lives of at least 100 million slum dwellers. The UN believes these goals can be attained by addressing the special needs of the least-developed countries, creating trade and market conditions that are more sympathetic to the least-developed countries, eliminating the debts of the least developed countries, providing job opportunities for young people, and by making technology accessible to the least-developed countries.[61]

The UN hopes to fund those goals through monetary contributions from developed countries, but some of those who initially offered to help this initiative have not been forthcoming. According to a UN 2007 progress report:

> The only donors to reach or exceed the United Nations target of 0.7 per cent of gross national income for development aid were Denmark, Luxembourg, the Netherlands, Norway and Sweden. Sixteen of the 22 member countries of the Development Assistance Committee (DAC) met the 2006 targets for official development assistance they set at the 2002 Monterrey Conference on Financing for Development.[62]

Also, mounting challenges that many of the countries in developing regions face hinder the MDGs. According to Jose Antonio Ocampo:

> Currently, only one of the eight regional groups cited in this report is on track to achieve all the Millennium Development Goals. In contrast, the projected shortfalls are most severe in sub-Saharan Africa. Even regions that have made substantial progress, including parts of Asia, face challenges in areas such as health and environmental sustainability. More generally, the lack of employment opportunities for young people, gender inequalities, rapid and unplanned urbanization, deforestation, increasing water scarcity, and high HIV prevalence are pervasive obstacles.[63]

If they are to fulfill the MDGs, developing countries will have to find ways to resolve the challenges that are within their reach. In the poorest countries, this would be impossible without the help of developed countries. According to Ocompo:

> Developed countries need to deliver fully on longstanding commitments to achieve the official development assistance (ODA) target of 0.7 percent of gross national income (GNI) by 2015. It requires, in particular, the Group of 8 industrialized nations to live up to their 2005 pledge to double aid to Africa by 2010 and European Union Member States to allocate 0.7 per cent of GNI to ODA by 2015. In spite of these commitments, ODA declined between 2005 and 2006 and is expected to continue to fall slightly in 2007 as debt relief declines.[64]

Experts point out that it will take approximately $150 billion in annual aid to meet the MDGs, but so far those nations that committed to donate have not given more than a total of $107 billion annually.[65] This is progress, but still a shortfall that could thwart the projections of the MDGs.

Nandy's Recommendations:

Nandy concludes that many of the factors of chronic poverty could in fact help to reduce poverty. Whether chronic or otherwise, poverty affects rural people the most because they tend to have limited options and less access to certain services that could raise their standard of living than do those in urban areas. This however, does not negate the poverty that also exists in urban slums and shantytowns.[66] This factor, Nandy argues, creates an opportunity to utilize a large workforce in the rural areas for enormous agricultural production. Very poor countries could use the extensive human resources in rural areas to produce enough food to feed themselves, and export, but they would have to be supplied with the material and technological resources that they would need to accomplish these goals.

Areas nearest to capital cities are better-served because traditionally more resources are directed into developing areas closest to capital cities. Thus, a minority is served while the majority of these countries are not served.[67] In this scenario, the poorer countries need to not only provide opportunities in the urban areas, but in the rural areas as well. The more people are put to work, the stronger their economy will be. Chronic poverty tends to follow a certain pattern along social-class lines. People working in agriculture tend to be more poverty-stricken than those in skilled manual labor and nonmanual professions.[68] Therefore, the governments of the poorer countries should seek to create a more just and equitable economic order and distribute the wealth throughout their populations, because it will benefit their overall economy far more than when the wealth is confined to a minority. Compensating agricultural workers closer to the rate of professionals would be an added incentive for people to take agricultural jobs. In that way, the stigma of working in the local agriculture sector would also dissipate.

Chronic poverty spreads across all genders and ages, but chronically poor women are more likely to be malnourished.[69] Therefore, these regions should take steps to make sure that mothers get the necessary nutrients and healthcare, because the more healthy children they produce, less the government will have to spend on sick mothers and children. When mothers give birth to healthy children and less people are sick, it is better for everyone because they are able to contribute more to society.

The United Nations Millennium Goals and Nandy's recommendation seem plausible. They seek to eliminate poverty and help to create more stable and progressive economies in extremely poor countries. Much of the help for these initiatives would have to come from the G8 nations. Each able citizen of the global community should be given a chance to play a role in the elimination of extreme poverty. In addition, we have to find ways to get to the root causes of poverty, rather than merely attending to the symptoms of poverty. Everyone should be empowered in such a way that they can avoid being poor. First, the developed countries should assume responsibility for their role in impoverishing the developing nations, and end their actions that perpetuate poverty. Second, the leadership and elites of these poorer countries should be held responsible by the global community for their actions that hinder the economic progress of their countries and nations. Third, infrastructures that generate ongoing economic resources for these nations should be implemented for the benefit of the local people, not merely foreign corporate interests and the oligarchy that often rules them.

E. Poverty Reduction Initiative

1. Hunger, Education, and Health

The United Nations (UN) 2007 Millennium Development Goals' (MDGs') progress report reveals that the proportion of people living on US$1 per day in Sub-Saharan Africa decreased slightly from 46.8% in 1990 to 45.9% and 41.1% in 1999 and 2004, respectively. In Southern Asia, the proportion of people in extreme poverty dropped from 41.1% in 1990 to 33.4% in 1999, and to 29.5% in 2004. Eastern Asia shows much more recent success than the previous regions, as the proportion of extreme poverty plummeted from 33% in 1990 to 17.8%, and 9.9% in 1999 and 2004, respectively. In Latin America and the Caribbean, however, the proportion of extreme poverty only reduced slightly from 10.3% in 1990 to 9.6% and 8.7% in 1999 and 2004, respectively. Southeast Asia shows much success from 1990 to 1999, but little progress from 1999 to 2004; the proportion of extreme poverty in this region fell from 20.8% in 1990 to 8.9% in 1999, and to 6.8% in 2004. North Africa has seen a decline in extreme poverty from 2.6% in 1990 to 2% and 1.4% in 1999 and 2004 respectively. In the transition countries of Southeastern Europe, extreme poverty fluctuates slightly from 0.1% in 1990 to 1.3% and 0.7% in 1999 and 2004, respectively.

In general, there has been some progress in reducing poverty throughout the developing regions, from 31.6% in 1990 to 23.4% and 19.2% in 1999 and 2004, respectively. The actual number of extreme poor has reduced from 1.25 billion in 1990 to 980 million in 2004, but with the global economic meltdown in 2007 and 2008, this will probably change for the worse. The report also reveals that income inequality is a major concern in East Asia, Latin America, the Caribbean, and Sub-Saharan Africa. Income inequality is highest in Latin America and the Caribbean, and the greatest proportion of hungry children is in Sub-Saharan Africa.[70]

Clearly, income disparity is among the factors that militate against poverty-reduction measures throughout the developing regions. Latin America, the Caribbean, and Sub-Saharan Africa have the widest income inequality gap. UN 2007 MDG's progress report shows that the poorest fifth of the people in Latin America and the Caribbean only account for 3% of their national consumption or income.[71] In 2008, the wealthiest 10% of Latin America and the Caribbean received over 40% of the total income generated by the region, while the poorest 10% received only 1%. This inequality gap is influenced by various factors, such as classism, elitism, place of birth, family background, race, gender, etc.[72] This indicates that the richest people are the ones primarily benefiting from any economic growth in these developing regions, evidence that there is a need for a just economic order.

Two of the factors that cause hunger to persist in developing regions are food distribution and failure to implement proper agricultural technology. There is enough food on earth to feed everybody, but the issue is that it is not distributed evenly. The problem is not with production, because the world has the ability and resources to produce enough food to feed everyone. Hence, distribution of food to poor countries and lack of advanced agricultural technologies to produce their own food are bigger problems. Singer states:

> The problem is not that the world cannot produce enough to feed and shelter its people. People in poor countries consume, on average, 400 lbs. of grain a year, while North Americans average more than 2,000 lbs. The difference is caused by the fact that in the rich countries we feed most of our grain to animals, converting it into meat, milk, and eggs.... If we stopped feeding animals on grains, soybeans, and fishmeal the amount of food saved would—if distributed to those who need it—be more than enough to end hunger throughout the world...These facts about animal food do not mean that we can easily solve the world [sic] food problem by cutting down on animal products, but they show that the problem is essentially one of distribution rather than production... Moreover, the poorer nations themselves could produce far more if they made more use of improved agricultural techniques.[73]

As it relates to education, there has been improvement in the number of children of primary-school-age now enrolled in schools in developing countries. This increase overall is from 80% in 1991 to 83% and 88% in 1999 and 2005, respectively. There is still a need to enroll the remaining 12%, which is still a wide margin when translated into real numbers. When one child is denied access to education, it is everyone's loss. While it is commendable that Sub-Saharan Africa has been making steady and significant progress in making sure that its children of primary-school age are in school, a striking 30% are still not attending school, and this puts this region at the bottom of the scale in comparison to other regions.[74]

Developing regions and the global community should make sure that 100% of its children attend and function in school. Education should no longer be a privilege but a right afforded to every child by their government and the global community. Just as everyone has a right to life, everyone should have a right to an education. The notion that some children should be educated and some should not because they do not show early intellectual prowess is false, and has deprived the world of prospects and promises that it will never know or realize. Just because a child appears slower than others due to issues such as malnutrition, a hostile home environment, illness, inability to pass standardized tests, and inability to learn by the methodology with which other children learn, does not mean that child is useless. It is not the child that is worthless and useless, rather a system that expects "one size to fit all," and condemns those who do not fit its worn-out paradigm. Educational systems should be modified to meet students' needs, not the other way around. Denying a child an education is an insult to human rationality, and strangely enough, some who consider themselves intellectuals and educated perpetuate this gross absurdity.

Also, developing regions must militate against elements that prevent girls and children from poorer or rural families from attending school. In some developing countries, one in five children old enough to attend secondary school is still attending primary school.[75] Children should attend school at their proper age; otherwise, remedial programs should be implemented to assist slower kids.

Despite a slight reduction in maternal and child mortality and some diseases over the past decade, there are still many health concerns in developing regions. The rate of child mortality per 1,000 live births was 106 in 1990 and 83 in 2005. It is estimated that 10.1 million children died in 2005 before reaching the age of five, primarily from preventable diseases. Other factors that contribute to the staggering increase in child mortality are AIDS, malaria, and measles, but the factors vary for each region. There is a dire need for people with the HIV virus to receive the antiretroviral therapy they need, but these drugs are not distributed to many patients. In 2006, 71% of those infected with the virus in the developing regions were not receiving antiretroviral therapy. Oftentimes the antiretroviral drug is too expensive and impoverished people cannot afford it.[76] Why pharmaceutical and drug companies cannot make acutely needed drugs more affordable to the poor?

2. Human Rights

Discrimination and crimes committed against humanity fueled by race, gender, class, ethnicity, and religion have terrified countless souls for centuries. The notion that someone is better than another because of their skin color, gender, class, ethnicity, tribal identity, or religious identity is not only absurd but false. Discrimination has had its day, and we must do everything we can to break this vicious monster around the world. During the Atlantic slave trade, millions of Black people were killed because they were considered to be less than human due to their race, and for centuries many were forced into the most vicious kind of slavery recorded in human history. In the Americas, countless Native Americans were massacred, and their livelihood and culture were destroyed because they were considered inferior. During the period of 1939–1945, Adolf Hitler's Nazi regime was responsible for the extermination of millions of Jews, and according to many sources, this was motivated by hate and prejudice.[77] From the 1990s to the present, we have seen various forms of ethnic cleansings that have led to genocide. The Rwanda genocide in 1994 led to the death of approximately 800,000 Tutsis alone, and around 1 million people overall, according to some estimates.[78] In Darfur, Sudan, since the late '90s, the number of people that have been murdered, displaced, starved, and infected with disease by the ongoing crisis exceeds 1.5 million. Many believe that this genocide is motivated by radical Muslim sentiments, and fueled by the Sudan government, to cleanse Sudan of native African Sudanese.[79]

The list of genocides and crimes committed against humanity is too much to exposit in this brief section, but how can we forget those mentioned above, and others such as the splitting of India in 1947, Indonesia 1965–66, Biafra 1968–71, Bangladesh 1970–71, the Vietnam War 1965–73, Cambodia 1975–79, Ethiopia 1984–85, Somalia 1991–92, Tibet 1951, and the struggle that developed in the Amazon among Indian tribes and Bosnia in the '90s.[80] Today, we have the ongoing Israeli-Palestinian conflict, Iraq and Afghanistan wars, and mounting terrorist attacks around the globe.

Due to the brevity of this section, below I will only discuss human trafficking, Dalit oppression in India, and gender discrimination.

Human trafficking is defined by the Human Rights Protocol, supplementing the United Nations Convention Against Transnational Organized Crime, as:

> The recruitment, transportation, transfer, harboring or receipt of persons, by means of threat or use of force or other forms of coercion, of abduction, of fraud, of deception, of abuse of power or of position of vulnerability or of the giving or receiving of payments or benefits to achieve the consent of a person having control over another person, for the purpose of exploitation. Exploitation shall include, at a minimum, the exploitation of the prostitution of others or other forms of sexual exploitation, forced labor or services, slavery or practices similar to slavery, servitude or the removal of organs.[81]

Approximately 600,000 to 800,000 persons are trafficked around the world annually.[82] The US State Department reports that 50,000 to 100,000 women and children are trafficked into the US alone each year from various countries around the world; half of those who are trafficked into the US are kept in bonded sweatshops or some form of domestic servitude.[83]

Victims of human trafficking are usually poor people from poor countries looking for economic opportunities elsewhere. There are instances in which persons are abducted, trafficked, and placed into forced labor or prostitution. Usually, traffickers come up with ways to lure their victims into trafficking by making lucrative offers to them. Human Rights Watch points out that:

> In a typical case, a woman is recruited with promises of a good job in another country or province, and lacking better options at home, she agrees to migrate. There are also cases in which women are lured with false marriage offers or vacation invitations, in which children are bartered by their parents for a cash advance and/or promises of future earnings, or in which victims are abducted outright.[84]

Trafficked victims are usually recruited by someone who knows them, like family members, friends, and neighbors; others are recruited by taxi drivers; and in very rare cases advertisements in local papers lure the victims.[85] These persons present very lucrative offers to potential victims that are often too good to resist because of the socioeconomic situation in their own countries. Oftentimes, these victims cannot get a job, afford to go to school, and buy food to eat. They take these job offers with the intention to migrate, work, earn money, and return home to help themselves and their family members, most of the time. The victims of trafficking never bargain to work in prostitution and servitude; they are usually forced into these roles. Usually these women and girls, and men and boys, are forced by their captors into bars, brothels, slavery on farms, factories, and restaurants.[86] Once traffickers obtain false documentation, make travel arrangements, and arrive with victims at their destination, the victim is put to work at the traffickers' pleasure. Victims usually get a rude awakening when they find out the circumstances under which they have to work and that they have no control over where they work, what work they are forced to do, how much they are paid, and their own lives.

Another frightening thing for the victims upon arrival at a trafficked destination is that they are usually indebted to their new owners, who bought them from their traffickers and may resell them at will to other persons, who sometimes resell them again and again. Each person in possession of them would tell them that they have to work to pay off their debt, the amount for which their owners have bought them, although they are often unable to do so, even after years of long hours of work each day.[87] After months and years of excruciating work, these victims earn very little, or sometimes no money at all, from their oppressors. When trafficked victims refuse to work, they are abused physically and forced to work even when they are sick. Coercive tactics are often used to keep victims in bondage and deter them from attempting to escape: deception, fraud, intimidation, isolation, death threats against victims and their family members back home, arrest by local law enforcement, confiscation of travel documents, constant surveillance, and threats of deportation.[88] Victims' living conditions are usually unhealthy, and they are improperly cared for and fed. To achieve the objective to exploit labor and service from their victims for monetary gain, traffickers exert absolute control over these people.[89]

The testimonies of trafficked victims are moving and sad. A woman in her mid-twenties from Ukraine told Human Rights Watch investigators in an interview after a brothel raid in March 1999:

> When I came to work here, they tricked me on the way. They told us that we would dance. They did a three month visa for me. We had a

visa and everything was fine at the first place. But when we wanted to leave, the owner sold us. They told me that I would be a dancer but then I had to be a prostitute. I have been here for over five months. At the first place, the owner...did not tell us that he had sold us. He just put us into a car. Then we came here and the owner here told us that we had been sold and that we had to work off our debt.... We could not leave. He said that we had to work off three more months even after we worked off our debt. He said that he would sell us to another man. He said that we had to work until the 8th of March. After that we still had to work... [The owner] from the first place sold us for 1,500 Deutschmarks [€769/U.S. $694].

Children are also victims of human trafficking, and two of the primary factors of child trafficking are poverty and lack of opportunities. Human Rights Watch interviewed scores of Togolese girls between the ages of three and seventeen who were trafficked internally and externally from Togo to places likes Nigeria, Benin, and Ghana. These girls recount chilling and graphic stories that involve horrific voyages, forced labor, sexual exploitations, and beatings.[91] Togolese boys are also victims of trafficking. They are trafficked from Togo to places like Benin and Nigeria, where they are forced to do long hours of difficult and uncompensated agricultural work. One boy in an interview with Human Rights Watch recounted his horrific voyage from Togo to Benin:

On the other side, another truck was waiting for us. It had no seats, so we had to stand up in the truck. We were 250 people in one truck, all standing. It was hot and we were falling on each other. The truck became so full that some boys had to sit on the edge. The boys on the edge would sometimes get hit by a tree and fall down—one boy fell from the truck and broke his leg. There was no hospital because we were in the bush, so we just picked him up and put him back on the truck. We drove in that truck for seven days, taking detours to avoid the soldiers. Sometimes we took the same route used to herd cattle from Nigeria to Benin. At night we got off the truck and slept in the bush.[92]

Clearly, human trafficking is vicious and dehumanizing; it is modern-day slavery and must be criminalized as such unequivocally by the global community. Redress should be given to trafficked victims. Oftentimes, when local law enforcement raids a brothel, they penalize the victims for breach of immigration laws and charge them with prostitution and other illicit acts, which they commit under duress. Such law-enforcement measures that criminalize the victims should be avoided. When victims testify, the government should provide them with protection and not merely deportation. Victims should be afforded the right to confidentiality, security of person, and justice, thus affirming the human dignity of every person.[93] Furthermore, governments should create policies and labor laws that protect migrant workers from abuse. Oftentimes, migrant workers are treated inhumanely by their employers. When they try to escape the cruel and inhumane treatment, they are forced to remain due to immigration laws, because fleeing from abusive working conditions means that one will fall out of legal immigration status and risks the possibility of arrest, detention, fines, and in some localities, imprisonment and caning.[94]

We now turn to Dalits oppression. India has what is called a caste system that goes back to the Vedic age, thousands of years ago; it is intricately woven into the social, political, and religious livelihood of that nation.[95] Yet India's caste system is one of the worst tragedies of our time, because it has consistently and persistently oppressed and marginalized more than 165 million of its people that are referred to as the Dalit caste.[96] India has five castes that are summarized here in order of the highest to the lowest.

1. The *Brahmins* are the priests, philosophers, and specialists in matters of life of the spirit.

2. The *Kshatriyas* are the nobles of feudal India, which involves kings, warriors, and vassals. Members of this caste are seen as the guardians of Indian society.

3. The *Vaishyas* caste consists of economic specialists, such as farmers and merchants.

4. The *Shudra* caste consists of manual laborers and artisans.

5. The *Dalits* are classified as untouchables or outcasts, and are relegated to carrying out all the tasks that are considered abhorrent to others in Indian society.[97]

India's caste system is supported by Hindu sacred writings—the Vedas, other sacred texts, and historical customs—that shaped their understanding of social roles and functions. India's rules dictating social roles are enumerated in the Code of Manu, which was compiled around 100 CE, and affirms the inhumane treatment of Dalits. The Code of Manu is described as follows:

> In it are laws governing all aspects of life, including the proper conduct of rulers, dietary restrictions, marriage laws, daily rituals, purification rites, social laws, and ethical guidance. It prescribes hospitality to guest and the cultural civilization of such virtues as contemplation, truthfulness, compassion, non-attachment, generosity, pleasant dealings with people, and self control. It condemns untouchables to living outside villages, eating only from broken dishes, and wearing only clothes removed from corpse…[98]

A person's caste cannot be revoked, according to this system; once born a Dalit, one is always a Dalit; people cannot work their way out their caste. Their caste is not only their social identity, but also their personal, familial, and cultural identity. Dalits are treated as the scum of the Indian society. Mahatma Gandhi disavowed this evil practice, renaming the Dalits *hirijan*, which is translated as "the children of God."[99] The "stigma of untouchability was legally abolished" in 1948, and in 1950 India's constitution was amended, abolishing untouchability in all forms, and incorporating numerous measures and laws to protect Dalits against caste-based abuses and discriminatory practices.[100] Dalits are still subjected to undue inhumane treatment, and barred from professional and government positions. According to government estimates of 2000, unemployment doubled among Dalits.

Furthermore, Dalit women tend to suffer more than men, in that they have to deal with the triple discrimination of being untouchable, poor, and female. Dalit women have to contend with the threat of sexual violence and trafficking. In some cases, Dalit women are auctioned off and sent to urban brothels. Dalits are subjected to segregation in schools, and are denied access to both public and private services. On a daily basis, Dalits face class-motivated abuses and killings, which violate their constitutional right to security of personhood and protection from state. Local law enforcement officers are often hesitant to protect Dalits from acts of looting, arson, torture, assault, tonsuring, stripping, and ridiculing of women. Dalits are frequent victims of crimes each day that they are hesitant to report, for fear of repercussions from upper-caste members to whom the government and local law-enforcement officers are sympathetic.[101]

Consequently, Dalits' civil, social, political, cultural, economic, and educational constitutional rights are constantly neglected and violated by their government, law enforcement, and upper-caste members. Dalits' rights to freedom of residence are denied because they are relegated to untouchable communities. Their right to marry and select the spouse of their choice is denied because inter-caste marriage often leads to punitive consequences, such as public beatings, lynching, murder, and rape of the couple and their relatives. Dalits' right to own property is constantly forfeited; on occasions, Dalits' property is taken away by force, and Dalits who resist are sometimes severely beaten or killed. Dalits' right to freedom of religion, thought, and conscience is still repressed. Dalits frustrated with the Hindu religion and caste system sometimes turn to Buddhism, Christianity, or Islam in rebellion and in hopes of a better life. In some Indian states, Dalits are forbidden from practicing any other religion, and those who do still experience elements of "castism." Dalits are denied their right to work wherever and however they want, and are subjected to menial tasks that nobody else wants.

In addition, many Dalits survive on less than US$1 dollar per day, placing them among the world's poorest people. Furthermore, more than 1.3 million Dalits are forced into manual scavenging, cleaning human waste from pit latrines. The inhumane treatment of Dalits, poor healthcare and working conditions, and denial of basic necessities and rights expose Dalits to serious and sometimes fatal health issues. More than 20% of Dalits lack access to safe drinking water, and only 10% live in housing with sanitation facilities.[102]

Clearly, India's government continues to fail the Dalits by not enforcing measures to protect their fundamental rights. The global community should hold them accountable. As Dalits push back by forming human-rights movements, getting active in their society, and making their voices heard in the global square, the global community should respond to them with love, compassion, and the empowerment that they seek.[103]

We now turn to gender discrimination. Globally, unemployment is still highest among women, and less women than men work, in nonagricultural jobs. The percentages of women working in nonagricultural jobs in 2005 were only 13% in Southern Asia, 20% in North Africa, 21% in Western Asia, 22% in Sub-Saharan Africa, 38% in Oceana, 39% in Southeast Asia, 41% in East Asia, and 42% in Latin America and the Caribbean. Women are not only marginalized in this sector in the developing regions, but in developed regions as well—in 2005, women only made up 47% of those working in the nonagricultural sector in developed regions.[104]

Income disparity between men and women is still staggering. More women do not get paid by employers, and fewer women work, whether as employees or employers. UN progress report shows that from 1990 to 2005, 60% of women worldwide contributed to the labor sector but did not earn any income in comparison to only 40% of men. This shows that women, more than men, continue to be denied the compensation they deserve for work done. Also, 22% of the world's employers are women, whereas 78% are men. Among employees, only 40% are women. In general, 41% of all people employed worldwide are females.[105]

Although women are making some progress politically, they still lag behind men in this regard. In 2007, women only made up 17% of single or lower houses of parliament worldwide, and 22% in the developed regions. Nonetheless, some countries are doing exceptionally well in empowering women to lead. In Rwanda, women occupy 49% of the parliamentary seats, followed by Sweden and Costa Rica, where women occupy 47% and 39% of parliamentary seats, respectively.[106] In recent years, various women served or are serving as heads of state—in Chile, Jamaica, Liberia, the Republic of Korea, Switzerland, Israel (as interim president),[107] Germany, and Brazil (most recently elected its first female president).

One cannot deny the abuse, suffering, and deprivation of many women around the world, simply because of their gender, and this is absolutely wrong. For example, some women are raped and used as "weapons of warfare" in places like Sierra Leone, Kosovo, the Democratic Republic of Congo, Afghanistan, and Rwanda. Some women are battered by their husbands at home at alarming rates, and in places such as Pakistan, South Africa, Peru, Russia, and Uzbekistan, this occurs with little or no government intervention.

Discriminatory laws prevent women from entering and retaining employment in places like Guatemala, South Africa, and Mexico. In the US, girls that are lesbian, bisexual, or transgender are sometimes attacked by their peers.[108]

In some parts of the world, women are considered unequal to men by their government, and legal authority for their decisions and reproductive healthcare is given to their husbands or male family members. Women are also restricted from full participation in the public sphere. These practices happen in countries like Morocco, Jordan, Kuwait, and Saudi Arabia. Furthermore, millions of women and girls in some parts of the world do not have control over their lives and what happens to their own bodies. Many females are forced to marry and have sexual intercourse with males whom they in no way desire. Women are at times sexually assaulted by jailers while in custody. In some cases, women are severely punished by the state for committing adultery, which recently played out in the Nigerian judicial system,[109] and also in Iran. Recently, a law was passed in Afghanistan that denies legal recourse to women raped by their husbands.

Citizens of the Global community should rise to the urgent call to combat the longstanding exploitation of girls and women everywhere:

> Our [categorical] duty as activists [for women's rights] is to expose and denounce as human rights violations those practices and policies that silence and subordinate women. We reject specific legal, cultural, or religious practices by which women are systematically discriminated against, excluded from political participation and public life, segregated in their daily lives, raped in armed conflict, beaten in their homes, denied equal divorce or inheritance rights, killed for having sex, forced to marry, assaulted for not conforming to gender norms, and sold into forced labor. Arguments that sustain and excuse these human rights abuses—those of cultural norms, "appropriate" rights for women, or western imperialism—barely disguise their true meaning: that women's lives matter less than men's. Cultural relativism, which argues that there are no universal human rights and that rights are culture-specific and culturally determined, is still a formidable and corrosive challenge to women's rights to equality and dignity in all facets of their lives.[110]

The inhumane treatment of girls and women anywhere and everywhere should be outlawed and have no place in human civilization. Consequently, as citizens of the world, we must militate against this tragedy and other forms of discrimination that dehumanize and oppress people. The notion that certain practices are relative and cultural should be reconsidered in many cases. Laws, practices, and customs that diminish the fundamental moral and legal rights of another in any way should not be tolerated and must be treated as crimes against humanity.

3. Nonviolence and Peacemaking

A fruit of the love imperative is nonviolence and peacemaking. The Christian view of nonviolence is supported by the teachings of Christ, which are consistent with the double-love command. In the Sermon on the Mount (Matt. 5–7) and throughout Christ's ministry, Christ completely denounces all forms of violence and commands that peacemaking efforts be employed even in the face of violence. Christ commands that we should "Do unto others as we would have them do to us," and that, "We should love our neighbor as we love ourselves." No one is comfortable with being treated violently. The Anabaptists were one of the first groups in the Christian tradition that sought to practice nonviolence and negate the use of violence, diverging from mainline Protestant and Roman Catholic churches that bought into the Just War theory, which advocates that war can be waged under certain circumstances.[111] The Just War theory in Christian thought goes back to Augustine and Aquinas. Augustine believes that a war is justified when it is for a just cause, when it is carried-out by the proper authority, and when its use is motivated by love. Aquinas later articulates a theory that he calls *jus ad bellum*, which holds that a war can be waged by the legitimate authority if the cause is just, if it is motivated by right intention, and serves the purpose of peace and common good.[112] Still, it is difficult to see how these Just War theories are consistent with Christ's teachings, when Christ lived and preached nonviolence even in the most dire of circumstances.

For example, when Christ was suffering the most violent death on the cross, He begged the Father to forgive those who were inflicting pain on him (Lk. 23:34).

In America, the Civil Rights Movement in the 1950s and '60s, with King invoked Christ's call to nonviolence to break the tyranny of prejudice and hate. King's philosophy of nonviolence was influenced by Christ's Sermon on the Mount and Mahatma Gandhi's successful nonviolent protest in India in the 1940s. King articulates:

> First, this [nonviolent action] is not a method for cowards; it does resist. The nonviolent register is just as strongly opposed to the evil against which he protests as is the person who uses violence.... A second point is that nonviolent resistance does not seek to defeat or humiliate the opponent, but to win his friendship and understanding.... A Third characteristic of this method is that the attack is directed against forces of evil rather than against persons who are caught in those forces.... A fourth point... concerning nonviolent resistance is that it avoids not only external physical violence but also internal violence of spirit.... Finally, the method of nonviolence is based on the conviction that the universe is on the side of justice. It is this deep faith in the future that causes the nonviolent register to accept suffering without retaliation...[113]

This principle, according to King, is rooted in *agape* love, the essence of love of God and neighbor. It is due to this unconditional love that Christ was able to love even those who persecuted Him.

Some of the Eastern religions have long subscribed to the idea and practice of nonviolence. The hallmark of Jainism is nonviolence, a principle that its adherents consider dear to their existence. *Ahimsa* or nonviolence in Jainism, means refraining from harm to humans, animals, insects, and plants to a certain extent.[114] Acarya Tulsi (1914–1997), a contemporary activist leader of Jainism, taught that monks should be engaged in world affairs, and brought Jainism into the broader dialogue on issues such as environmental degradation and nuclear proliferation. In 1945, Tulsi outlined nine basic universal principles that should be used in the application of nonviolent action. This effort was influenced by Tulsi's concern over the prolongation of the Second World War and the urgent need for peace. Gandhi, after receiving a copy of these principles, was reportedly saddened that they were not published long before.

Tulsi's nine principles of nonviolence are: 1) Nonviolence should be propagated widely around the world, emphasizing antipathy and loathe for violence and death. This will allow peace to be cultivated in the hearts of humankind. 2) The four origins or root causes of unrest, dispute, or discord are anger, pride, deceitfulness, and discontent. Therefore, humans should militate against these to attain peace. 3) Education should be a basic right afforded to everyone, and the object of education should not be for material gains but for the development of the inner self. Consequently, the powers that be should strain every effort to make education accessible to all. 4) The foundation and goal of any government should be justice, equity, and good conduct. Therefore, government should never be for the purposes of exploitation and unjust reasons. 5) Scientific discoveries should never be utilized for material gains and the purpose of war. 6) Universal fraternity should be advocated instead of nationalism, and economic and political conflict should be avoided. 7) Greed, power struggles, acts of jealousy, and rivalry should be resisted forcefully. Armed conflicts are usually caused by attempts to seize another's land or property. 8) Acts of injustice and oppression of the weak and marginalized should not be practiced by an individual, nation, or state, who instead should exercise justice, impartiality, and humanity. 9) Religious freedom should be granted to all people. Consequently, no one should force one's faith upon others through acts of coercion and undue influence. Faith should be transmitted through education and honest preaching.[115]

It is clear that love leads to peace, not war, and in order to achieve peace in the wake of wars, terror attacks, and conflicts around the globe, the law of love should be given a chance to transform human nature and structures. The efforts and resources spent on waging wars and conflicts around the globe are astronomical in comparison to those spent on promoting love of neighbor. There cannot be any real and lasting peace without love. How can you commit acts of violence against someone whom you truly love unconditionally? When love takes precedence, nonviolence is the natural action and reaction in any given circumstance.

Finally, there are some who think that violence and warfare flow out of and lead to love when waged by the proper authority or for the object of love, but this could not be less consistent with the love imperative, because love always proceeds toward and results in nonviolence and peacemaking. The nonviolent life, teaching, and ministry of Jesus Christ exemplified the love imperative.

Concluding Remarks

Out of goodwill, people have been giving to help provide food and basic necessities for the poor around the globe, but many are still in poverty. We need to help the extreme poor to "fish" for themselves rather than just giving them "fish". This does not mean that people should cease to give "fish", but there is a more dire need for the implementation of measures and programs that harness the resources of these regions for the good of the poor. Clearly, there might be disagreements about the methods used to alleviate poverty, but all should share the common goal to rid the world of extreme poverty. Differences in style should not halt any progress toward fulfilling the needs of the majority in those nation-states. Efforts should be made to enlighten the people about their choices so that everyone feels a part of their country and its progress. While the world is helping the localities to achieve their goals, it should not circumvent local people and ignore their needs.

Hunger, education, health, human rights and peace-making must be primary in any initiative to reduce or eliminate global poverty. Education must be the chiefest of these issues. An effort that focuses on one of these elements in isolation of another might be good and helpful—as it meets the particular need that it sets out to address—but it will not fully address the issue of extreme poverty. Whenever there is a concentrated effort, in an extremely poor context, on these five elements by just one organization or multiple organizations— there is bound to be a serious dent in absolute poverty.

Solving global poverty is the collectively global loving thing to do. It will make life better for everyone. We must bear in mind that extreme poverty is a form of socioeconomic injustice, which is categorically evil. Socioeconomic injustice brings unhappiness to its victims and everybody else. The global community cannot be truly free and happy when scores of fellow humans are in dire poverty. Although some unjust people may pretend to be happy and be convinced that they receive pleasure from their exploitation of the poor, they are not truly happy because they live in terror of their own conscience, however they may try to suppress it. Although some people appear conscienceless, their conscience is not dead, as it is alive to the dictates of their nature. When the human ecology's proper order is disrupted by socioeconomic injustice, everyone suffers its effects—the victims, oppressors, and spectators alike. The socioeconomic monsters that humans create are not kind to anyone and may appear only to affect its intended victims, but in the fullness of time, all will be suffocated by these perversions until they are permanently discredited and abandoned. Extreme poverty is a threat to the happiness of everyone on the planet. This threat must be taken seriously, by putting an end to global poverty. It is the loving and good thing to do.

Notes

[1] Minujin, Alberto, Jan Vandemoortele, and Enrique Delamonica, "Economic Growth, Poverty and Children," *Environment and Urbanization* 14.2 (October 2002): 23–43, 25. "The poverty line of US $1 per day is usually considered the international line for measuring and comparing the incidence of poverty in low-and middle-income nations. This line is based on studies in the 1980s in ten low-income countries, including Bangladesh, India, Kenya and Tanzania. The price of a minimal "basket of necessities" was around US$1 per day per person at 1985 purchasing power."

[2] Ibid., 25; *see also* World Bank's website, http://www.worldbank.org/poverty/data/trends/income.html.

[3] Ibid.

[4] Ibid., 26.

[5] Nandy, Shailen, "'Misunderstanding' Chronic Poverty?: Exploring Chronic Poverty in Developing Countries Using Cross-sectional Demographics and Health Data," *Global Social Policy* 8.1 (April 2008): 45–79, 48, 49; Klasen, S., "Poverty, Inequality and Deprivation in South Africa: Analysis of the 1993 Saldru Survey," *Social Indicators Research* 41.1 (1997): 51–94; Klasen, S., "Measuring Poverty and Deprivation in South Africa," *Review of Income and Wealth* 46.1 (2000): 33–58.

[6] Minujin, "Economic Growth," 27, 28.

[7] Ibid., 28.

[8] Ibid., 28.

9. U.S. Census Bureau, "Poverty Thresholds Income, Poverty, and Health Insurance Coverage in the United States," (2009), http://www.census.gov/prod/2010pubs/p60–238.pdf.

10. United Nations, *World Summit for Social Development Programme of Action –Chapter 2*, Copenhagen 1995, http://www.un.org/esa/socdev/wssd/text-version/agreements/poach2.htm.

11. Nandy, "'Misunderstanding' Chronic Poverty?" 50.

12. Ibid., 52.

13. Ibid., 48.

14. Ibid., 49.

15. Minujin, "Economic Growth," 32.

16. Nandy, "'Misunderstanding' Chronic Poverty?" 33.

17. Ibid.

18. Ibid.

19. Singer, Peter, "Rich and Poor," in *Morality and Moral Controversies: Readings in Moral, Social, and Political Philosophy*, ed. John Arthur, 7th ed. (Upper Saddle River, NJ: Pearson Prentice Hall, 2005), 478.

20. Minujin, "Economic Growth," 33.

21. Ibid.

22. Shore, Rima, *Rethinking the Brain: New Insights into Early Development* (New York: Families and Work Institute, 1997), 15, 27.

23. Minujin, "Economic Growth," 39.

24. Ibid., 40.

25. Ibid., 41.

26. Geisler, *Love Your Neighbor*, 71–75.

27. Singer, "Rich and Poor," 478.

28. Ibid., 478–79.

29. Ibid., 479.

30. Ibid.

31. Ibid., 480.

32. Ibid., 481.

33. Ibid.

34. Ibid., 481–83.

35. Landon, Michael, "The Challenges of Poverty to the North American Church," *Restoration Quarterly* 47.2 (2005): 105–15.

36. Palmberg, Mai, "Colonialism Made Africa Poor and Dependent," in *Problems of Africa: Opposing Viewpoints*, ed. Janelle Rohr (Minnesota: Greenhaven Press, 1986), 17.

37. Ibid.

38. Ibid., 18

39. Ibid.

40. Ibid., 19.

[41] Ibid.

[42] Ibid., 19–20.

[43] Ibid., 20.

[44] Ibid.

[45] Ibid., 21.

[46] Ibid., 22.

[47] Ibid., 23.

[48] Danaher, Kevin, "Colonial Policies Cause Famine," in *Problems of Africa: Opposing Viewpoints*, ed. Janelle Rohr (Minnesota: Greenhaven Press, 1986), 118.

[49] Ibid., 118.

[50] Ibid.

[51] Ibid.

[52] Ibid., 119.

[53] Ibid., 119–20.

[54] Ibid., 120.

[55] Bauer, P. T., "Colonialism is not Responsible for Africa's Problems," in *Problems of Africa: Opposing Viewpoints*, ed. Janelle Rohr (Minnesota: Greenhaven Press, 1986), 24.

[56] Ibid., 25–27.

[57] Ibid.

[58] Ibid.

[59] Rodney, Walter, *How Europe Underdeveloped Africa* (Washington, DC: Howard University Press, 1981), 33–70.

[60] Bauer, "Colonialism," 30.

[61] United Nations, *United Nations Millennium Declaration*, A/55/L.2 (September 2000), http://www.un.org/millennium/declaration/ares552e.htm (accessed July 14, 2008).

[62] United Nations, *United Nations Millennium Declaration Goals Report 2007*: 1–36, 28, http://www.un.org/millenniumgoals/pdf/mdg2007.pdf. Since the utilization of the 2007 progress report in this work, there have being subsequent progress reports that are not included in this text.

[63] Ibid., 4.

[64] Ibid., 5.

[65] Christianity Today, "How We Fight Poverty," *Christianity Today* 51.12 (December 2007): 1–2, 1, downloaded at http://www.christianitytoday.com/ct/2007/december/17.20.html.

[66] Nandy, "'Misunderstanding' Chronic Poverty?" 71.

[67] Ibid.

[68] Ibid.

[69] Ibid.

[70] *Millennium Declaration Goals Report 2007*, 6–8.

[71] Ibid.

[72] World Bank, *America Latina and the Caribbean Regional Brief*, http://web.worldbank.org/WBSITE/

External/countries/lacext/o (accessed July 23, 2008). World Bank, *Inequality in Latin America & the Caribbean: Breaking with History? http://web.worldbank.org/WBSITE/EXTERNAL/COUNTRIES/ LACEXT/0,* (accessed Novemeber 10, 2010); World Bank, *Leveling opportunities, key to Latin American Development* web.worldbank.org/WBSITE/EXTERNAL/COUNTRIES/LACEX - 44k. (accessed Novemeber 10, 2010). Lopez, J. Humberto, Guillermo Perry, "Inequality in LatinAmerica: Determinants and Consequences," *Policy Research Working Paper/The World Bank* 1.1 (2008): 1–39; *and* Paes de Barros, Ricardo, Francisco H. G. Ferreira, José R. Molinas Vega, and Jaime Saavedra Chanduvi, *Measuring Inequality of Opportunities in Latin America and the Caribbean,* (Washington DC: World Bank, 2009), 1.

[73] Singer, "Rich and Poor," 478.

[74] *Millennium Declaration Goals Report 2007*, 10–11.

[75] Ibid.

[76] Ibid., 15–21.

[77] Destexhe, Alain, *Rwanda and Genocide: In the Twentieth Century,* trans. Alison Marschner (London: Pluto Press, 1995), 27. *See also* Fischel, Jack R., *The Holocaust* (Westport, CT: Greenwood Press, 1998); McDonough, Frank, *The Holocaust* (New York: Palgrave Macmillan, 2008); LaCapra, Dominick, *History and Memory After Auschwitz* (Ithaca, NY: Cornell University Press, 1998); Bloxham, Donald and Tony Kushner, *The Holocaust* (Manchester: Manchester University Press, 2005).

[78] Melvern, Linda, *Conspiracy to Murder: The Rwandan Genocide* (New York: Verso, 2004), 9, 10, 250. The Hutus were determined to exterminate the Tutsis, whom they viewed as their inferior oppressors. Some reports show that in 1972, about 200,000 Hutus were killed in neighboring Burundi when they rose up against Tutsi rule. Many blame the Europeans for sowing seeds of discord among Rwandans by putting a wedge between Hutus and Tutsis that eventually resulted in the massacre of 1994. For further reading on this subject, *see* Rittner, Carol, John Koth, and Wendy Whitworth eds., *Genocide in Rwanda: Complicity of the Churches?* (St. Paul, MN: Paragon House, 2004); Destexhe, *Rwanda and Genocide*; *and* Eltringham, Nigel, *Accounting for Horror* (London: Pluto Press, 2004).

[79] Prunier, Gerard, *Darfur: A 21st Century Genocide* 3rd ed. (New York: Cornell University Press, 2008), 148–58; Galchinsky, Michael, *Jews and Human Rights* (Lanham, MD: Rowman & Littlefield Publishers, 2008), 84.

[80] Destexhe, *Rwanda and Genocide*, 15–20.

[81] Patten, Wendy, "U.S.: Efforts to Combat Human Trafficking and Slavery: Human Rights Watch Testimony Before the U.S. Senate Judiciary Committee," *Human Rights Watch* (July 6, 2004), http://www.hrw.org/en/news/2004/07/06/us-efforts-combat-human-trafficking-and-slavery (first accessed August 15, 2008).

[82] Ibid.

[83] Ralph, Ragan E., "International Trafficking of Women and Children: Testimony before the Senate Committee on Foreign Relations Subcommittee on Near Eastern and South Asian Affairs," *Human Rights Watch* (February 22, 2000), http://www.hrw.org/backgrounder/wrd/trafficing.htm (accessed August 15, 2008).

[84] Ibid.

[85] Vandenberg, Martina, *Hopes Betrayed: Trafficking of Women and Girls to Post-Conflict Bosnia and Herzegovina for Forced Prostitution* vol. 14.9D (New York: Human Rights Watch, November 2002), 15.

[86] Patten, "US Efforts to Combat Human Trafficking".

[87] Vandenberg, "Hopes Betrayed," 17, 18.

[88] Ralph, "International Trafficking of Women and Children".

Chapter Fourteen: Global Poverty   211

[89] Ralph, "International Trafficking of Women and Children;" Patten, "US Efforts to Combat Human Trafficking."

[90] Jefferson, LaShawn R., "Bosnia and Herzegovina: Traffickers Walk Free," *Human Rights Watch* (November 16, 2002), http://hrw.org/english/docs/2002/11/26/bosher4425_txt.htm (accessed August 15, 2008).

[91] Cohen, Jonathan, *Borderline Slavery: Child Trafficking in Togo* vol. 15. 8 (A) (New York: Human Rights Watch, April 2003), 8–28.

[92] Ibid., 29, 31.

[93] Patterson, "US Efforts to Combat Human Trafficking."

[94] Varia, Nisha, "International Trafficking in Persons: Taking Action to Eliminate Modern Day Slavery," *Human Rights Watch* (2007), http://www.hrw.org/en/news/2007/10/17/international-trafficking-persons-taking-action-eliminate-mo (first accessed August 15, 2008).

[95] Fisher, Mary Pat, *Living Religions*, 5th ed. (New Jersey, Prentice-Hall, 2002), 88.

[96] Barbour, Stephanie, Tiasha Palikovic, Jeena Shah, and Smita Narula, *Hidden Apartheid: Caste Discrimination Against India's "Untouchables"* vol .19.3C (New York: Human Rights Watch & The Center for Human Rights and Global Justice, NYU School of Law, February 2007), 2.

[97] Fisher, *Living Religions*, 87.

[98] Ibid.

[99] Ibid.

[100] Ibid.; "Hidden Apartheid," 37, 90.

[101] "Hidden Apartheid," 9, 13, 42.

[102] Ibid., 8–14, 103, 113.

[103] Ibid.

[104] *Millennium Declaration Goals Report 2007*, 12.

[105] Ibid., 13

[106] Ibid.

[107] Ibid.

[108] "Women's Human Rights," *Human Rights Watch*, http://www.hrw.org/women or http://www.hrw.org/en/node/82134 (first accessed August 15, 2008).

[109] Ibid.

[110] Ibid.

[111] Gonzalez, *A History of Christian Thought*, vol. iii., 86–102.

[112] Hill, *Faith, Religion & Theology*, 435–37.

[113] Washington, James, *A Testament of Hope: The Essential Writings and Speeches of Martin Luther King, Jr.* (New York: HarperCollins Publishers, 1991), 7–9.

[114] Chapple, Christopher Key, "Jainism and Nonviolence," in *Subverting Hatred: The Challenge of Nonviolence in Religious Traditions*, ed. Daniel L. Smith-Christopher (Maryknoll, NY: Orbis Books, 1998), 13, 14.

[115] Kumar, Muni Prashant, don Muni Loc Praksh "Lokesh," "Anuvrat Anushasta Saint Tulsi: A Glorious Life with a Purpose," *Anuvibha Reporter* 3.1 (October–December 1997): 42, cited in Chapple, "Jainism and Nonviolence," 20–21.

CHAPTER FIFTEEN

Church and State Relation

A proper church-and-state relationship can impact global poverty in a significant way that brings hope and liberation to millions. One cannot ignore the enormous influence, whether for good or ill, both the church and the state have on scores of people on a daily basis. Arguably, some people believe that these two institutions have helped to create, and in some ways maintain, some of the problems that persist in the world today. For example, extreme poverty and the factors arising from it, in part can be traced back to the legacy of colonialism that the Western church and state once embraced. Some church traditions for centuries have also taught and perpetuated gender discrimination that marginalized women. In some church groups today, women are not permitted to be a part of the hierarchy or play certain roles due to their gender. Most international denominations have never been governed by anyone of color, yet in some cases those denominations have majority nonwhite membership.

During the slave trade, slaves were taught on the plantations that Whites were superior to Blacks and other races. Slaves were even admonished by churches to obey their masters despite the tyranny and inhumanity with which they were being treated. In the past, some in the church have also authorized burning at the stakes those who were deemed infidels and apostates; carried out massacres of Muslims in their crusades or holy wars. Many indigenous people and there culture were hurt by some Western missionaries who projected superiority to other people elsewhere, thus causing more harm than good, and the spread of ethnocentrism instead of Christianity. These and other failures of the church are unequivocally contrary to Christ's command to "love God and neighbor." One should not see Christianity as evil and irrelevant to addressing contemporary social, economic, political, human-rights, and peacemaking challenges because of the failures of some in the church.

Throughout the centuries, we have seen various models of church-and-state relations. One model articulates that the church and the state should be separated, while another reasons that both institutions should be aligned with each other. Some models dictate that the church should dominate the state and vice versa, and others integrate two or more of the previous models and their variances.[1]

Despite the various models, the one that seems to stand out in the contemporary modern Western worldview is the separation of church and state. Arguably, one cannot conclude that the separation of church and state is entirely attainable in a context where faith is deemed valuable. For example, people often espouse that the US Constitution stipulates that there should be a separation of church and state, but it seems almost impossible for anyone to be elected to public office in the United States without professing that he/she is a person of faith, in most cases Christian. On the one hand, it seems plausible that the church and state should be separated because, in the past, having the state aligned with the church created many problems, resulting in the subversion and repression of many people, other religions, and even Christian movements that were not in line with the status quo. On the other hand, the church and state do have enormous impact on people, and together both could attain much in working toward a common goal.

David Levin argues that throughout history, the church and state, or the religious and political, have always been indistinguishable, and their separation is only a fairly recent construct that developed in Western societies since the Protestant reformation.[2] If it is interpreted that the alliance of church and state was the norm in antiquity, however, this argument seems to contradict the position of some prominent early Christian writers. To illustrate, St. Augustine in the eighteenth book of *The City of God* articulates a two-kingdom theory, whereby the church reflects the spiritual or heavenly kingdom and the state the temporal kingdom (the world), which spans from the time of Abraham to the end of the ages.³ The separation of church and state that this espouses appears to be only a partial, not absolute separation, because there are ways in which the church and state of his day worked together. The Reformers, such as Martin Luther, John Calvin, and some modern scholars, emphasized this Augustinian functional dichotomy of the church-and-state relation. Calvin articulates a two-sword theory, the church having the Word as its sword and the state ruling with the literal sword that facilitates law and order in a society.⁴ Calvin, along with other Reformers, helped to give impetus to the ideology of separation of church and state, which today dominates North American political consciousness.⁵ Dietrich Bonhoeffer points out that both the church and state emanate from God, with separate functions, yet both accomplish the objectives of the same Lord.⁶

According to Walter Altmann, both the church and state (whether aligned or separated) participate in the injustice and oppression that exist in some contexts,⁷ and as a result, he offers a model of church-and-state relation that focuses on justice for the poor and oppressed, which is a significant theme of the message of the kingdom of God.⁸ Both institutions helped to develop structures that in some cases oppress those who are most vulnerable. Therefore, both the church and state could be seen as institutions of hope and despair. Nevertheless, the reign of God challenges any oppressive structure created by any institution, because liberation is its objective. Both institutions can work together to forge justice and equality for the marginalized of society.

The document of the Parliament of World Religions expands this dialogue by bringing representatives from all the religions of the world together to help forge principles on how to solve global crises. The Parliament of World Religions convened in 1993 in Chicago, with more than 6,500 representatives from the various religions of the world, to discuss global crises such as poverty, violence, drugs, corruption, crime, destruction of families, and environmental devastation.⁹ One external factor common to all these religions is that their followers are affected by global crises. Another commonality is that they all emphasize the golden rule in their moral codes: "Do unto others as you would have them do to you." This maxim was used to craft the four irrevocable commitments that all the religions support in the final declarations.

These principles are: commitment to cultivate a culture of nonviolence and respect for life, solidarity and a just economic order, tolerance and truthfulness, and equal partnership between men and women.[10] Furthermore, the parliament was careful to point out that their attempt was neither to merge all the world's religions into one entity nor to formulate a global ideology to which all religions must subscribe.

The church, in aligning with the state to address contemporary socioeconomic injustice, should not lose its prophetic voice. In the biblical text, the prophets often played a major role in the political life of the ancient Israelites in both the Northern and Southern kingdoms, but they never abandoned their prophetic message. The word, action, and utterance of God affect all manner of life, and the ancient Israelites were to abide by God's covenant. In fact, the covenant between them and God defined the core of their existence, and the church, through Jesus Christ, shares this covenant. T. R. Hobbs argues, "It is understandable that the prophets' speaking out (on behalf of God) on matters of national policy appears political from our point of view. But every aspect of Israel's life was seen by them as being under the judgment of God."[11] Hobbs further articulates that,

> All the prophetic pronouncements in 1 and 2 Kings relate to the political life of the people, since the political life is the arena in which the ideology (covenant) is to be worked out in practice... [and that] mistreatment of one's own people, especially the poor and marginalized, is not only a social scandal, but a religious sin.[12]

Religion and politics were fundamental frameworks in which the prophets provoked and invoked the consciousness of God in ancient Israel and Judea. The political and religious are seen as one entity modeling the core of the covenant, "love of God and neighbor."

The church's prophetic voice is at times offensive to the state, particularly when it challenges its unjust laws and practices. J. Severino Croatto points out that Jesus died a political death, simply because he challenged and counteracted the political order of His day:

> The key to understanding the trial of Jesus is not Pilate, but the Sanhedrin...We have seen that Jesus' deeds and word, orientated to the recovery of humankind and its natural values, aroused the fury of

the power groups—high priests, elders, scribes, Pharisees—and motivated their decision to eliminate him. Jesus' praxis—action and theory together, in mutual interdependency—was unmasking the superstructural and ideological universe that the leaders of Israel controlled, and whose axis of viability was the law understood as "tradition..."[13]

Furthermore, Jesus was sentenced as a religious subversive who threatened the peace and stability of the existing religious structure that was political in nature. According to Croatto:

> Formal proceedings against Jesus are instituted later, before the Sanhedrin (Mark 14.53–59)...Jesus is condemned as a *religious subversive,* on grounds of having threatened to destroy and rebuild the temple and, especially, that he claimed to be the Christ, the Son of God.[14]

Therefore, the underlying reasons for Jesus' indictment are "...all his deeds and words critical of the religious status quo, and of the authority of the leaders who are passing judgment upon him."[15] Clearly, like the prophets of old, Jesus' prophetic utterance offended the religious and political leaders of His day, which led to His execution, and the same fate is often handed down to those who challenge the unjust structures of our day. Still, this should not shake our will to stand up for justice and equality wherever it is lacking.

Concluding Remarks

Clearly, the current global crises require the help and partnership of both the church and state, because there are ways in which the state must help, and the same is true for the church. A caveat that should be inserted is that one should not expect religious creeds to become public policy or public policy to become scripture. Therefore, both the church and state could find common ground in addressing global crises, but this goal must be the good of humanity, particularly in addressing socioeconomic injustice. The mission of any church-and-state relationship should be to work categorically for the happiness of the people in the most loving way.

Notes

1. Altmann, Walter, *Luther and Liberation: A Latin American Perspective*, trans. Mary M. Solberg (Eugene, OR: Wipf and Stock Publishers, 2000), 69–83.

2. Levine, David H., *Religion and Politics in Latin America* (Princeton, NJ: Princeton University Press, 1981), 20, 21.

3. Augustine, St., *The City of God*, trans. Marcus Dods (New York: Random House, 1950), 610, 668. In addition, Augustine's church-and-state dichotomy seems to reflect the teachings of Christ in the Gospels and Pauline theology. For example, when Christ was asked if it was permissible to pay taxes to Caesar, Christ responded that people were to Give to Caesar what is due to him, and to God the things that are due to God (Matt. 22:15–22). Furthermore, when Pilate asked Jesus if He was the King of the Jews, Jesus replied that His kingdom was not of this world; and that if His kingdom was of this world, His men would have fought to prevent Him being surrendered to the Jews. But His kingdom is not of this world's system (John 18:36). The Apostle Paul acknowledged the role of the state and admonished the early Christians to obey the state because civil authority was appointed by God (Romans 13:1–7). These texts, therefore, acknowledge the existence and function of both spiritual and civil authorities (church and state, or the religious and the political). They do not, however, indicate that the church and state are one and the same, but that they are of the same Lord. For further dialogue on Church and State (or religion and politics) in the Synoptic and Pauline traditions, and antiquity, see the following: Herzog, William R., "Dissembling, A Weapon of the Weak: The Case of Christ and Caesar in Mark 12:13–17 and Romans 13:1–7," *Perspective in Religious Studies* 21.4 (1994): 339–60; Feinberg, Paul D., "The Christian and Civil Authority," *TMSJ* 10.1 (Spring 1999): 87–99; Wozniuk, Vladmir, "In Pursuit of a Politics of Holiness: Reconciling Hellenic and Hebraic Political Wisdom in the Acts of the Apostles," *Journal of Church and State* 45.2 (Spring 2003): 283–304; Kroger, Daniel, "Paul and the Civil Authorities: An Exegesis of Romans 13:1–7," *Asia Journal of Theology* 7.2 (1993): 344–66; Ferguson, Everett, "Early Christian Martyrdom and Civil Disobedience," *Journal of Early Christian Studies* 1.1 (1993): 73–83; and Leadbetter, Bill, "Constantine and the Bishop: The Roman Church in the Early Fourth Century," *The Journal of Religious History* 26.1 (February 2002): 1–14.

4. VanDrunen, David, "The Two Kingdoms: A Reassessment of the Transformationist Calvin," *Calvin Theological Journal* 40.02 (2005): 248–66.

5. Ibid.

6. Bonhoeffer, Dietrich, *Ethics* (New York: Simon & Schuster, 1955), 327–48.

7. Altmann, *Luther and Liberation*, 75–78.

8. Ibid.

9. Küng, Hans and Karl-Josef Kuschel, eds., *A Global Ethic: The Declaration of the Parliament of the World's Religions* (New York: Continuum International Publishing Group, 2003), 8, 17–19. For an historical overview and the development of the Parliament of World's Religions, from its inception in 1893 when it had its first convocation to its second convocation in 1993, *see* 77–105.

10. Ibid, 24–34.

11. Hobbs, T. R., *Word Biblical Themes: I & II Kings* (Dallas: Word Publishing, 1989), 32; *see also* Deut. 18:18.

12. Ibid., 32–33.

13. Croatto, J. Severino, "The Political Dimension of Christ the Liberator," in *Faces of Jesus: Latin American Christologies*, ed. Jose Miguez Bonino (Maryknoll, NY: Orbis Books, 1984), 112–13.

14. Ibid., 113.

15. Ibid.

EPILOGUE

The core of Christianity is love of God and neighbor. As a result of God's love for humanity, Christ came to redeem human fallen nature from being dominated by its evil inclination and restores it to love, so that we may yield to love God and neighbor. When we initially receive God's love, we are converted from sin to grace (born again). In other words, when people heed God's love through the Spirit's conviction, they are born-a-new in God's love. The image and likeness of God innately in us is thus restored—this is conspicuous in the fruits that this renewed love in us bears in our lives and world. Christian conversion, therefore, is a response to God's love and a commitment to continue steadfast in this love. The love of God in us continues to be perfected through ongoing Christian formation and transformation; thus we are moved from one stage to another to achieve perfect love.

Physiological and psychological maturation does not dictate the born-again believer's spiritual growth and development, as the Spirit's working is not confined to those. This, however, does not alter humans' natural progression toward physical death, but it redeems the fallen soul. It guarantees the soul immortal love and life eternal. There is a responsibility on each believer to live his/her life in the present to inherit this promised eternal bliss that God's love affords. At the core of personal spirituality and piety should be that propulsion, daily, to live the fruits of the Spirit and to avoid the works of the flesh, and to continue in entire sanctification (perfect love) as prophet, priest, and king.

The gifts of the Spirit are given to believers to perform Christian service. We serve one another in love with our gifts and callings—thus making neighbor's life better. There are diverse gifts and manifestations, but all are given by Christ and the Spirit to serve neighbor. When we serve neighbor in love, we demonstrate love for God. The Christian believer is called to care for and demonstrate Christ's love to all people, regardless of their differences, not just fellow Christians.

Love will not allow us to sit by and not care for the impoverished, victimized, and hurting around us. The temptation is to leave issues like poverty to the state or government thereof, but love obligates us to care unconditionally. While it is not an option for the church to bond with the state in distorted politics, it is the church's responsibility to hold the state responsible for its policies that bring pain and suffering to others, regardless of their race, gender, nationality or social stratification. There is a fierce urgency for the church to partner with the state to solve contemporary issues like global poverty. All that Christians do individually and corporately in the home, church, and society should be for love.

APPENDIX

A. Responsibility and Relationality

The double-love command brings us back full circle to our original obligation to volitionally love God and neighbor as self; and to be good stewards of all that God entrusted in our care. In the Genesis account, God instructed Adam to "have dominion over the fish of the sea, over the birds of the air, and over every living things that moves on the earth" (Gen. 1.28). Some seem to interpret this authority wrongly—thinking that it means to dominate and exploit—whereas it is to care for and preserve God's creation (Gen. 2.15). When neighbor is exploited—God is exploited. When creation (i.e. earth, sea, and air) is exploited—humans are also exploited—for on these God allows us to depend for survival.

H. Richard Niebuhr, in his responsibility model, points out that the pattern and idea of responsibility has to do with action, effect, interpretation, and response. Implying that when a person encounters some action—divine, human, material or immaterial—he/she responds to this experience in the way he/she understands and interprets the effects of such experience.[1] If Niebuhr's argument holds, each person has a responsibility to respond to the actions and subsequent effects that invade his/her life. We might not have absolute control over the stimuli (intrinsic or extrinsic) that affect our lives but we do have the power to guide the way we interpret and respond to impressions on our lives. The result of our response is perhaps more powerful than that which impacts our lives (negatively or positively). The key here is how we responsibly interpret and respond. Guided by the maxim of love, a person should be able to make responsible decisions in light of his/her relationships: God, self, neighbor, and creation in general.

Curran expands on Niebuhr's responsibility model by incorporating relationality. By relationality, Curran means humans living consistent within their multiple relationships with God, self, neighbor, and creation. Curran's critique of Niebuhr's responsibility model is that it does not allow a person to initiate action, rather persons respond to some stimuli. Curran maintains that we should initiate as well as respond to the action of others in light of our multiple moral relationships.[2] Unconditional love should be that which influences human vertical (upward), inner-personal, and horizontal (interpersonal and intrapersonal) relationships.

As mentioned in Chapter One, love of neighbor does not mean the neglect of self—for we can only love neighbor in as much as we love ourselves. Other loves such as filial (friendship) and erotic (romantic) should flow out of agape love or unconditional love that is intrinsic to the double love command—when unconditional love is at their core these other loves are most excellent.

When one seriously considers the state of romance in our context it appears fickle; it seems easily altered by different factors and situations. Oftentimes, when romance wanes in a relationship, once loving partners ended up in rancorous fights and sometimes separation. I often wonder how once-loving partners could become enemies. Regardless of the things that may have led to the degeneration of a relationship: how could love change to dislike? This leads to the speculation that the bond of romance is not as strong as some think. It seems to be more capricious than many are willing to admit. Romantic love can be selfish, jealous, erratic, possessive, and mutualistic; yet it can be the most wonderful thing for many.

It seems as though when friendship and romance are not built on agape love, they are short lived. Unconditional love gives humans the capacity to love even in dire circumstances. So when the romance fades and the friendship wanes, if the foundation of the relationship is unconditional love, it should remain strong and unshakable. In times of emotional and relational turbulence only unconditional love can navigate us safely. This leads to the conclusion that the foundation of any lasting relationship must be unconditional love. While we should strive to love everyone, even our enemies, this must be even stronger for those with whom we share our lives. The unconditional question should precede the romantic one, but for many it is the other way around. Can I love someone romantically should come after the unconditional question is resolved. Perhaps romance can go on for a while without unconditional love, but it will become anemic and perhaps weakened if not buttress by unconditional love. A relationship lacking unconditional love is like a beautiful house that is built upon the sand and glitters while the sun shines but starts coming apart as soon as it begins to rain heavily; even before the storm arrives.

It seems natural for people to trust those who are more like them: having the same origin, ethnicity, racial identity, religious persuasion, or political ideology—and mistrust others—but the double-love command encourages fairness. People seem more apt to mistrust, dissociate, and fear those with whom they do not share common traits and are often more comfortable with people with whom they do share similar traits. Sometimes, people blame and despise people who are different from them for things that they often overlook in someone of their own origin, tradition or liking. The double-love command, however, runs counter to xenophobia; it encourages the love of neighbor regardless of conflicting peculiarity and likability. The double-love command identifies neighbor as all people, those near and far. Therefore, to treat another with disdain because the person seems exotic is unlike the attitude of Christ, who showed that it is possible to love people who are different. This is evident in His association with the outcasts of His day including lepers, sinners, tax collectors, and prostitutes. Unmarried women, widows (to a lesser extent), children, and slaves were also considered lesser members of society in the Greco-Roman context, but Jesus treated them with love, to the dismay of the establishment of His day. The Jewish religious and civic leaders marveled at how a man of Jesus' status, a rabbi, would mingle with and give preferential care to those who were labeled inferior—this they used as an opportunity to call Jesus derogatory names.

If we are to be true to the double-love command, we cannot love based on race, culture, ethnicity, religiosity, or political ideology, among other peculiarities. Love of neighbor, therefore, demands that the same manner of love and goodwill that we have for those in our relational circle, we should have for others. The love that Christ had for His inner circle and people of His origin and culture is the same He demonstrated for all people. Christ died for the salvation of all people, not a select few as some would like to think. We should categorically love people first, then debate and/or tolerate their differences if necessary.

Some people often said that they put their country or nation first, which seems natural, but is nationalism in conflict with the double-love command? Is our primary horizontal responsibility to a particular country, or is it to people? Probably, lack of nationalism is part of why several countries in the developing regions are so devastated over the course of time. A sensible dose of nationalism might just be what they need to rise to the challenge to make their nations great. A nation bonding together as one people could enable them to harness and distribute vast resources they sometimes have, equitably. It always seems odd, though, that a continent like Africa with such vast wealth of natural resources is the world's poorest and most devastated. One cannot ignore the legacy of colonialism and the various setbacks from such system that the people of this continent have endured, but their struggle seems to persist like none other. The strength and genius of these people to survive despite centuries of systematic oppression and hardship must be commended; but in the twenty-first century absolute success and prosperity must be their reward. The urgent need, however, is not for more nationalistic states, for gross inequity and human atrocity persist even in the most nationalistic states; rather nation states that put people first.

The love imperative emphasizes love for people. While I do not expect to see a world without nation states adored by patriots, we should strive for the happiness and well-being of all people, everywhere. A person in a remote location shares a common bond with people everywhere—member of the human race—and citizen of God's global community. Whether we accept it or not, peoples of the world rise and fall together, this is apparent in contemporary global challenges—which impact us all. Lasting peace, prosperity and security, lies in fostering a world in which people are loved, regardless of their differences; love affords each one a chance to acquire basic goods for survival and opportunity to succeed in life. The notion that one person is superior to another and therefore is more deserving of essentials to live a good life is not only false, but barbaric at its core. The severe lack and abject poverty of a child in a remote part of the world should be enough to stoke our passion, release our compassion, and results in renewed action for a just social and economic order.

Love should be the standard by which we govern ourselves and are judged. The goal of any rule or law should be love. Deterrence, retribution, or restraint should not be the primary goal of any rule—those sometimes bring the worse out of people—rather it should be love because love begets love.

The measure of a person should be love: how much you love and with what intensity you fulfill your obligation to love—this duty can only flow out of a life that cultivates and practices the greatest virtue—love. The criteria by which we are often evaluated—wealth, appearance, accomplishment, etc.—are merely materialistic—these often feed into the selfishness and greed that contradict the love command.

B. Obligation and Care

The term obligation can be defined as a duty, something that is required of us morally, socially, familially, legally, etc. Moral obligations are typically duties of commission or omission. That which we must endeavor to do and/or refrain from doing (specific things or series of actions) to attain certain goals, virtues or goods. Moral obligations are often overriding because they are often final and supersede. They are also universal in nature, because our moral obligation is not just to a select or preferred few but to humanity. Social obligations are those duties that we carry out in relation to our peers and social networks. Familial obligations are those people have towards their household or family. Legal obligations are those acted upon due to some contractual or covenantal arrangement.[3] There are various types of obligations moral, social, legal, intellectual, and familial obligations[4] but here we will confine obligation to two general categories natural and ethical obligations. Natural obligation is that which we feel compel to do out of mere sentimentality (feeling), and ethical obligation out of a sense of duty. Unlike ethical obligation, with natural obligation there might not be institutional consequence or reward for the action or characteristic that we are expected to display, except conflict with our own conscience for the most part. Conscience impacts both natural and ethical obligations. Natural obligation is only bound to conscience, but ethical obligation is further adjudicated by institutional moral, social, familial, and legal norms.

Does love obligates us to care? Christ's love imperative (inclusive love) obligates us to love God and neighbor unconditionally. This command gives no reason not to love. It seems logical that if one loves, one also cares. As caring would be a fruit of the love we have for another. Also, it seems plausible to care naturally for those you love, but it is possible to care ethically and not love. The one who administers care to another in an institutional caregiving context does not necessarily care because of love, but moreso because his/her job requires it. For example, on the job a physician might feel obligated to administer care to a patient who he/she has no relation with, but might later drive by, on the street, this same person experiencing a heart attack.

Two general kinds of care seem to obligate us, natural and ethical. The former flows out of the love we feel for another and the latter out of duty. The double-love command is applicable to both kinds of care. If we love unconditionally as the love imperative admonishes us to do—we would care naturally—it is almost impossible to love and not care. As it relates to the ethical dimension, there are times when we care not because we feel love for that person but because it is our divine duty to care. This makes care both pathological and practical. On the one hand, you love and care for another because of the affection you feel for that person. On the other hand, you care because it is your duty to do so.

Notes

[1] Niebuhr, H. Richard, *The Responsible Self: An Essay in Christian Moral Philosophy* (New York: Harper & Row, Publishers, 1963), 65.

[2] Curran, *The Catholic Moral Tradition Today*, 73

[3] Evans, C. Stephen, *Kierkegaard's Ethic of Love: Divine Commands and Moral Obligations* (Oxford: University Press, 2004, 1-2.

4 For further readings on types/models of obligation see Schneider, Hebert W. "Moral Obligation," *Ethics* 50.1 (Oct., 1939): 45-56; Mitchell, William, "Moral Obligation," *Mind* 11.41 (Jan. 1886): 35-48; Greenwood, David, "Moral Obligation in the Sermon on the Mount," *Theological Studies* 31.2 (1970): 301-09; Miller, Caleb, "An Anabaptist Theory of Moral Obligation," *Mennonite Quarterly Review* 71.4 (1997): 571-93; Herman, Stewart W., "Luther, Law, and Social Covenants: Cooperative Self-Obligation in the Reconstruction of Lutheran Social Ethics," *Journal of Religious Ethics* 25.2 (Fall 1997): 257-75; Johnson, Conrad D., "Moral and Legal Obligation," *The Journal of Philosophy* 72.12 (Jun 1975): 315-33; Gilbert, Margaret, "Agreements, Coercion, and Obligation," *Ethics* 103.4 (Jul. 1993): 679-706; Herman, Stewart W., "Luther, Law, and Social Covenants: Cooperative Self-Obligation in the Reconstruction of Lutheran Social Ethics," *Journal of Religious Ethics* 25.2 (Fall 1997): 257-75; Frye, A. Myrton, "Intellectual and Moral Obligation," *The Journal of Philosophy* 29.17 (August 1932), 449-56; Routledge, Robin, "Hessed as Obligation: A Re-examination," *Tyndale Bulletin* 46.1 (1995), 179-96; Judish, Julia E., "Balancing Special Obligations with the Ideal of Agape," *Journal of Religious Ethics* 26.1 (Spr 1998): 17-46.

BIBLIOGRAPHY

Aikin, Daniel L. "Conversion." In *Holman Illustrated Bible Dictionary*, edited by Chad Brand, Charles Draper, and Archie England. Nashville, TN: Holman Bible Publishers, 2003.

Aker, Benny C. "Charismata: Gifts, Enablements, or Ministries?" *Journal for Pentecostal Theology* 11.1 (2002): 53–69.

Albrecht, Daniel E. "Pentecostal Spirituality: Looking Through the Lens of Ritual." *Pneuma* 14.2 (1992): 107–25.

Altmann, Walter. *Luther and Liberation: A Latin American Perspective*, translated by Mary M. Solberg. Eugene, OR: Wipf and Stock Publishers, 2000.

Aquinas, Thomas. *Summa Theologiae*, edited by Timothy McDermott. Westminster, MD: Christian Classics, 1989.

Aristotle. "Nicomachean Ethics," In *Morality and Moral Controversies: Readings in Moral, Social, and Political Philosophy*, edited by John Arthur. 7th ed. Upper Saddle River, NJ: Pearson Prentice Hall, 2005.

Arrington, French. *Encountering the Holy Spirit*. Cleveland, TN: Pathway Press, 2003.

Augustine, St. *Saint Augustin's Anti-Pelagian Works*, vol. v, translated by Peter Holmes and Robert E. Wallis. Grand Rapids, MI: William. B. Eerdmans Publishing Company, 1994.

_____. *City of God*, edited by Marcus Dods. NY: Random House, 1950.

_____. *Saint Augustine Confessions*, translated by R.S. Pine-Coffin. NY: Penguin Books, 1961.

_____. *Teaching Christianity*, vol. 1.11, edited by John Rotelle. New York: New City Press, 1990.

Baker, Frank. *John Wesley and the Church of England*. Nashville, TN: Abingdon Press, 1970.

Barbour, Stephanie, Tiasha Palikovic, Jeena Shah, and Smita Narula. *Hidden Apartheid: Caste Discrimination Against India's "Untouchables"* vol. 19.3 C. New York: Human Rights Watch & The Center for Human Rights and Global Justice, NYU School of Law, February 2007.

Barth, Karl. *Church Dogmatics*, vol. 1.2, translated by G. W. Bromiley and T. F. Torrance. Edinburgh: T & T Clark, 1963.

Balcer, J. M. "Athenian Episkopos and the Achaemenid 'King's Eye'." *AJP* 98 (1977): 252–63.

Bauer, P. T. "Colonialism is not Responsible for Africa's Problems." In *Problems of Africa: Opposing Viewpoints*, edited by Janelle Rohr. Farmington Hills, MN: Greenhaven Press, 1986.

Bauer, Walter. *A Greek-English Lexicon of the New Testament and Other Early Christian Literature*, edited by William F. Arndt, F. Wilber Gingrich, and Fredrick W. Danker. Chicago: University of Chicago Press, 1979.

Berding, Kenneth. "Confusing Word and Concept in 'Spiritual Gifts': Have We Forgotten James Barr's Exhortations?" *JETS* 43.1 (March, 2000): 37–51.

Bernier, Paul. *Ministry in the Church: A Historical and Pastoral Approach*. Mystic, CT: Twenty-Third Publications, 2003.

Bloch-Hoell, N. *The Pentecostal Movement: Its Origin, Development, and Distinctive Character*. Oslo: Universitetsforlaget, 1964.

Bloxham, Donald, Tony Kushner. *The Holocaust*. Manchester: Manchester University Press, 2005.

Bonhoeffer, Dietrich. *Ethics*. NY: Simon & Schuster, 1995.

Borsch, F. "Apt Teachers: Bishops as Teachers and Theologian." *ATR* 79 (1997): 102–44.

Bouley, Allan, ed. *Catholic Rites Today*. Collegeville, MN: The Liturgical Press, 1992.

Branick, Vincent P. "Wisdom, Pessimism, and 'Mirth'."*Journal of Religious Ethics* 34.1 (2006): 69–87.

Browning, Don S. "Fulfillment and Obligation in Modern Psychologies." *Anglican Theological Review* 68.4 (1986): 287-301.

Bryant, Darrol. "Conversion in Christianity: from without and from within." In *Religious Conversion: Contemporary Practices and Controversies*, edited by Christopher Lamb and M. Darrol Bryant. New York: Cassell, 1999.

Breshears, Gerry. "The Body of Christ: Prophet, Priest, King?" *Journal of the Evangelical Theological Society* 37.01 (March 1994): 3–26.

Brugger, Walter, ed. *Philosophical Dictionary*, translated by Kenneth Baker. Spokane, WA: Gonzaga University Press, 1974.

Burkes, Shannon. *Death in Qoheleth and Egyptian Biographies of the Late Period*. Atlanta: Society of Biblical Literature, 1999.

Carver, Frank G. "Biblical Foundations for the 'Secondness' of Entire Sanctification." *Wesleyan Theological Journal* 22 (1987): 7–23.

Chance, Bradley. "Fellowship." In *Holman Illustrated Bible Dictionary*, edited by Chad Brand, Charles Draper, and Archie England. Nashville, TN: Holman Bible Publishers, 2003.

Chapple, C. Key. "Jainism and Nonviolence." In *Subverting Hatred: The Challenge of Nonviolence in Religious Traditions*, edited by Daniel L. Smith. Maryknoll, NY: Orbis Books, 1998.

Charette, Blaine. *Restoring Presence: The Spirit in Matthew's Gospel*. Sheffield: Sheffield Academic Press, 2000.

Christianity Today, "How we Fight Poverty." *Christianity Today* 51.12 (2007). Downloaded at http://www.christianitytoday.com/ct/2007/december/17.20.html?start=1.

Cohen, Jonathan. *Borderline Slavery: Child Trafficking in Togo* vol. 15. 8 (A). New York: Human Rights Watch, April 2003.

Clapper, Gregory S. "From the 'Works of the Flesh' to the 'Fruit of the Spirit:' Conversion and Spiritual Formation in the Wesleyan Tradition." In *Conversion in the Wesleyan Tradition*, edited by Kenneth J. Collins and John Tyson. Nashville, TN: Abingdon Press, 2001.

_____. *John Wesley on Religious Affections: His Views on Experience and Emotion and their Role in the Christian Life and Theology*. Metuchen, NJ: Scarecrow Press, 1989.

_____. "Orthokardia: The Practical Theology of John Wesley's Heart Religion." *Quarterly Review* 10.1 (Spring 1990): 49–66.

Clemmons, Ithiel. "True Koinonia: Pentecostal Hopes and Historical Realities." Presented at the Eleventh Annual meeting of the Society for Pentecostal Studies—on the campus of East Coast Bible College, Charlotte, NC. *Pneuma* 4.01 (November 12, 1981): 45–56.

Coffey, David. "The Incarnation of the Holy Spirit in Christ." *Theological Studies* 45.3S (1984): 466–80.

___. "Spirit Christology and the Trinity." In *Advent of the Spirit: An Introduction to the Current Study of Pneumatology*, eds. Bradford Hinze, D. Lyle Dabney Milwaukee, WI: Marquette University Press, 2001.

Collins, Gary. *Christian Counseling: A Comprehensive Guide*. Nashville, TN: Thomas Nelson Publishers, 2007.

Croatto, J. Severino. "The Political Dimension of Christ the Liberator." In *Focus of Jesus: Latin American Christologies*, edited by Jose Miguez Bonino. Maryknoll, NY: Orbis Books, 1984.

Curran, Charles E. *The Catholic Moral Tradition Today*. Washington, DC: Georgetown University Press, 1999.

Danaher, Kevin. "Colonial Policies Cause Famine." In *Problems of Africa: Opposing Viewpoints*, edited by Janelle Rohr. Farmington Hills, MN: Greenhaven Press, 1986.

Davis, E. F. *Proverbs, Ecclesiastes, and the Songs of Songs*. Louisville, KY: Westminster John Knox Press, 2000.

Degrazia, David, Thomas Mappes, and Jeffery Brand-Ballard. *Biomedical Ethics*. 7th ed. NY: McGraw-Hill Higher Education, 2006.

Deiss, Lucien. *Springtime of the Liturgy: Liturgical Texts of the First Four Centuries*. Translated by Matthew J. O' Connell. Collegeville, MN: The Liturgical Press, 1979.

Destexhe, Alain. *Rwanda and Genocide: In the Twentieth Century*, translated by Alison Marschner. London: Pluto Press, 1995.

Devettere, Raymond J. *Practical Decision Making in Health Care Ethics*. 3rd ed. Washington, DC: Georgetown University Press, 2010.

Di Berardino, Angelo. "Patterns of Koinonia in the First Christian Centuries." In *The Ecumenical Constitution of Churches*, edited by Jose Oscar Beozzo and Giuseppe Ruggieri. London: SCM Press, 2003.

Dockery, David S. "King, Christ As." In *Holman Illustrated Bible Dictionary*, edited by Chad Brand, Charles Draper, and Archie England. Nashville, TN: Holman Bible Publishers, 2003.

Downey, Michael. "Ministerial Identity: A Question of Common Foundations." In Ordering the Baptismal Priesthood, edited by Susan K. Wood. Collegeville, MN: Liturgical Press, 2003.

Duffy, Stephen. "Genes, Original Sins and The Human Proclivity to Evil." *Horizons* 32.2 (2005): 210–34.

Eaton, M. A. *Ecclesiastes*. Leicester: IVP, 1983.

Eltringham, Nigel. *Accounting for Horror*. London: Pluto Press, 2004.

Erikson, Erik. *Childhood and Society*. New York: W. W. Norton and Co., 1985.

Evans, C. Stephen. *Kierkegaard's Ethic of Love: Divine Commands and Moral Obligations*. Oxford: University Press, 2004.

Euben, J. Peter. "Walzer's Obligations." *Philosophy and Public Affairs* 1.4 (Summer 1972): 438-59.

Faupel, D. William. *Everlasting Gospel: The Significance of Eschatology in the Development of Pentecostal Thought*. Sheffield: Sheffield Academic Press,1996.

Fee, Gordon. "Paul and the Trinity: The Experience of Christ and the Spirit for Paul's Understanding of God." In *The Trinity: An Interdisciplinary Symposium on the Trinity*, edited by Steven Davis, Daniel Kendal, and Gerald O'Collins. Oxford: Oxford University Press, 1999.

Feinberg, Paul D. "The Christian and Civil Authority." *TMSJ* 10.1 (Spring 1999): 87–99.

Ferguson, Everett. "Early Christian Martyrdom and Civil Disobedience." *Journal of Early Christian Studies* 1.1 (1993): 73–83.

Fischel, Jack R. *The Holocaust*. Westport, CT : Greenwood Press, 1998.

Fisher, M. Pat. *Living Religions,* 7th ed. Upper Saddle River, NJ: Pearson Prentice Hall, 2008.

Fisher, Mary Pat. *Living Religions*, 5th ed. Upper Saddle River, NJ: Prentice-Hall, 2002.

Fisher, M. Pat, Lee W. Bailey. *An Anthology of Living Religions*. Upper Saddle River, NJ: Pearson Prentice Hall, 2008.

Fitzmyer, Joseph. "The structured ministry of the church in the Pastoral Epistles." *Catholic Biblical Quarterly* 66.4 (October 2004): 582–96.

Fletcher, Joseph. *Situation Ethics: The New Morality*. Louisville, KY: Westminster John Knox Press, 1966.

Flinn, Frank K. "Conversion: up from Evangelicalism or the Pentecostal and Charismatic Experience." In *Religious Conversion: Contemporary Practices and controversies*, edited by Christopher Lamb and M. Darrol Bryant. NY: Cassell, 1999.

Fowler, James W. "Perspectives on the Family from the Standpoint of Faith Development Theory." *The Perkins Journal* 33.1 (Fall 1979): 1–19.

_____. *Stages of Faith: The Psychology of Human Development and the Quest for Meaning*. New York: Harper Collins Publishers, 1981.

Fox, M. V. "The Meaning of Hebel for Qoheleth." *JBL* 105 (1968): 407–27.

Francis, Mark. "Liturgy and Assembly." In *Handbook for Liturgical Studies* vol. ii, edited by Anscar J. Chupungco. Collegeville, MN: The Liturgical Press, 1998.

Frye, A. Myrton. "Intellectual and Moral Obligation." *The Journal of Philosophy* 29.17 (August 1932): 449-56.

Galchinsky, Michael. *Jews and Human Rights*. Lanham, MD: Rowman & Littlefield Publishers, 2008.

Gause, R. Hollis. *Living in the Spirit: The Way of Salvation*. Cleveland, TN: Pathway Press, 1980.

Geisler, Norman L., Ryan P. Snuffer. *Love Your Neighbor*. Wheaton, IL: Crossway Books, 2007.

Gelpi, Donald. *Committed Worship: A Sacramental Theology for Converting Christians* vol. 1. Collegeville, MN: The Liturgical Press, 1993.

_____. *Charism and Sacrament: a Theology of Conversion*. NY: Paulist Press, 1976.

Gilbert, Margaret. "Agreements, Coercion, and Obligation." *Ethics* 103.4 (Jul. 1993): 679–706.

Gilbert, Marvin. *The Holy Spirit and Counseling*. Peabody, MA: Hendrickson Publishers, 1985.

Gonzalez, Justo L. *A History of Christian Thought*, vol. 3. Nashville, TN: Abingdon Press, 1975.

Gordis, R. *Koheleth—The Man and His World*, 3rd augmented edition. NY: Schocken Books, 1968.

Gordon, D., C. Pantazis. "Measuring Poverty: Breadline Britain in the 1990s." In *Breadline Britain in the 1990s*, edited by D. Gordon and C. Pantazis. Aldershot: Ashgate Publishing, 1997.

Grannell, Andrew. "The Paradox of Formation and Transformation." *Religious Education* 50.3 (Summer 1985): 384–98.

Green, Joel. "To Turn from Darkness to Light (Acts 26.18): Conversion in the Narrative of Luke-Acts." In *Conversion in the Wesleyan Tradition*, edited by Kenneth J. Collins and John H. Tyson. Nashville, TN: Abingdon Press, 2001.

Greenwood, David. "Moral Obligation in the Sermon on the Mount." *Theological Studies* 31.2 (1970): 301–09.

Grenz, Stanley. *Theology for the Community of God*. Grand Rapids, MI: William B Eerdmans Publishing Company, 2000.

Hahnenberg, Edward P. *Ministries: A Relational Approach*. New York: A Herder & Herder Book, The Crossroad Publishing Company, 2003.

Haight, Roger. "The Case for Spirit Christology." *Theological Studies* 53.2 (1992): 257–87.

Hanrahan, Clare. *Global Resources*. NY: Greenhaven Press, 2008.

Harper, Steve. *Devotional Life in the Wesleyan Tradition*. Nashville, TN: Upper Room, 1983.

Hartman, Robert H., ed. *Poverty and Economic Justice: A Philosophical Approach*. NY: Paulist Press, 1984.

Harrington, Daniel J., James F. Keenan. *Jesus and Virtue Ethics: Building Bridges Between New Testament Studies and Moral Theology*. Maryland, IL: Sheed & Ward, 2002.

Hauerwas, Stanley. "Politics of Charity." *Interpretation* 31.3 (1977): 251–62.

Held, Virginia. *Feminist Morality: Transforming Culture, Society, and Politics*. Chicago: University of Chicago Press, 1993.

Herman, Stewart W. "Luther, Law, and Social Covenants: Cooperative Self-Obligation in the Reconstruction of Lutheran Social Ethics." *Journal of Religious Ethics* 25.2 (Fall 1997): 257–75.

Hiebert, D. Edmond. "An Exposition of 1 John 1.1–4." *Bibliotheca Sacra* 145.0578 (April–June 1988): 197–210.

Hill, Bennett D. *Church and State in the Middle Ages*. NY: John Wiley and Sons Inc., 1970.

Hill, Brennan R., Paul Knitter and William Madges. *Faith Religion & Theology*. Mystic, CT: Twenty-Third Publications, 2003.

Herzog, William R. "Dissembling, A Weapon of the Weak: The Case of Christ and Caesar in Mark 12.13–17 and Romans 13.1–7." *Perspective in Religious Studies* 21.4 (1994): 339–60.

Hobbes, Thomas. "Leviathan: Morality as Rational Advantage." In *Morality and Moral Controversies*, edited by John Arthur. Upper Saddle River, NJ: Pearson Prentice Hall, 2005.

Hobbs, T. R. *Word Biblical Themes: I & II Kings*. Dallas: Word Publishing, 1989.

Holladay, William Lee. *The Root Subh in the Old Testament*. Leiden: Brill, 1958.

Jackson, Thomas. *The Works of John Wesley*. Grand Rapids, MI: Baker Book House, 1979.

Jefferson, LaShawn R. "Bosnia and Herzegovina: Traffickers Walk Free," *Human Rights Watch* (November 16, 2002), http://hrw.org/english/docs/2002/11/26/bosher4425_txt.htm (FIRST accessed August 15, 2008).

Johns, Cheryl. *Pentecostal Formation: A Pedagogy among the Oppressed*. Sheffield: Sheffield Academic Press, 1998.

Johnson, Conrad D. "Moral and Legal Obligation." *The Journal of Philosophy* 72.12 (Jun 1975): 315–33.

Judish, Julia E. "Balancing Special Obligations with the Ideal of Agape." *Journal of Religious Ethics* 26.1 (Spr 1998): 17–46.

Kant, Immanuel. "The Fundamental Principles of the Metaphysics of Morals." In *Morality and Moral Controversies*, edited by John Arthur. Upper Saddle River, NJ: Pearson Prentice Hall, 2005.

Keller, B. "1 Timothy 5.17– Did All Presbyteroi Proclaim God's Word?" *Wisconsin Lutheran Quarterly* 96 (1999): 43–69.

Klasen, S. "Poverty, Inequality and Deprivation in South Africa: An analysis of the 1993 Saldru Survey." *Social Indicators Research* 41.1 (1997): 51–94.

____. "Measuring Poverty and Deprivation in South Africa." *Review of Income and Wealth* 46.1 (2000): 33–58.

Kroger, Daniel. "Paul and Civil Authority: An Exegesis of Romans 13.1–7." *Asia Journal of Theology* 7.2 (1993): 344–66.

Kumar, Muni Prashant, Don Muni Loc Praksh "Lokesh". "Anuvrat Anushasta Saint Tulsi: A Glorious Life with a Purpose."*Anuvibha Reporter* 3.1 (October–December 1997): 33–36.

Küng, Hans. "The Charismatic Structure of the Church: From the Church and Ecumenism." *Concilium* 4 (1965): 41–61.

Küng, Hans, Karl-Josef Kuschel, eds. *A Global Ethic: The Declaration of the Parliament of the World's Religions*. New York: Continuum International Publishing Group, 2003.

LaCapra, Dominick. *History and Memory After Auschwitz*. Ithaca, NY: Cornell University Press, 1998.

Land, Steven. *Pentecostal Spirituality: A Passion for the Kingdom*. Sheffield: Sheffield Academic Press, 2001.

Landon, Michael. "The Challenges of Poverty to the North American Church." *Restoration Quarterly* 47.2 (2005): 105–15.

Laubach, F. "epistrepho, metamelomai." In "Conversion, Penitence, Repentance, Proselyte," *The New International Dictionary of New Testament Theology*, edited by Colin Brown. Grand Rapids, MI: Zondervan, 1981.

Leadbetter, Bill. "Constantine and the Bishop: The Roman Church in the Early Fourth Century." *The Journal of Religious History* 26.1 (February 2002): 1–14.

Levine, David H. *Religion and Politics in Latin America*. Princeton, NJ: Princeton University Press, 2000.

Loder, James. *The Transforming Moment*. Colorado Springs, CO: Helmers & Howard Publishers, 1989.

Lopez, J. Humberto, Guillermo Perry. "Inequality in LatinAmerica: Determinants and Consequences." *Policy Research Working Paper/The World Bank* 1.1 (2008): 1–39.

Lovin, Robin W. *Christian Ethics*. Nashville, TN: Abingdon Press, 2000.

Maggiani, Silvano. "Liturgy and Aesthetic." In *Handbook for Liturgical Studies*, edited by Anscar J. Chupungco. Collegeville, MN: The Liturgical Press, 1998.

Mansfield, Robert. *Spirit and Gospel in Mark*. Peabody, MA: Hendrickson Publishers, 1987.

Martyr, Justin, St. *Writings of Justin Martyr*. Hermigild Dressler, Robert Russell, Thomas Halton, William Tongue, and Josephine Brennan, eds. WA, D.C: The Catholic University of America Press, 1965.

Matthaei, S. Higgins. "Rethinking Faith Formation." *Religious Education* 99.1 (Winter 2004): 56–70.

McDonough, Frank. *The Holocaust*. New York: Palgrave Macmillan, 2008.

McDonnell, Kilian. "The Ideology of Pentecostal Conversion." *Journal of Ecumenical Studies* 5.01 (1968): 105–26.

McDonnell, Kilian, George T. Montague. *Christian Initiation and Baptism in the Holy Spirit: Evidence from the First Eight Centuries*. Collegeville, MN: The Liturgical Press, 1964.

McInerny, Ralph. *Ethica Thomistica*. Washington, DC: The Catholic University of America Press, 1997.

____. *St. Thomas Aquinas*. Notre Dame, IN: University of Notre Dame Press, 1982.

McKim, Donald, ed. *Westminster Dictionary of Theological Terms*. Louisville, KY: Westminster John Knox Press, 1996.

Melina, Livio, Carl A. Anderson. *The Way of Love*. SF: Ignatius Press, 2006.

Meier, J. P. "*Presbyteros* in the Pastoral Epistles." *CBQ* 35 (1973): 323–45.

Melvern, Linda. *Conspiracy to Murder: The Rwandan Genocide*. NY: Verso, 2004.

Menzies, Robert P. *Empowered for Witness: The Spirit in Luke-Acts*. Sheffield: Sheffield Academic Press, 1994.

Middlemas, Jill. "Ecclesiastes Gone 'Sideways.'" *The Expository Times* 118.5 (2007): 216–21.

Mill, John Stuart. "Utilitarianism." In *Morality and Moral Controversies: Readings in Moral, Social, and Political Philosophy*, edited by John Arthur. 7th ed. Upper Saddle River, NJ: Pearson Prentice Hall, 2005.

Miller, Caleb. "An Anabaptist Theory of Moral Obligation." *Mennonite Quarterly Review* 71.4 (1997): 571–93.

Mills, Watson E. *Mercer Dictionary of the Bible*. Macon, GA: Mercer University Press, 1990.

Minujin, Alberto, Jan Vandemoortele, and Enrique Delamonica. "Economic Growth Poverty and Children." *Environment and Urbanization* 14.2 (October 2002): 22–43.

Mitchell, William. "Moral Obligation." *Mind* 11.41 (Jan. 1886): 35–48.

Molnar, Paul D. "Love of God and Love of Neighbor in the Theology of Karl Rahner and Karl Barth." *Modern Theology* 20.4 (October 2004): 567–99.

Moltmann, Jurgen. *The Coming of God*, translated by Margaret Kohl. Minneapolis: Fortress Press, 1996.

____.*The Trinity and the Kingdom*. N Y: Harper and Row, 1981.

Montagu, Ashley. *Anthropology and Human Nature*. NY: McGraw-Hill Book Company, 1957.

Murphy, Ronald. E. *Ecclesiastes*. Dallas: Word, 1992.

____. *The Tree of Life: An Exploration of Biblical Wisdom Literature*. New York: Doubleday, 1990.

Nandy, Shailen. "'Misunderstanding' Chronic Poverty?: Exploring Chronic Poverty in Developing Countries Using Cross-Sectional Demographics and Health Data." *Global Social Policy* 8.1 (2008): 45–79.

Niebuhr, Reinhold. *Moral Man and Immoral Society: A Study in Ethics and Politics*. New York: Charles Scribner's Sons, 1934.

____. *The Nature and Destiny of Man*, vol. 1. New York: Charles Scribner's Sons, 1964.

Niebuhr, H. Richard. *The Responsible Self: An Essay in Christian Moral Philosophy*. New York: Harper & Row, Publishers, 1963.

Noddings, Nel. *Caring*. Berkeley: University of California Press, 2003.

Ocampo, Jose Antonio. Foreword to *United Nations Millennium Declaration Goals Report 2007*. New York: United Nations, 2007.

Oden, Thomas C. *John Wesley's Scriptural Christianity: A Plain Exposition of His Teaching on Christian Doctrine*. Grand Rapids, MI: Zondervan Publishing House, 1994.

O'Meara, Thomas. *Theology of Ministry*. NY: Paulist Press, 1983.

Osborn, George, ed., *The Poetical Works of John and Charles Wesley*. London: Wesleyan-Methodist Conference Office, 1869.

Outler, Albert C., ed. *John Wesley*. NY: Oxford University Press, 1964.

Palmberg, Mai. "Colonialism Made Africa Poor and Dependent." In *Problems of Africa: Opposing Viewpoints*, edited by Janelle Rohr. Farmington Hills, MN: Greenhaven Press, 1986.

____. *The Struggle for Africa*. NY: Zed Books, 1983.

Paes de Barros, Ricardo, Francisco H. G. Ferreira, José R. Molinas Vega, and Jaime Saavedra Chanduvi. *Measuring Inequality of Opportunities in Latin America and the Caribbean*. (WA, DC: World Bank, 2009).

Pannenberg, Wolfhart. *Jesus, God and Man*. PA: Westminster Press, 1968.

Patten, Wendy. "U.S.: Efforts to Combat Human Trafficking and Slavery: Watch Testimony Before the U.S. Senate Judiciary Committee." *Human Rights Watch* (July 7, 2004):1–5. http://hrw.org/english/doc/2004/07/15/usdom9075 (accessed August 15, 2008).

Percy, Martyn. "Sweet Rapture: Subliminal Eroticism in Contemporary Charismatic Worship." *Theology & Sexuality* 6 (1997): 71–106.

Perdue, Leo. G. *Wisdom & Creation: The Theology of Wisdom Literature*. Nashville, TN: Abington Press, 1994.

Perkins, Pheme. "Koinonia in 1 John 1.3–7: The Social Context of Division in the Johannine Letters." *Catholic Biblical Quarterly* 45.04 (1983): 631–41.

Pieper, Josef. *Death and Immortality*. NY: Herder and Herder, 1969.

Plato. *Phaedo*, translated by D. Gallop. NY: World's Classics, 1993.

Poellet, Michael. "Ecclesial Darwinism and the Collapse of Koinonia." *Consensus* 15.1 (1989): 47–62.

Poewe, Karla. "Charismatic Conversion in Light of Augustine's Confessions." In *Religious Conversion*, edited by Christopher Lamb and Darrol Bryant. NY: Cassell, 1999.

Porter, L. "The Word *episkopos* in Pre-Christian Usage." *ATR* 21 (1939): 103–42.

Powers, David. "Priesthood Revisited: Mission and Ministries in the Royal Priesthood." In *Ordering the Baptismal Priesthood: Theologies of Lay and Ordained Ministry*, edited by Susan K. Woods. Collegeville, MN: Liturgical Press, 2003.

Prunier, Gerard. *Darfur: A 21st Century Genocide* 3rd ed. NY: Cornell University Press, 2008.

Rad, Gerhard Von, *Wisdom in Israel*. Nashville, TN: Abingdon, 1972.

Rahner, Karl. *The Spirit in the Church*. NY: Seabury Press, 1970.

_____. *Theological Investigations* vol. 6, translated by Karl-H Kruger and Boniface Kruger. London: Darton, Longman & Todd, 1974.

Ralph, Ragan E. "International Trafficking of Women and Children: Testimony before the Senate Committee on Foreign Relations Subcommittee on Near Eastern and South Asian Affairs. *Human Rights Watch*: 1–11(February 22, 2000), http://www.hrw.org/backgrounder/wrd/trafficing.htm (accessed August 15, 2008).

Ratzinger, Joseph [Pope Benedict XVI]. *Introduction to Christianity*, translated by J. R. Foster. NY: Herder and Herder, 1970.

Rauschenbusch, Walter. *A Theology for the Social Gospel*. Louisville, KY: Westminster John Knox Press, 1997.

Ridge, Michael. "Hobbesian Public Reason." *Ethics* 108 (April 1998): 538–68.

Rittner, Carol, John K. Roth, and Wendy Whitworth, eds. *Genocide in Rwanda: Complicity of the Churches?* St. Paul, MN: Paragon House, 2004.

Rodney, Walter. *How Europe Underdeveloped Africa*. Washington, DC: Howard University Press, 1982.

Rosato, Phillip. "Spirit Christology: Ambiguity and Promise." *Theological Studies* 38.3S (1977): 423–49.

Routledge, Robin. "Hessed as Obligation: A Re-examination." *Tyndale Bulletin* 46.1 (1995): 179–96.

Runes, Dagobert D. *The Dictionary of Philosophy*. NY: Philosophical Library, 1942.

Sanders, Jack T. "Wisdom, Theodicy, Death, and the Evolution of Intellectual Traditions." *Journal for the Study of Judaism* 36.3 (2005): 263–77.

Sanders, Thomas G. *Protestant Concepts of Church and State*. NY: Anchor Books, Doubleday & Company, 1965.

Sandnes, Karl Olav. "Equality Within Patriarchal Structures: Some New Testament perspectives on the Christian fellowship as a brother- or sisterhood and a family." In *Constructing Early Christian Families*, edited by Halvor Moxnes. New York: Routledge, 1997.

Schnackenburg, Rudolf. *The Moral Teaching of the New Testament*. NY: Herder and Herder, 1956.

Schneider, Hebert W. "Moral Obligation." *Ethics* 50.1 (Oct., 1939): 45–56.

Schoeps, H. J. *Jewish Christianity: Factional Disputes in the Early Church*. Philadelphia: Fortress Press, 1969.

Schrage, Wolfgang. *The Ethics of the New Testament*, translated by David Green. PA: Fortress Press, 1988.

Seamone, Donna Lynne. "Body as Ritual Actor and Instrument of Praise: Verna Maynard's Experience as Praise Leader in the Kitchener Church of God." *Journal of Ritual Studies* 12.1 (Summer 1998): 17–26.

Seymour, William J. "The Azusa Street Papers." *The Apostolic Faith Mission Publications*. (1906–08).

Shaw, William. "Relativism in Ethics," in *Morality and Moral Controversies*, edited by John Arthur. Upper Saddle River, NJ: Pearson Prentice Hall, 2005.

Skehan, Patrick. W., trans. *The Wisdom of Ben Sira*. New York: Doubleday, 1987.

Shields, Martin A. "Ecclesiastes and the End of Wisdom." *Tyndale Bulletin* 50.1 (1999): 117–39.

Shore, Rima. *Rethinking the Brain: New Insights into Early Development*. New York: Families and Work Institute, 1997.

Singer, Peter. *Practical Ethics*. NY: Cambridge University Press, 1979.

____. "Rich and Poor." In *Morality and Moral Controversies: Readings in Moral, Social, and Political Philosophy*, edited by John Arthur. 7th ed. Upper Saddle River, NJ: Pearson Prentice Hall, 2005.

Slote, Michael. *The Ethics of Care and Empathy*. NY: Routledge, 2007.

____. Slote, Michael. "Agent-Based Virtue Ethics." *Midwest Studies in Philosophy*, 20.1 (September 1995): 83–101.

Stanlick, Nancy. "Hobbesian Friendship: Valuing Others for Oneself." *Journal of Social Philosophy* 33.3 (Fall 2002): 345–59.

Stephanou, Eusebius."Charismata in the early church Fathers." *Greek Orthodox Theological Review* 21.02 (June 1976):125–46.

Thomas, J. C. *Ministry & Theology*. Cleveland, TN: Pathway Press, 1996.

____. *Foot-washing in John 13 and the Johannine Community*. Sheffield: Sheffield Academic Press, 1991.

Tillich, Paul. *Systematic Theology*, vol. 3. Chicago: The University of Chicago Press, 1963.

Torrell, Jean-Pierre. *Aquinas's Summa*, translated by Benedict Guevin. Washington DC: The Catholic University of America Press, 2005.

Tyson, John H. "John Wesley's Conversion at Aldersgate." In *Conversion in the Wesleyan Tradition*. Nashville, TN: Abingdon Press, 2001.

United Nations. *United Nations Millennium Declaration, A/55/L.2* (September 2000). http://www.un.org/millennium/declaration/ares552e.htm (accessed July 14, 2008).

_____. *The Millennium Development Goals Report 2007*: 1–36. Downloaded at http://www.un.org/millenniumgoals/pdf/mdg2007.pdf

_____. *World Summit for Social Development Programme of Action—Chapter 2*. Copenhagen, 1995. Downloaded at http://www.un.org/esa/socdev/wssd/text-version/agreements/poach2.htm.

U.S. Census Bureau. "Poverty *Thresholds Income, Poverty, and Health Insurance Coverage in the United States*." (2009). Downloaded at http://www.census.gov/prod/2010pubs/p60-238.pdf

Vandenberg, Martina. *Hopes Betrayed: Trafficking of Women and Girls to Post-Conflict Bosnia and Herzegovina for Forced Prostitution* vol. 14.9 (D). New York: Human Rights Watch, November 2002.

VanDrunen, David. "The Two Kingdoms: A Reassessment of the Transformationist Calvin." *Calvin Theological Journal* 40.02 (2005): 248–66.

Varia, Nisha. "International Trafficking in Persons: Taking Action to Eliminate Modern Day Slavery." *Human Rights Watch* (2007), http://www.hrw.org/en/news/2007/10/17/international-trafficking-persons-taking-action-eliminate-mo (accessed August 15, 2008).

Vorgrimler, Herbert. *Sacramental Theology*. Collegeville, MN: The Liturgical Press, 1992.

Walter, Ullman. *A History of Political Thought in the Middle Ages*. Baltimore, MD: Penguin Books, 1970.

Wan, Yee Tham. "Bridging the Gap Between Pentecostal Holiness and Morality." *AJJS* 4.2 (2001): 153–80.

Washington, James. *A Testament of Hope: The Essential Writings and Speeches of Martin Luther King, Jr.* NY: HarperOne, 1991.

Whybray, R. N. "Qoheleth, Preacher of Joy." In *Wisdom: The Collected Articles of Norman Whybray*, edited by K. J. Dell and M. Barker. Aldershot: Ashgate, 2005.

Wilken, Robert Louis. "Christian Formation in the Early Church," an essay in *Educating People of Faith*, edited by John H. Van Engen. Grand Rapids, MI: Eerdmans, 2004.

Williams, Eric. *Capitalism & Slavery*. London: Andre Deutsch, 1987.

Winn, Albert C. "The Holy Spirit and the Christian Life." *Interpretation* 33.01 (January 1979): 47–57.

Winston, David. *The Wisdom of Solomon*. NY: Doubleday, 1979.

"Women's Human Rights." *Human Rights Watch.* Http://www.hrw.org/women or http://www.hrw.org/en/node/82134 (first accessed August 15, 2008).

World Bank. http://www.worldbank.org/poverty/data/trends/income.html

_____. *Inequality in Latin America & the Caribbean: Breaking with History? http://web.worldbank.org/WBSITE/EXTERNAL/COUNTRIES/LACEXT/* (accessed November 10, 2010).

_____. *Leveling opportunities, key to Latin American Development* web.worldbank.org/wbsite/external/countries/lacex-44k. (accessed November 10, 2010).

_____. "America Latina and the Caribbean Regional Brief." http://web.worldbank.org/WBSITE/External/countries/lacext/o (accessed July 23, 2008).

Wozniuk, Vladmir. "In Pursuit of a Politics of Holiness: Reconciling Hellenic and Hebraic Political Wisdom in the Acts of the Apostles." *Journal of Church and State* 45.2 (Spring 2003): 283–304.

INDEX

Aboriginal Traditions, 95
Adam and Eve, 59
   Adamic Nature, 104
Africa, 173-174, 182-188, 190-192, 194, 201-202, 207-209, 224
   Antifarmer Coalition, 184
Afterlife, ix, 89, 91-101, 169
Agape, 24, 38, 204, 222, 227
Agricultural Production, 189
Albrecht, Daniel, 129-132, 134-135
Animal Instincts, 38
Aquinas, St. Thomas, vi, 33, 43-45, 47-48, 61-62, 161, 180, 203
   Thomistic Thought, 44
Aristotle, 52-55, 60-62
   Aristotelianism, 60-62
Asia, 173-175, 185-188, 190-191, 201, 210
Atlantic Slave Trade, 186, 194
Augustine of Hippo, St., v, 6, 14, 33-36, 38, 45-46, 60, 62-65, 70, 75-76, 105, 170, 203, 214-215, 218
   Confessions, 63-65, 70, 75
   City of God, 214, 218
Awakenings, 66-68
   The First Awakening, 66
   The Second Awakening, 66-67
   The Third Awakening, 67
   The Fourth Awakening, 68
Barth, Karl, 3, 9-12, 15, 30, 144-145

Basil of Caesarea, St., 146
Bauer, P. T., 185-187, 209
Berardino, Angelo Di, 145-147, 155
Brugger, Walter, 36-37, 46-47
Buddhism, 68, 94-95, 200
Calvin, John, 144, 215, 218
Caribbean, 173, 185, 191, 201, 209-210
Chance, Bradley, 137, 139, 154
Charismata, 113-115, 119
Charismatics, ix, xi-xii, 61, 69-71, 75-76, 109, 111, 113-115, 118-119, 121, 124-139, 150, 162, 165
   Charismatic Movement, xi-xii, 61, 69-70, 118, 162
Charisms, 69-70, 107-109, 113-118, 125, 130, 169
   Extraordinary Charisms, 70, 113, 115-116, 130
   Leadership Charisms, 109, 115
Christian Conversion, ix, 59, 65-66, 73-75, 219
Christian Initiation, 71, 111, 119
Christian Situationism, 17
Chrysostom, St. John, 124
Church, x, xi, 58, 62, 64-65, 69, 75, 82-83, 106, 109, 111, 114-117, 119, 121-135, 138-155, 158-159, 163, 165, 169-171, 178, 203, 208, 210, 213-218, 220
   Church and State, x, 58, 171, 213-218

Early Churches, 69, 138-155
Clemmons, Ithiel, 149, 155
Collins, Gary, 13, 15
Colonialism, 181-187, 208-209, 213, 224
    Neocolonialism, 181-182
Commonwealth, 40-42
Confucianism, 68
Conversion, ix, xi, 9, 57, 59-76, 89, 142, 152, 164-165, 169, 219
    Classic Conversion Experiences, 62-65
Creation, 6, 29, 55, 98, 107, 160-161, 164-165, 221-222
Crimes Against Humanity, 20, 194, 203
Croatto, J. Severino, 216-218
Curran, Charles, 157, 160-162, 164-165, 222, 226
Dalits, 20, 171, 194, 198-201, 211
    Caste, 20, 198-201, 211
    Oppression, 20, 171, 194, 198-201
    Untouchables, 198-200, 211
Danaher, Kevin, 184-185, 209
Death, ix-x, 4, 40, 51, 57, 85, 89, 91-101, 104, 106, 108, 113, 123, 140, 158, 169, 179, 181, 194, 196, 204-205, 216, 219
Developed Countries, 180, 183, 187-188, 190
Developing Countries, 175, 179, 181, 183, 185, 187-188, 192-193, 207
Development Aid, 183, 188
Discrimination, 45, 152, 171, 194, 198, 201, 203, 211, 213
Downey, Michael, 108, 111
Duffy, Stephen, 37-38, 47

Education, x, 13, 89, 165, 173-175, 177, 186-187, 190-193, 200, 205-206
Egalitarianism, 141-142, 149-150, 152
Egoism, 33, 39-43, 45
Ekklesia, 121-123
Epicurus, 92
Epistrephe, 60, 74
Equality, 39, 123, 149, 152, 154-155, 189, 203, 215, 217
Erikson, Erik, 79-81, 83-85, 90
Eschatology, vi, 7, 35, 67, 69, 98, 108, 123, 159-160, 162, 165
Europe, 149, 182, 184-186, 188, 191, 209, 210
Evil, v-vi, ix, 4, 13, 34-39, 43-45, 47, 57, 59-60, 63, 68, 105-106, 140, 158, 160-161, 199, 204, 207, 214, 219. *See also* Sin
    Human Proclivity to, 37, 47
Faith, ix-xii, 1, 3, 6, 9, 12, 45-46, 50, 57-170, 204, 205, 211, 215
    Justification by, 64, 157-158, 161-162, 164
Faupel, William, 158-159, 165
Fee, Gordon, 167, 169
Fellowship, ix-x, 80, 85, 89, 128, 137-155, 169
Fiorenza, Elizabeth, 141
Fivefold Gospel, 157-162
Fletcher, Joseph, 17-18, 26, 28-29
Flinn, Frank, 61-62, 66-69, 75-76
Formation, ix-x, 71, 74, 77-90, 133, 165, 169, 219
Fowler, James, 78-86, 89-90
Francis, Mark, 121-122, 124, 133

Index

Fundamental Goodness, x, 13, 31, 34, 45-46, 105, 161

G8, 190

Gandhi, Mohandas K. (Mahatma), 77, 85, 199, 204-205

Gause, R. Hollis, 103-105, 110

Gelpi, Donald, 72-74, 76

Global Crises, x, 28, 214, 217

Good Samaritan, 4-5, 169

Gordis, R., 95-96, 100

Gordon, A. J., 67, 159

Grannell, Andrew, 77-78, 89

Greco-Roman World, 152, 223

Grenz, Stanley, 60, 70, 74, 76, 125-126, 133

Hahnenberg, Edward, 117, 119

Happiness, ix, 18, 22, 31, 39, 45-46, 49-55, 94, 164, 207, 217, 224

Hiebert, D. Edmond, 139, 154

Hinduism, 94-95

Hobbes, Thomas, 5, 33, 39-43, 45, 47

> Hobbesian School of Thought, 5, 41-42

Hobbs, T. R., 216, 218

Holiness, xi, 67, 104, 106-107, 110, 158-159, 164-165, 218

Holladay, William, 60, 74

Holy Spirit, v-vi, ix-xi, 6, 8, 10-12, 57-58, 66-67, 69-72, 79, 89, 98, 103-108, 110-111, 113-119, 125-128, 130-133, 137-138, 143-145, 149, 153-154, 157-160, 162-165, 167-170, 219-220

> Baptism in, xi, 69, 71-72, 104, 111, 119, 130, 157-160, 162, 164
>
> Being Born Again, 57, 61, 66, 71, 79-84, 86, 88, 219
>
> Fruits of, x-xi, 57, 103-104, 110, 219
>
> Gifts of, ix-xi, 6, 52, 58, 89, 107-110, 113-119, 145, 162, 169, 219
>
> Spiritual Blessings, 128, 138

Hospitality, 150-151, 155, 199

Human Inclination, 38, 44

Human Nature, ix-x, 13, 28, 31, 33-49, 54, 59-60, 77-78, 89, 101, 105, 160-161, 205

Human Rights Watch, 195, 197-198, 210-211

Immortality, 37, 41, 57, 94-99, 219

India, 20, 194, 198-201, 204, 207, 211

Individualism, 93, 147-148, 150, 153

Inequality, 19-20, 191, 207, 210

Initiation, 71, 76, 111, 119

Injustice, 19-20, 31, 40, 46, 96, 171, 183, 205, 207, 215-217

Islam, 95, 201

Jainism, 94, 204, 211

Jesus, x-xi, 3-6, 8-11, 13, 18, 24-25, 45, 47, 60, 63-64, 66, 69, 71-74, 79, 86, 97, 104, 106-7, 113, 117, 123, 126, 138-140, 145, 150-151, 154, 157, 159-160, 164, 168, 170, 206, 216-218, 223

Judgment, 7, 22, 68, 81-82, 84, 95-95, 97, 159, 216-217

Justice, 18-19, 21, 24, 26, 29, 38, 40, 44, 46, 104, 178, 181, 187, 198, 204-205, 211, 215, 217

Justification. *See* Faith, Justification by

Justin Martyr, 123, 133

Kant, Immanuel, 17-19, 23, 27, 29

> Kantian School of Thought, 19, 23

King, 57, 107-109, 111, 121-122, 125, 218-219
King, Martin Luther, 85, 204, 211
Koinonia, 137-155
    Agent of, 143, 145
    Elements of, 150-153
    Factors that Hinder, 147-150
    Instrument of, 145-147
    Models of, 141-142
Küng, Hans, 111, 115, 119, 218
Latin America, 173, 175, 185, 191, 201, 210, 218
Laying on of Hands, 128, 134
Loder, James, 86-87, 89-90
Luther, Martin, 62, 64-65, 75, 158, 211, 215, 218, 227
    Turmerlibnis experience, 64
Mason, Charles H., 149
McDonnell, Killian, 69, 76, 111, 119
Metanoeo, 60
Middlemas, Jill, 49, 55, 99
Mill, John Stuart, 18, 29
Millennium, 67-68, 147, 157-159, 162, 164
Minujin, Alberto, 174-175, 177, 207-208
Molnar, Paul, 11-12, 15, 30
Moltmann, Jürgen, 92-93, 99, 101
Montagu, Ashley, 36, 47
Mortality, 91-95, 186-187, 193
Murphy, Ronald, 51, 55
Nandy, Shailen, 174, 187, 189-190, 207-209
Natural Law, vi, 33, 43-45
Niebuhr, Reinhold, 35-36, 46, 221-222, 226

Nonviolence, 38, 203-206, 211, 216
Nozick, Robert, 179-180
Ocampo, Jose, 188
Overpopulation, 180, 184
Palmberg, Mai, 181-184, 208
Parliament of World Religions, 215-216, 218
    Four Irrevocable Commitments, 215-216
Parousia. See Second Coming
Pastoral Epistles, 109, 111, 141
Paul, Apostle, vi, 5-7, 9, 62-65, 79, 86, 92, 97, 99, 103-109, 113-116, 118, 123, 138-142, 148-149, 151-152, 167, 169, 218
Peacemaking, x, 171, 173, 203-206, 214
Pelagius, 34
Pentecostalism, ix, xi-xii, 61, 68-71, 75-76, 118-119, 121, 129-135, 149-150, 155, 157-165
    Pentecostal Mode and Sensibilities, 129-132
Perdue, Leo, 51, 55
Perkins, Pheme, 139-140, 154
Plato, 52, 60-62, 98, 101
    Neoplatonism, 60-61
    Platonism, 60-61
Poewe, Karla, 70, 76
Politics, 52-53, 55, 68, 72-74, 84-85, 88, 171-218, 220, 223
    Socio-Politics, 72-74, 84-85, 171-218
Poverty, x, 38, 41, 58, 93, 171, 173-211, 213, 215, 220, 225
    Child Poverty, 176-177
    Chronic Poverty, 176-189, 207-209
    Economic Dependence, 182-183

Index

Global Poverty, 173-211, 213, 220
Human Trafficking, 171, 194-195, 197-198, 210-211
Hunger, x, 173, 184-187, 190-193, 206
Poverty Reduction, x, 175, 187, 190-207
Preferential Option for the Poor, 38, 178
Unequal Exchange, 182-183
US$1 per day, 174-175, 187, 190, 200

Priest, 57, 62, 64, 103, 107-111, 117, 124, 198, 217, 219.

Promised Land, 122

Prophet, 3, 7, 13, 57, 60, 107-111, 115, 124, 126, 143-144, 168, 178, 181, 216-217, 219

Protestant, 61, 64-66, 69, 117, 126, 131, 134, 148, 161, 203, 214

Qahal, 121-123

Qoheleth, 49-51, 54-55, 91-92, 95-96, 100

Qumran, 97

Rahner, Karl, 3, 5, 7-12, 14-15, 30, 85, 111
Anonymous Christianity, 8-9, 85

Rapture, 68, 93, 100, 133, 159-160

Rauschenbusch, Walter, 36, 46

Relativism, 17, 20-21, 29, 202-203

Religion and Politics. *See* Church and State

Repentance, 39, 60, 67, 69, 71, 74

Resurrection, 96-99, 123, 138, 150, 160-161, 164

Ridge, Michael, 41-42, 47

Rodney, Walter, 186, 209

Roman Catholic, 62, 64-65, 75, 117, 128, 134, 148, 160-161, 165, 203

Runes, Dagobert, 33-34, 46

Salvation, v, x, 8, 25-26, 61, 65, 69, 70, 79, 110, 113, 127, 148, 158, 161, 164, 167, 169, 224

Sanctification, xi, 57, 71, 103, 106-107, 110, 157-158, 160-162, 164, 219
Entire Sanctification, xi, 57, 106, 110, 219

Sanders, Jack, 95-96, 99-101

Sandnes, Karl, 141-142, 152, 154-155

Savior, 8, 66, 69, 71, 81, 148

Schafer, Klaus, 141

Schleiermacher, Friedrich, 144

Schnackenburg, Rudolf, 5-6, 14

Schrage, Wolfgang, 3-5, 14

Second Coming, 67-68, 92, 128, 138, 158-160, 162

Self-Preservation, 37, 40-41, 43, 45, 153

Sermon on the Mount, 4-5, 106, 110, 126, 138, 151, 203-204, 227

Seymour, William, xi, 69, 71-72, 76, 149-150, 158

Shields, Martin, 51, 55

Sideways: the Movie, 49-50

Sin, v, x, 13, 33-39, 57, 59-60, 63, 65-67, 69, 71, 73-74, 92, 104-106, 110, 113, 127-128, 140, 158, 160-161, 164-165, 216, 219, 223. *See also* Evil
Carnal Nature, 59, 105
Disobedience, v, 34, 59, 92
Genesis Account, v-vi, 37, 59, 67, 100, 161, 220
Original Sin, 33-39, 67, 105, 161, 165

Works of the Flesh, 57, 104-106, 110, 165, 219

Singer, Peter, 179, 180, 192, 208, 210

Situation Ethics, 17-19, 29

Slavery, 152, 194-196, 198, 210-211

Sociobiologists, 37-39

Spirit. *See* Holy Spirit

Spirituality, ix-x, 57, 89, 103-117, 124, 130, 132, 134-135, 157, 163, 165, 169, 219

Spirituality and Piety, ix-x, 57, 89, 103-117, 124, 169, 219

Stanlick, Nancy, 42-43, 47

Synoptic Gospels, 3, 10, 123, 167

Third World, 179, 183-184

Tillich, Paul, 145

Torah, 3-4, 13, 126

Transcendental Efficacy, 129-130

Transformation, ix-xi, 67, 70-71, 74, 77-90, 117, 158, 169, 218-219

Transformational Logic, 86-89

United Nations, 176, 187-190, 195, 208-209
- General Assembly, 176
- Millennium Development Goals, 187-190

Wesley, John, vi, 62, 64-65, 75, 104, 106, 110-111, 134, 157-158, 162-165
- Aldersgate Street, 64-65, 164
- John Wesley's Quadrilateral, 162

Whybray, R. N., 51, 55

Winn, Albert, 143-145, 154

Worship, ix-x, 76, 80, 89, 105, 107-108, 121-135, 151, 169.

www.ingramcontent.com/pod-product-compliance
Lightning Source LLC
Chambersburg PA
CBHW071655090426
42738CB00009B/1531